HELMI'S SHADOW

HELMI'S SHADOW

A JOURNEY OF SURVIVAL FROM RUSSIA TO EAST ASIA TO THE AMERICAN WEST

DAVID HORGAN

UNIVERSITY OF NEVADA PRESS | *Reno & Las Vegas*

University of Nevada Press | Reno, Nevada 89557 USA
www.unpress.nevada.edu
Copyright © 2021 by David Horgan
All rights reserved
All photos courtesy of the author unless otherwise noted.
Cover by TG Design
China frame © Chartgraphic / Adobe Stock

The quotation from Sgt. Edward Saylor on page 102 is from *Yank, the Army Newspaper*, July 8, 1942, reprinted in *Destination Tokyo* by Stan Cohen, Pictorial Histories Publishing Co., 1983. Used with permission.
The epigraph on page vii from Jill Lepore is used with her kind permission.
The epigraph from Soren Kierkegaard (1813-1855) on page vii is from his 1843 journals, IV A 164.

LIBRARY OF CONGRESS CATALOGING-IN-PUBLICATION DATA
Names: Horgan, David, 1951- author.
Title: Helmi's shadow : a journey of survival from Russia to East Asia to the American West / David Horgan.
Description: Reno : University of Nevada Press, [2021] | Includes bibliographical references. | Summary: "Helmi's Shadow is an intimate true story of a stateless Russian-Jewish mother and daughter, the author's grandmother and mother who, with determination and good luck, managed to survive decades of hardship in the hidden corners of war-torn Asia, finally landing after the Second World War in the unlikely safe harbor of Reno, Nevada, to become bona fide citizens for the first time. The book is also a loving memoir of growing up under the wings of these remarkable women in a unique American family, told through the author's eyes as both a child and young adult" —Provided by publisher.
Identifiers: LCCN 2021008820 | ISBN 9781647790202 (paperback) | ISBN 9781647790219 (epub)
Subjects: LCSH: Koskin, Rachel, 1896-1991 | McCorkle, Helmi, 1923-2002. | Women refugees—United States—Biography. | Jewish refugees—United States—Biography. | Refugees—United States—Biography. | Stateless persons—Biography. | LCGFT: Biographies.
Classification: LCC CT275.K6257 H67 2021 | DDC 362.87089/924092 [B]—dc23
LC record available at https://lccn.loc.gov/2021008820

The paper used in this book meets the requirements of American National Standard for Information Sciences-Permanence of Paper for Printed Library Materials, ANSI/NISO Z39.48-1992 (R2002)

FIRST PRINTING

Manufactured in the United States of America

Frontispiece: Helmi Koskin, 1947

For Beth and Tai

History is the shadow cast by the dead.
JILL LEPORE

~

Life can only be understood backward,
but it must be lived forward.
SOREN KIERKEGAARD

Contents

PART TWO. AMERICA

Preface

THIS IS AN INTIMATE STORY about my family, not a scholarly history. Nevertheless, I have made every effort to describe events, places, and people as accurately as possible. My intent is to create a portrait of the highly unusual lives of my mother and grandmother, set against some of the most tumultuous events of the twentieth century.

The book is divided into two parts, matching the two halves of that century. Part One, covering 1896 to 1946, begins in the city of Odessa, in the former Russian Empire, where my grandmother Rachel (pronounced Rah-*shell*) was born; moves across Asia to Harbin, a Russian-controlled city in northeast China; continues over the East China Sea to Kobe, Japan, where my mother, Helmi, was born; moves back again to Shanghai for most of the 1920s and 1930s; and finally returns to Kobe for the entirety of the Second World War. Through several decades of hardship, upheaval, and violence, mother and daughter lived as stateless Jews and perpetual refugees, denied the rights of citizenship anywhere. Along with other distinctions, they were among the select few who were bombed by both the Japanese and the United States. They slipped through the cracks of history and survived.

I was told, growing up, that Rachel was Russian but came from China, and that Helmi came from Japan with no nationality at all. They spoke to each other in English, Russian, and Yiddish and proudly declared themselves Jews, though this had little to do with religion. They both resisted talking about the past, but after considerable prodding they proved to be excellent storytellers. The information about Helmi's early years contained in this account comes from interviews I conducted with her late in her life. Her memory was sharp, her tales vivid and detailed, and I have striven to be faithful to the stories she recounted. All incidents and conversations, plus the letter from Helmi to Rachel on page 136, are reconstructed from these interviews. My grandmother Rachel, whom we and everybody else knew as Baba, had her own dramatic flair for relating incidents from long ago. By the time they both died, I possessed an abundance of personal information and a host of jumbled, colorful, and often frightening anecdotes. Yet large pieces of the historical puzzle remained missing. I had little understanding, for instance, of how stateless Russian Jews could have come to be stranded in Asia during the years between the two world wars, or the circumstances that made it possible for some to survive when so many did not.

To answer such questions, and to confirm the stories I had been told by these remarkable women, I conducted additional research. Included is a bibliography listing the most important sources I have used for corroboration of details and events described in Part One.

Part Two is composed mainly of my own memories and takes place almost entirely in Reno, Nevada, where both Helmi and Rachel resided after the Second World War and spent the rest of their lives, and where I was born. This half of the book paints a picture of family life from my own perspective growing up under the protective wings of these two resilient women.

I believe their stories are well worth telling. I believe it is especially important to tell the stories of those who, for their own reasons, never finished telling the stories themselves.

~

ADDITIONAL NOTE: In Part One, I have used the modern pinyin system for rendering a number of Chinese names and places in English, instead of the Wade-Giles system that was common when Rachel and Helmi lived in Shanghai. The pinyin system is closer to Mandarin pronunciation and has become widely used. Thus, Huangpu River instead of Wangpoo River, Hongkou instead of Hongkew, Suzhou instead of Soochow, Beijing instead of Peking, Zhapei instead of Chapei, etc.

HELMI'S SHADOW

Prologue

Kobe, Japan, August, 1945

ON A SWELTERING SUMMER DAY, just before noon, a petite young woman sat in a crowded streetcar that rolled along the industrial waterfront of Kobe, Japan's main international seaport. The streetcar's progress was painfully slow. Mounds of rubble were heaped all around, the result of recent American carpet bombings that had killed thousands of people and destroyed large swaths of the city. Entire blocks down near the harbor had been leveled, and to the young woman it seemed miraculous that the streetcar could even still operate.

Her hair was dark, nearly black, and although Kobe was the city of her birth she was not Japanese. Her name was Helmi Koskin, and she was Russian Jewish, part of a small community of foreigners who had survived in Japan throughout the Second World War. She was on her way to one of the waterfront black markets where fresh fruits and vegetables, though officially unavailable, might yet be for sale. She and her mother, with whom she lived in a small boardinghouse that her mother managed, had subsisted mostly on rations of moldy white rice and beans for the past four years of war.

Suddenly the streetcar lurched to a stop in the middle of a block, and the conductor gestured impatiently for everyone to get off. Helmi joined the other passengers filing into the street. It was probably just a blockage on the tracks. No one moved with any particular urgency. Weariness and resignation were in every face. Sirens had sounded several times in recent days, but no American bombers had appeared over Kobe for over a month. Everyone understood that Japan was on its knees. Tokyo, the capital city, had been ravaged repeatedly by firebombings, as had most

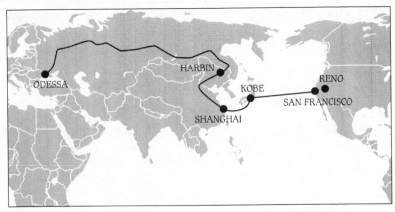

The journey of Rachel and Helmi, 1905 to 1947. Map by Kirk Johnson.

other major cities. Word was circulating that a week ago some kind of new bomb—one bomb dropped from a single plane—had obliterated the city of Hiroshima, only 150 miles to the east. Another, three days later, supposedly had done the same to Nagasaki, a bit further away. In between these horrors, the Soviet Union, fresh from fighting the Nazis, finally declared war on Japan. Would Russians soon be dropping bombs, too? No one knew what to believe anymore. As she stepped onto the sidewalk, Helmi looked upward at the hazy sky, wondering if it was Kobe's fate also to be wiped off the map. But there was nothing in the sky, and no sound of a plane.

Traffic all around had stopped, and people had congregated on the sidewalk, maintaining an odd silence. Some were gathered around a table set outside a storefront, on which a large console radio had been placed. The radio suddenly crackled to life, as did the loudspeakers mounted on rickety poles that normally broadcast air-raid sirens. There were no sirens now, just the crackling static, but everyone around her appeared intent on listening. Then a voice began broadcasting, tinny and peculiarly high-pitched. She strained to listen, but she could understand nothing. She had lived in Kobe long enough to learn conversational Japanese, but this voice spoke in an unfamiliar dialect. She couldn't even tell whether it was a man's voice or a woman's. People glanced at each other with shocked expressions, but no one looked at her. The voice from the speakers went on for several minutes and then abruptly stopped, and all was quiet again. For a few seconds nothing happened and no one moved, as if the world had been frozen. Then, slowly, people shuffled to life again on the sidewalks; cars and trucks and bicycles started moving up the street; and passengers made their way back to the streetcar. Faces remained stunned. Hardly anyone spoke. A few had begun to weep. She overheard a word, spoken in a whisper: Showa. This is what they called their emperor. Was the voice his? What in the world could he have to say? As far as she knew, he had never before addressed the populace. Had he announced new restrictions? Would there be the great invasion of the mainland that many had feared?

It wasn't until later, when she finally returned home with a few meager vegetables, that she learned the news, from an English-speaking Japanese neighbor. Indeed it was the emperor, speaking directly to his people for the first time in his life. His speech had a title, "The Jewel-Voice Broadcast," and it had been delivered in the arcane dialect used for rare royal decrees. The message was simple: Japan had surrendered to America.

Helmi Koskin was twenty-two years old in 1945. She saw that everything now would change. It would be a different world—whether better or worse, she couldn't tell, although it was hard to imagine things getting much worse. She had long hoped for her life to be different. She had hoped to live in a place where she could feel she belonged. Her first languages were Russian and English, yet she had never lived in a place where either of these was the native tongue. Although her birthplace was Japan, her mother had raised her in Shanghai, across the South China Sea, under impoverished conditions. The Japanese had bombed their tenement there during the invasion of China, before the Second World War even began. After fleeing back to Japan, they had endured more privation and more bombs. Their house was one of the few on their block still standing. They had no citizenship anywhere. They had no true home.

Throughout the war the Japanese had relentlessly publicized the idea that Americans were vicious barbarians, and that if war ever came to the mainland people would be slaughtered mercilessly, tortured, even eaten alive. Helmi Koskin never believed this. For as long as she could remember, she had harbored an image of America gleaned from books and movies and music, and from a few actual Americans she had met. If America would stop raining down bombs, then she believed in her heart that things would get better. If the war was really over, then maybe she could finally find a place to call home.

PART ONE

~

THE FAR EAST

Exile—Odessa to Harbin

Rachel Koskin (*far right*), with (*left to right*) her sisters, Anna and Rebekah; her younger brother, Israel; and their mother, Feiga (Fanny), in Harbin, about 1908. Rebekah and Israel later perished in the Soviet gulag. Courtesy of Marianne Carthew.

Pogrom

Odessa, 1905

MY GRANDMOTHER, Rachel Koskin, known to me as Baba, was born in the Ukrainian city of Odessa, a famously beautiful port on the Black Sea, in 1896. Ukraine in the early twentieth century belonged to the Russian Empire under Tsar Nicholas II. Baba's parents, Solomon and Feiga Cooper, were middle-class Jews. Solomon may have been a doctor in Odessa, although my mother, Helmi, always expressed doubts about this, as she did about most of what her mother said about the past, or about anything else. Where this western-sounding surname came from my mother never knew, and my grandmother never said. It turns out that "Cooper" was a fairly common name among Jews in Russia and other eastern European countries in the nineteenth and early twentieth centuries. Its origin is different from that of the Anglo-Saxon "cooper," which means a barrel maker. The Russian "cooper" probably comes from *kuper*, meaning coppersmith. In any case, Baba lived in Odessa until 1905, when her family escaped from persecution, along with many other Jews, eastward across Asia on the newly completed Trans-Siberian Railway to the remote frontier city of Harbin in northeastern China. She was nine years old.

In October 1905, Tsar Nicholas, as part of a last-ditch effort to stave off revolution among the masses, issued a proclamation granting certain limited political liberties to the Russian citizenry, including the right to stage civil protests. This became known as the October Manifesto. The Russian economy was in a serious recession, and throughout the empire there was rampant social and economic discontent. And, as was so often the case during periods of instability in many parts of the Western world, much of the blame had been put on the Jews. Since the mid-nineteenth century, anti-Jewish riots in Russia occurred with mind-numbing regularity—violent events in which mobs of citizens, often abetted by the government or the military, attacked Jews in their homes and businesses, murdering them indiscriminately and destroying or stealing their property. The city of Odessa was an important shipping port with a substantial Jewish population and had been the site of many such anti-Jewish riots, known as pogroms, from a Russian word meaning "beating," "smashing," or "destruction." The tsar's new declaration was widely interpreted in certain quarters as a license to once again attack the Jews.

Most Russian Jews lived in the southwestern part of Imperial Russia known as the Pale of Settlement, the area that today makes up Poland and Ukraine. The Jewish citizens may have had hopes that the strict conditions under which they lived might actually be relieved by the new declaration of civil rights, but within days of the tsar's October Manifesto, a new wave of pogroms began. On October 18, 1905, one of the bloodiest attacks in many decades occurred in the city of Odessa. During that single night, as many as 2,500 Jews were murdered out of a total Jewish population of approximately 140,000. Rachel and her family were among those who barely escaped being killed.

~

ONCE, WHEN I WAS HOME in Reno on a break from college in the early 1970s, I went to visit my grandmother, Baba, for lunch in her apartment, where she had lived alone for several years. She seemed tinier than ever, shrinking physically as well as mentally. Always a tense and anxious person, she had become ever more nervous and fearful. She was in her mid-seventies by then, and with her deteriorating mental state we knew that she would not be living on her own much longer. Every time I saw Baba in those days, she would reel me in for an obligatory slobbering wet kiss and then seize my arm with a viselike force—my brother and I called it The Death Grip—and pull me in closer.

"Davidochka," she said, looking deep into my eyes, "tell me the truth. Is Helmi happy?" My mother had recently remarried. My father had died four years earlier. Baba still wasn't on board with the idea of her daughter having a new husband.

"Oh, yes!" I replied, with customary enthusiasm. "She is very happy."

Baba wasn't buying it.

"Oy, Davidochka." Her voice dropped an octave or two, to its lowest register, her trademark conspiratorial baritone. Her eyes grew fierce. "How can we be sure?"

What she meant was, *how can I be sure she is happy with her new husband, who is a stranger to me, if I can't see her every single second?*

This kind of conversation had become one of the rituals of our visits, and I was used to it.

"Oh yes," I reassured her, "she's happy as a clam!"

I knew full well she would never take my word for it. There wasn't much logic to her thinking—perhaps her fearful nature was simply getting the best of her. In the years to come, she would continue to become more and more suspicious of the world and everyone in it until she slowly floated away from reality altogether.

It was time to change the subject. "What's for lunch?" I asked, loud and perky. "Sure smells good!"

"Oy, lunch!" she shouted, and dashed back into her tiny kitchen. It didn't matter what she was making, there was invariably something forgotten or overlooked: soup boiling over, toast burning, omelet turning crusty. Her cooking had become very simple. She didn't make piroshke or borscht or any of her other signature dishes anymore. I felt sorry for her now in a way that I never had before. Today it was merely a grilled cheese sandwich starting to smoke on the stove.

I helped her salvage the sandwich, and we finally sat down. She had set up a folding TV tray for me in front of the couch and she pulled up a kitchen chair on the opposite side of the tray. In this way we were sitting very close, which is what she liked. All she was having was a cup of tea.

I had come with an agenda. After some chitchat about my college classes and my roommates, I thought I'd make another stab at gaining information about her life. Since I had begun college, my own view of the world had widened, and my interest in our family history had intensified.

I said, "Baba, I'd really like to know more about your past."

Silence. She looked away, then got up and headed back to the kitchen. "Would you like another sandwich? I'll make you another nice sandwich."

"No, no, I'm fine." I pressed on. "But I truly am interested. Russia, China, anything at all." She came back and finally gazed me square in the eye, then sat down again.

"David," she said, "all right. I will tell you one story. From this you will learn something about me, okay?"

"Yes!" I said, I hoped without too much eagerness. This was a rare chance, and I didn't want to spoil it.

"All right. Because you want to know, I will tell you about how I came from Russia to China. From Odessa to Harbin, when I was a little girl, not yet ten years old."

The story she told me was interspersed with many hesitations and trips back and forth to the kitchen to make sure I was getting enough to eat and drink.

She was at home in Odessa with her family in their upstairs apartment. It was evening. They had heard during the day stories of gangs roaming the streets, drunk, violent, attacking Jewish families, murdering them, stealing their possessions. There had been stories like this before, but never in their neighborhood. On this night, they heard shouting in the street below. From their balcony they could see, far up the street, a mass of people. A mob was coming down the street. Some were carrying torches, some were carrying clubs. People were screaming. Suddenly there was pounding on the door of their apartment. Her parents weren't sure whether to answer, but someone was calling out their name. Finally her father opened the door, and there was a neighbor, one of their non-Jewish neighbors. This person gave to her parents a picture, a framed religious image. This was an icon, a Christian icon. They were to hang it on their door and leave it there. And so this was done. The mobs came down the street, and all night there was shouting and screaming. This was called a pogrom, this killing and attacking of Jews. The children hid in the bedrooms, but could not sleep. But no one else came to their door. In the morning they found out that many people had been attacked and many had been killed. But her family was spared because of the icon given to them by their neighbor. The mobs had been drunk on vodka, given to them by the army, the Tsar's Army. This was what they heard from their neighbors. And very soon, perhaps within only a few days, they packed all their belongings and got on a train. They left Odessa and traveled across all of Russia, across Siberia, to China. This was a place where they were free to go. To Harbin, a city where Russians could live, where Jews could be safe. And this is where she grew up, in Harbin.

Telling me all this, Baba made no mention of the October Manifesto or anything else related to the Russian politics of that bygone era. She spoke slowly, almost dreamily.

"So that is all," she said, rising from her seat again. "This is why I am a Russian, a Russian old lady from China." She went to the kitchen and opened the refrigerator.

"Did you ever go back to Odessa?" I called out to her.

She came back carrying two bowls. "Here," she said. "We will have dessert together. I have made you some Jell-O." She set the bowls down on the TV tray.

"Of course I never went back," she said. "No one ever went back. If they did, they disappeared. Like that, gone, in the wink of any eye. And now, no more questions. We eat our nice Jell-O, and you tell me more about your college. Go on, eat. Eat!"

And so I obeyed.

When I went home afterward, I related Baba's story to my mother. Had she heard all this before? I understood by now that, apart from the other hardships in my mother's life, being Baba's only child had not been easy.

Yes, she had heard it before, or a version of it.

"Listen to me," Helmi said. "You can see what's happening to her, can't you? She's starting to lose her marbles. Not exactly starting, I might add. As far as I'm concerned, this began long ago. These days she is going downhill fast. She has always had a great imagination. Now sometimes she is in a world of her own, a complete fantasy world. She's a great one for drama. Yes, she grew up in Harbin. Yes, her parents always said they were from Odessa. But all this with the late-night mob, and the torches, and the killing, and the icon on the door? Who's to say? If I were you, I would take it all with a grain of salt."

I knew my mother was right. Baba was beginning to lose her grip on reality. We could all see it. And so I followed Helmi's advice and took this story, and others that Baba occasionally doled out, with many grains of salt.

It wasn't until decades later, long after she was gone, that I finally read detailed accounts of the October 1905 Odessa pogrom. Mobs did in fact rage down the streets of the city, fueled by vodka provided by the Tsarist military, on the very day after the October Manifesto was issued. The Jews were treated as scapegoats for a litany of economic and social ills. People were murdered in their homes, slaughtered viciously. Icons of Christian saints were used to mark the doors of non-Jewish families who lived in the predominantly Jewish neighborhoods. Horrible atrocities were committed. Bodies were piled in the streets. Baba said she was not yet ten years old at the time of these events; in fact, when the Odessa pogrom occurred she was exactly nine years old. It doesn't seem unlikely that she would retain a memory of this terrible night for the rest of her life. The power of this memory might help explain what my mother meant when she said that Baba had begun to lose her marbles long ago. It would help explain why she was such an anxious, nervous, easily frightened person, and why she had to be hospitalized several times because of emotional breakdowns. We grew up making fun of her, imitating her, laughing at her. Her quirks of behavior, her weird fears and superstitions, were hilarious to us.

Even now my brother and I, after more than half a century, sometimes still speak to each other in the mock Russian accent we first adopted for fun as smart-alecky little boys. We had no understanding when we were growing up that she might have lived through horrors beyond our imagining. She left no documentation or proof of these things. All we can do now is wonder and speculate, as we merge our own memories and impressions with what there is of a historical record.

This is how we attempt to tell the stories of our forebears, and perhaps even come to know them better, once they are gone from us.

The Paris of the Orient

Harbin, 1920

HARBIN WAS FOUR THOUSAND MILES east of Odessa, in the northern district of China known as Manchuria, near the eastern Russian border. By the second decade of the twentieth century Harbin had grown from a tiny fishing village into a sophisticated metropolis, known as the Paris of the Orient and sometimes the St. Petersburg of the East—a city unique in all of Asia, built on Chinese territory but containing a largely Russian population, including a number of prosperous Jews, and governed under Russian jurisdiction. This came about through an unusual set of circumstances.

In 1895, the Tsarist Russian government leased a fifteen-mile-wide strip of land across the width of Manchuria to extend the Trans-Siberian Railroad through Asia, as part of a secret and short-lived defense pact between Russia and China. By 1898 this last leg of the Trans-Siberian, known as the China-Eastern Railroad, was under construction by Russian engineers, and it was completed by 1904. China granted both economic and territorial concessions to Russia along the route of the railroad, and in an effort to rapidly populate the area and help establish a strong economic foothold, the Tsarist government made an unprecedented concession to its Jewish population. Persecuted for decades throughout the Russian empire, Jews suddenly were given the right to travel to Manchuria and settle in Harbin with few restrictions.

The logic was twofold. Jews would be removed from places within the Russian Empire where they were not wanted and, at the same time, the Jews' supposed "economic talents" would be introduced into a frontier region that Imperial Russia was eager to exploit. For a brief period, roughly fifteen years, this plan worked very well. Harbin became the administrative hub of the eastern railroad, and the city quickly grew from a small cluster of Chinese fishing villages nestled on the banks of the Songhua River into a thriving Russian-populated metropolis. The tsar's official "invitation" to travel eastward, coupled with the rise in virulent antisemitism in Ukraine and the other western Russian provinces, produced a substantial exodus of Jews from Russia to China, and Harbin is where many of them ended up.

In 1902, Harbin's Jews numbered only around 200. By the Jewish population's peak in the 1920s, in a city whose total population was around 100,000, they numbered over 20,000, most living comfortably and relatively free of persecution. The population was eventually bolstered by an influx of non-Jewish "White Russians," Tsarist supporters fleeing the Bolshevik Revolution. For their part, the Chinese populace in the area, one of the Chinese empire's least-developed border regions, welcomed the Russians, Jews and non-Jews alike, at least in the first two decades, because of the economic boom they brought about. For the Jews, Harbin became one of the few places on the Eurasian continent where they could live in freedom. This mutually beneficial relationship would last into the 1920s, despite periods of armed conflict among the nations—Russia, Japan, and China—whose economic and territorial interests converged, and frequently clashed, in that part of the world.

In the spring of 1906, the train journey from Odessa to Harbin on the Trans-Siberian railroad took eleven days. Nine-year-old Rachel Cooper and her family were transplanted to what must have seemed a wilderness. The train, powered by a belching steam engine, chugged across the vast Siberian landscape at fifteen miles per hour. They traveled second class, with sleeping berths stacked three high and no meals provided, so they brought their food with them. Somewhere up ahead, closer to the engine, was a first-class section, including a dining car outfitted with linen and silver and a separate parlor car equipped with its own grand piano, reserved for well-to-do Russians with financial interests in the newly accessible Far East. Outside the window, as they traveled east, the towns and train stations grew smaller, the distance from the home the Coopers had known greater and greater. With every mile the horizon seemed to grow more barren and treeless.

From the Odessa station the train plodded through the towns of Donetsk and Volgograd, then along the thousand-mile northern border of Kazakhstan to the city of Omsk; followed the Mongolian border to the village of Irkutsk at the southern tip of Lake Baikal, whose waters produced a famously pure vodka; and finally, after ten days, reached the Manchzhuriya Station (later renamed Manzhuli), situated on the Inner Mongolian grasslands at the Manchurian border. They had seen sheep-herders living in yurts, herds of camels, and many miles of emptiness. Now, at their brief stop in Manchzhuriya, an open boxcar was added at the rear, and a hundred or more Chinese clambered aboard to ride in the open air for the remaining seven-hour trip to Harbin. The train, now in Chinese territory, continued on the Russian-controlled rails, completed only two years before, which cut diagonally across Manchuria to the port of Vladivostok, the far Russian outpost on the coast of the Sea of Japan. Halfway through Manchuria's great central prairie, the tracks crossed the Songhua River flowing south, and the train reached its destination at last—Harbin, the former Chinese fishing village, now a virtual Russian colony. It was a harsh place, a far cry in every way from Odessa. In summer, in place of mild breezes off the Black Sea, there was a relentless hot wind filled with stinging dust that seemed to coat everything. In winter, howling Arctic blizzards and subzero temperatures were the rule.

Rachel's father soon established a modest medical practice in Harbin, serving the rapidly expanding Jewish community, many of whom, like the Cooper family, had brought along their savings, possessions, and intact families. Here they could freely own property, conduct business, and attend schools without adhering to strict quotas. The price they paid for these freedoms was relocation on foreign soil at the far end of the Asian continent. And within another twenty years, the cost would be even greater. The respite would prove temporary.

The only surviving photograph of Solomon Cooper is severely damaged, taken in a Harbin studio around 1912. It shows him posing comfortably in a light-colored summer suit, seated with his three teenage daughters standing behind him in white, high-collared dresses and large fashionable hats. The youngest daughter, Rachel, perhaps sixteen years old, holds a Chinese fan below her waist. Rebekah, the tallest of the three, rests a hand on her father's shoulder. Anna, the oldest daughter, has a forthright gaze that foretells the capable nature she would demonstrate in years to come. Solomon's perfectly bald head shines as if polished, and one eyebrow is raised in a manner that possibly conveys amusement, although it's hard to tell if he's actually smiling, since his

Left to right: Anna, Rebekah, and Rachel with their
father, Solomon, in Harbin, about 1915.

mouth is obscured by an enormous jet-black mustache across the entire
width of his face. He holds a hat casually between his knees. He looks
happy to be in the company of his daughters. They seem sophisticated
young women. They have gone through Russian-administered *gymnasi-
ums* in Harbin, and among their classes have been mandatory language
studies, including the study of English, in which they are now nearly
fluent. This is a skill which will prove of great value in the near future.

One other family photo exits from the Harbin years, taken several years earlier, this time of the three daughters along with their little
brother, Israel, who appears to be about six years old, together with their
mother, Feiga, whom they called Fanny. The girls are in dark winter
dresses, and their brother, seated at his mother's knee, his hair cut very
short, is wearing small leather boots and a child's military-style tunic
with a large belt buckle, in the Russian fashion of the day. My future
grandmother, Rachel, perhaps eleven or twelve, holds a stem of lilies
gracefully across her lap. With her dark eyebrows and delicate features,
she is the prettiest of the daughters. She looks off to one side, unsmiling,

Rachel, in Harbin, about 1920.

distracted by some private thought. Again, Anna aims a direct, sensible gaze at the camera. Rebekah, standing tall in the back, wears an open, dreamy look on her face. By 1930 both she and her brother Israel would disappear into the Soviet gulag, never to be heard from again.

Rachel's parents may have been religious Jews, but she herself, at least later in life, was not. As she grew into a young woman, the city of Harbin also grew, becoming a thriving commercial and cultural center dominated by Russian culture, with opera and concert halls, Russian Orthodox churches and Jewish synagogues, and numerous nightclubs and restaurants. Although built on leased land deep within China, by 1916 Harbin had the largest population of Russians, including a substantial number of Russian Jews, of any urban center outside Imperial Russian territory. The tsar's design for a strong Russian presence in Manchuria had been fulfilled. Not for long, however. By the early 1920s, the defeat of the Russian army and navy by the Japanese in the Russo-Japanese War of 1904–1906 and Japan's own rapidly expanding colonial ambitions brought Manchuria increasingly under the political control of Japan. By 1931 Japan's annexation of the region would be complete, and Manchuria would become the puppet state of Manchuko. Additionally,

China's own Manchu Dynasty had fallen in 1911 to Sun Yat-sen's repub-
lican forces, leading to years of vicious infighting among Chinese rival
political factions, gangsters, and warlords. The Russian moment was not
destined to last.

By 1920, Rachel Cooper, age twenty-four, had become an attractive
and vivacious young woman, making the most of Harbin's nightclubs,
cabarets, and ballrooms. In one of these nightspots she met a Finnish
pearl trader named Edward Koskin, who had shortened his name from
Koskinen. He may have been a newspaper editor in Finland who fled
after the failed leftist revolution there—or so Helmi remembered being
told when she was young. His business interests in the Far East took
him back and forth between Harbin and Kobe, a major commercial seaport in Japan, where he was based. In Harbin, he patronized the lively
nightlife scene, as did most international visitors. He liked to dance.
Rachel was a lively and attractive young woman who also enjoyed dancing. In the few photographs that have survived, she has sparkling eyes
and a beguiling smile, with hair tightly curled in the 1920s flapper style.

～

DURING ONE OF MY LAST VISITS with her in the 1980s, I once again
asked Rachel—Baba—to tell me something of her past. She was residing in a nursing home by then. The conversation began, as it often did
during those late visits, with her in a state of confusion. She always recognized me, but she had plenty of trouble keeping track of other details.
On this occasion, she was particularly perplexed by a recent visit from
Helmi.

"Davidochka," she declared huskily, "it's so good of you to come." She
grabbed my arm and pulled me closer. She was seated on the edge of
her bed, and I was perched in a chair beside her. Her face had begun to
sprout whiskers around the chin, and it occurred to me to ask the nurse
later why she wasn't given a shave. Her voice dropped to a conspiratorial
whisper: "Listen to me. *She* has been here again."

"Who?" I said, feigning innocence, though I knew exactly who. "You
mean Helmi?"

"Yes, that one. Her. She says stupid things."

"Like what?"

"She says she is my daughter. Just imagine. Such an old lady! And she
claims to be *my* daughter. This is ridiculous. This must stop."

By now I knew better than to try to correct her, to avoid making her upset. Helmi had warned me not to argue with her, and I had learned to heed the warning.

"Well," I said, attempting to change the subject, "I'm living in a new place, with a couple of nice roommates." This was a lie. Actually, I was living with my girlfriend.

"Oh, that's nice," she said. "How many servants do you have?"

I couldn't help laughing. This was a new angle. "No servants," I said. "Nope. Not one. But do I ever wish." Then it occurred to me that maybe something from the past might be bubbling up here. I sensed a potential inroad. "Did you have servants? When you were young?—well, I mean, back in China, when you grew up?"

"Oh, yes," she said. "Certainly. Many servants. Chinese servants." She said this in a tone that conveyed mild annoyance, as if I were being dense. She gazed into the air somewhere above my head.

"That's great," I said. "Tell me more."

She looked at me sharply.

I tried to tamp down my eagerness. "Tell me anything you want."

Suddenly she smiled, and leaned over close. "Davidochka, do you want to know a secret?" Her breath was hot and smelled terrible, as if her dentures had been soaking in formaldehyde.

"Yes, I do," I said.

"I went to parties." Her voice was soft, conspiratorial. "I was very popular. I knew how to make a grand entrance." She leaned back triumphantly and laughed.

"How would you make your entrance?"

"I would go to a party, and I would make sure to always be late. Everyone else was there already. But I would wait, for the right moment. There would be a piano. And I would wait, and then I would run into the room, just so, and then jump! I would jump, up onto the piano!"

"That's fantastic," I said, and I meant it.

"Oh, yes. What an entrance. Everyone would remember me afterward. Then we would sing, and dance also. Oh, what an entrance I made."

I had never heard this story before, but it didn't occur to me for a second that she might be making it up. I felt at that moment, and still do today, that it was coming straight from her memory bank.

"What else?" I asked, breathlessly. "Please tell me more, Baba." I knew I was displaying too much eagerness, but I couldn't help it.

The sparkle in her eyes faded, and she eyed me with suspicion. For one brief moment I had been an ally, but now I was once more on the side of the untrustworthy.

"It's time to eat, I think," she said. "Come, take me to where we eat." And that was all I got. The subject was closed. It was time for lunch in the dining room. Not long after this visit, the curtain closed even further across her consciousness, and I never again had a chance to talk with her about her past. She lost track of who I was, and she showed no more interest in divulging any secrets.

Perhaps she met Edward Koskin, the Finnish businessman, not in a nightclub but at one of those parties. Perhaps he was charmed by her flamboyant entrance. He was an older man, in his early forties, a sophisticated traveler, an expatriate Finn in the Far East passing through Harbin to sell Japanese pearls. She, an impressionable and high-spirited young beauty in her mid-twenties, the daughter of Jewish colonists in Manchuria, was searching for a sense of identity in a foreign land. Perhaps such a party took place at the stately art deco Hotel Moderne, one of Harbin's most glamorous gathering places, built and owned by Russian Jews, or in another of the city's many Russian ballrooms or banquet halls.

Rachel might well have been employed for a time as a shopgirl in one of the large Jewish-owned department stores on Kitaiskaya Street. But after meeting Edward Koskin, she embarked on what her Harbin family probably viewed as an impetuous, even reckless, adventure—she followed him to Japan in 1921, settling in Kobe where his business interests were centered. She was twenty-five years old. Two years later, still unmarried, she and Edward had a daughter, giving her the Finnish name Helmi, which means *pearl*. A single family portrait survives, showing a tall, handsome man with pale eyes and a kind aspect, fifteen or so years older than the proud young mother beside him. Together they sit in a Kobe photo studio, holding between them a chubby baby girl, who stares with a clear and open gaze at the camera. This is how Helmi came to be born stateless: Japan was not a country that granted citizenship to foreigners born there. The new Soviet state had likewise revoked the citizenship of all Russians living abroad. So neither Rachel nor her

Rachel, Edward Koskin, and baby Helmi, in Kobe, 1923.

daughter were citizens of any country. This didn't seem to matter to them. Likewise, it didn't matter that Rachel had not married Edward. She took his name anyway, Koskin, and also bestowed it on their new daughter. The photograph clearly shows a happy family unit.

The baby, Helmi, who would one day become my mother, was born on July 15, 1923. Six weeks later, on September 1, at two minutes before noon, an earthquake lasting several minutes was felt in Kobe. No damage occurred locally. It would be three more days before a full account of what occurred would be published or broadcast. When the news came, it was hard to believe. The quake, centered near the population centers of Tokyo and Yokohama, 260 miles to the east, had reduced both of those cities to rubble. Combined with subsequent firestorms fed by typhoon-force winds, the quake killed over 240,000 people. It was the worst natural disaster in Japan's history. The tragic stories that emerged were as horrendous as they were numerous. Forty thousand unlucky souls were burned alive instantly when they were trapped by a firestorm that engulfed a gigantic abandoned warehouse where they had sought shelter. Many drowned by leaping off of bridges to escape the conflagration. Countless thousands more were crushed in their homes, office buildings, and hotels. False rumors spread rapidly that Koreans had somehow been responsible for setting the fires, and before order could be restored, more than six thousand innocent people of Korean descent were murdered by mobs of Japanese wielding knives and clubs, who seemed to have gone collectively insane. My grandmother, young, high-spirited, and nervous-tempered, as well as estranged from the rest of her family, unmarried, and sitting in Kobe with her new infant daughter to care for, would be strongly affected. No doubt she felt vulnerable and frightened. She would be reminded of the time in her own childhood when her family escaped death at the hands of a mob and fled Odessa for Harbin. She would be reminded that pain and terror can come out of nowhere and shatter a temporarily happy and safe existence.

Within three years, much more would change for Rachel. By 1926, war clouds would be gathering on the horizon in all directions, Edward would be gone, and she and her little daughter, Helmi, would be left on their own.

Telegram

Harbin, 1926

IN THE SUMMER of 1926, my grandmother Rachel, one month from her thirtieth birthday, journeyed from Japan with her now three-year-old daughter back to Harbin, China, where she had grown up, in order to introduce Helmi to her family. Edward Koskin, the Finnish man with whom she had fallen in love and who had fathered her child in Japan, stayed behind in Kobe to attend to his pearl-trading business. Rachel had not seen her parents in three years, and she hoped to repair their relationship.

Rachel and Helmi sailed by steamship to Port Arthur on the Chinese mainland, and then across Manchuria by way of the China Eastern Railroad. By this time, the liberal city of Harbin was in the process of another political transformation. Japan had embarked on an aggressive imperial expansion into the Asian mainland, exerting increased political and economic control, making life more difficult for the Russian immigrants who had founded the city. Within another ten years the Japanese would take full control of the Russian-built railroad, and Manchuria would become the puppet state of Manchukuo, part of Japan's rapidly expanding empire.

Harbin's Jews were now finding that life was not as free and open as it had been in the first two decades of the century. Since the Russian October Revolution, many White Russians had fled eastward and poured into Harbin and the other eastern frontier cities in large numbers, bringing with them their religious beliefs and cultural predilections, including a deep and virulent strain of antisemitism. The brief golden moment for Jews in the Far East was coming to an end. Even here in Manchuria, far beyond the borders of the new Soviet Union, persecution was increasing once again.

By the time of Rachel's return visit to Harbin with little Helmi, in 1926, her older sister Anna had married a man named Mr. Fishman and, with her own young daughter, called Olga—Helmi's first cousin—had moved south to Shanghai. Shanghai was China's most cosmopolitan city and had become a major center of international economic activity and yet another haven for refugees and expatriates of all kinds, including Jews. Within a few more years Rachel's two other siblings, Rebekah and Israel, would develop sympathies for the Russian Revolution, thinking, as many Jews did at the time, that the Communist order would foster a more hospitable atmosphere in the new Soviet Union. Eventually these two traveled back to the Soviet Union from Harbin, under a supposedly "open" Soviet policy of repatriation for Russian Jews. And, like hundreds of thousands of their countrymen, both Jews and non-Jews, Rebekah and Israel perished in Joseph Stalin's labor camps.

In the mid-1970s, nearly fifty years later, Rachel, now living in the United States and the only surviving member of her immediate family, received an official letter from the meticulous record-keepers in the Soviet government informing her that her sister Rebekah, who had died in a Stalinist labor camp, had left a small estate, which Rachel was entitled to recover. The catch was that she needed to appear in person in order to claim the estate. By now suffering from full-scale dementia along with her regular anxieties, she listened calmly as Helmi read the letter out loud to her. She believed, not unreasonably, that a person who traveled to the Soviet Union for such a purpose might never be allowed to return and might also die in Siberia. She sat up, looked her daughter straight in the eye, and declared, "You couldn't drag me there." The so-called inheritance would remain unclaimed. The Soviet letter was thrown in the trash.

Yet in 1926, when Rachel took her daughter from Japan back to visit Harbin, there was still an intact family, parents and siblings, to greet them. The meeting was no doubt joyous, despite Rachel having run off three years earlier with Edward Koskin. Helmi was a lively and cherubic little girl who charmed all who met her. The joy, however, would be short-lived. Within a week of Rachel and Helmi's arrival in Harbin, word was received by telegram that back in Japan, Edward Koskin, while walking in the hills overlooking Kobe harbor, had collapsed and died of a heart attack. His body was found by some Japanese hikers.

At first the news was withheld from Rachel. Seventy years later, long after Rachel's death, Helmi learned from her cousin Olga about this delay. Even as a young woman, Rachel was high-strung and volatile, and the family had been afraid of the traumatic effect on her of the news of Edward's death. A major factor adding to the difficulty of these events was the fact that Rachel and Edward had never married. Whether or not Rachel suffered any shame for not being a proper widow, it certainly meant that she was not entitled to any inheritance from Edward Koskin, despite having adopted his last name under the pretense of being married. She was now a single mother with no means of income. For a time Rachel and Helmi stayed in Harbin with Rachel's parents, but Solomon and Feiga were not in a position to provide much support. Solomon's medical practice had begun to shrink. And Harbin had become crowded with thousands of new refugees, Tsarists fleeing the Russian Revolution, bringing with them their virulent antisemitism. Soon they outnumbered Jews ten to one, and Harbin was no longer the haven it had been.

What to do? Where to go? With Helmi's father gone, it made no sense to return to Kobe. Rachel had no prospects there. Meanwhile, Harbin was descending into near-chaos. Nearly every morning the newspapers reported bodies found in the gutters. In the streets Tsarists and Communists murdered each other, Japanese and Chinese murdered each other, and various Chinese factions—supporters of the new republic, supporters of the old imperial order, and followers of the war lords—also took turns murdering each other. Nobody was being nice to the Jews. As ever, there were plenty who hoped to make them scapegoats for the various troubles. Department stores and other Jewish businesses were closing. A single Jewish mother such as Rachel had few prospects for supporting herself and not much future to look forward to in Harbin. In truth, she was in a state of desperation.

Word came of a good place to go, another haven of relative freedom: the western-controlled treaty port of Shanghai to the south. It was the new open city. Rachel's older sister Anna, by now a single mother herself with her own young daughter to support—having divorced the aforementioned Mr. Fishman—wrote from Shanghai to offer Rachel and four-year-old Helmi a place to stay. Anna may have been husband-less now, but she was far from helpless. She was a tough, enterprising young woman and had found a way to sustain herself. Making use of her own excellent English, she rented a Shanghai tenement building from an American landlord and was subletting most of the rooms for income. And so, in the spring of 1927, Rachel accepted her sister's invitation. She carried her daughter, not yet three years old, to the Harbin station and took the train south to Shanghai. There was nowhere else to go.

Refugee—Harbin to Shanghai

The Garden Bridge, Shanghai, August 14, 1937, looking south toward the riverfront Bund. The bridge is crowded with Chinese refugees escaping the Japanese attacks in the northern Hongkou neighborhood. Courtesy of the Hoover Institution Library and Archives, Randall Chase Gould papers, Album fH, Stanford University.

Soothing the Barbarian

Shanghai, 1927

In the 1920s Shanghai was unlike any other city in the Far East: it was the richest and most powerful urban center in all of Asia, yet not truly an Asian city. Its workforce was overwhelmingly poor and Chinese, but the wealth that built and maintained its economic engines was Western. Shanghai was the largest trading port in the Far East, but its trade was almost entirely controlled by British, European, and American banks and businesses. Even its municipal government was a polyglot of international control—separate districts answering to the laws of different nations, and in some areas to no laws at all. It was one of the few major ports in the world that required no entrance visa or passport from immigrants. Anyone could freely come to Shanghai from anywhere. Consequently, the city was a haven for those who, for one reason or another, found themselves stateless.

Shanghai, in Chinese, means "above the sea." The city was, in fact, built barely above sea level on former swampland beside the Huangpu River, which continues north for ten miles to join the delta of the Yangtze, China's great river and the trade route to its vast interior. In a mere eighty years it had grown from a modest Chinese trading port into a sprawling international metropolis. China's defeat in the Opium Wars of the nineteenth century had resulted in the granting of free-trade agreements to Britain, France, and the United States. Shanghai was the largest of five designated "treaty ports," created for the benefit of the western colonial powers as a result of the Chinese policy of appeasement known as "soothing the Barbarian."

The opium trade was the foundation of an explosively expanding economy. The city's downtown skyline of imposing structures that hugged the curve of the river, huge banks with colonnades and clock towers alongside luxurious hotels with copper spires, was mostly erected in the bustling decade between 1920 and 1930. The broad boulevard fronting the river, formerly a mud towpath, was called the Bund. The name, taken from a Hindustani word meaning "waterfront embankment," was given by traders from the East India Company in the early nineteenth century. The rest of the city spread out behind the river, its residents representing every stratum of the human economic scale. Stately mansions lined the broad leafy boulevards of the French Concession west of the Bund, providing luxurious homes to Western diplomats and business moguls, wealthy drug dealers, and gangsters, while north of the river, and further out along a vast network of ditches and smaller tributaries, were spread wide expanses of narrow streets and alleys where much of the city's population, Chinese and foreigners alike, dwelled in various levels of poverty. Along the ditch banks and bordering the railroad lines, numerous shantytowns had sprung up, made up of tiny shacks and makeshift hovels. Here, as well as on homemade rafts, junks, and sampans floating in the creeks and in flimsy shelters thrown up in the gutters and alleys, lived Chinese coolies and beggars, the poorest of the poor.

Rachel Koskin, a single mother not yet thirty, and Helmi, her toddler daughter, were among the many Shanghai immigrants with no citizenship, no documentation, no papers, no passport. The Bolshevik Revolution in Russia had eventually resulted in those who had considered themselves Russian nationals but who had lived outside Russian borders—in Russian-controlled Manchuria, for instance—being stripped of their Russian citizenship. This meant that Rachel's entire family in Harbin became stateless. And so, Helmi and her mother, both now stateless, came to Shanghai, most likely by train directly from Harbin, to join Rachel's older sister Anna and Anna's daughter, Olga, who was nine years older than Helmi. The open port of Shanghai was considered a place of refuge, just as the frontier city of Harbin had been twenty years before. It was one of the last such places in all of Asia.

Anna and Olga lived in the Hongkou district of Shanghai, close to the Huangpu River near where it made a sharp bend to the east in the heart of the city. The neighborhood was known to the foreign population as Wayside. Their tiny apartment was on the third floor of a brick tenement building at the corner of Congping Road and Broadway, the district's main thoroughfare, one block from the riverfront docks. Hongkou made up the northern half of what was designated the International Settlement, governed jointly by American and British interests ever since the loss of Chinese sovereignty over the city. Originally settled by Chinese refugees from the countryside during China's many decades of dynastic civil strife, the Hongkou district was now to a large degree occupied by the most destitute class of international refugees, many of whom were Russian. Some were Jews, and many more were the formerly Tsarist White Russians. In time, still more Jewish refugees would pour into Shanghai, following the wide-scale persecutions of the 1930s in Europe. The wealthier residents of Shanghai lived elsewhere—the shaded avenues of the French Concession, or the bustling streets of the southern half of the International Settlement nearer the Bund, on the opposite side of Suzhou Creek. These were the places with modern luxuries like toilets and hot tap water. And chauffeurs and gardeners.

When she was asked much later, at age seventy-five, to describe where she had grown up, Helmi merely said, matter-of-factly, "It was a slum." Pressed to elaborate, she shrugged and said, "You know what a slum is," then quickly added, "Well, actually, I suppose you don't. So, imagine the filthiest conditions you can think of. Whatever you can dream up, I guarantee Shanghai was worse."

Helmi's first language was English. Her mother spoke English well, although with a thick Russian accent. Helmi's Finnish father, Edward Koskin, had also been fluent in English as well as several other languages. Rachel insisted on speaking English to Helmi from the very beginning, knowing full well that it was the most common language among foreigners everywhere in the Far East, including in Shanghai. Languages came naturally to Helmi, and she grew up speaking fluent Russian as well as English. Around the house, she also learned to understand Yiddish from her mother and her Auntie Anna. Later on, in school, she would excel in both French and German. No one in the family learned Chinese. It was rare for any foreigner in Shanghai, rich or poor, to learn the difficult language of the native population. With the Chinese, foreigners spoke Pidgin English ("pidgin" being a Chinese slang term for "business"), comprising mainly English words with a smattering of Chinese, Indian, and Portuguese. This hybrid dialect had evolved over nearly a century to become a useful common denominator for communication with the Chinese citizenry who, after all, made up 90 percent of the city's population.

It was clear that Helmi was an exceptionally bright child. She learned to read at a very early age, despite the fact that Rachel held her back from going to school until the age of nine. Sixty-five years later, Helmi said she always understood this was because of her supposedly fragile health and the persistent cough she had as a young girl. All her life Rachel was terrified of germs and disease. The apartment in Shanghai had cold water but no toilet, and Helmi was made to use her own chamber pot, separate from the one shared by everyone else in the household. Every morning the "night soil" was collected and carted away by the Chinese "honey pot" man. Rachel also subscribed to some peculiar dietary beliefs. Young Helmi was required to consume a quarter-pound of butter a day, Rachel apparently having concluded that this was beneficial for her daughter's proper development. As a result the little girl grew quite chubby, even as her chronic cough persisted.

There were other reasons for keeping Helmi at home in Shanghai. Rachel no doubt feared for her daughter's safety in a city that was steadily becoming more dangerous. Bankers, businessmen, warlords, racketeers, opium dealers, murderers, thieves, petty crooks, revolutionaries, and reactionaries, representing virtually every nation on earth and every political persuasion, vied against each other for power and profit, frequently with violent results. Throughout the late 1920s and 1930s, pitched battles between various gangs and warring factions were frequently waged in the streets of Shanghai. For a single mother with meager financial resources who was responsible for the safety and welfare of a young daughter and who shared a cramped flat with another single mother in one of Shanghai's grimy waterfront neighborhoods, life must have been daunting. Rachel had her own memories of growing up under harrowing circumstances. If she feared for the life of her daughter amid the chaos of the Shanghai streets and therefore chose to keep her at home most of the time, it would not be hard to understand why.

By the 1920s Shanghai had become a flashpoint for conflicts that within the next two decades would engulf the world. The year 1925 marked a change in relations between the Chinese and the coalition of colonial powers that had shared economic and political control of the city, and by extension the rest of China. This was a year of massive anti-imperialist strikes by Chinese workers—which began in Shanghai and

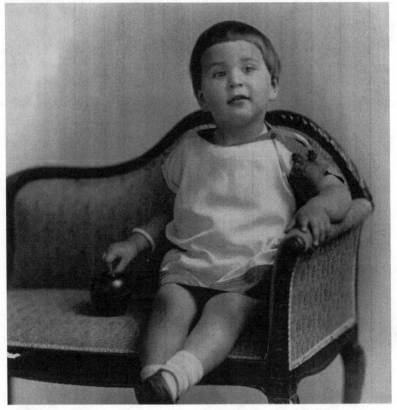

Helmi, in Kobe, 1925.

then spread to other cities—against the powerful colonial interests, particularly the Japanese and the British, with the goal of abolishing the foreign concessions. Beginning in May of that year, strikes, demonstrations, and protests occurred frequently, with the inevitable violent reprisals. Trade and shipping would shut down, military forces would take to the streets, and it was considered unsafe for foreigners to be out on the sidewalks in certain districts.

By 1928, a year after Helmi and Rachel arrived to live with Anna and Olga, permanent steel-gated barricades had been erected on many streets to separate the International Settlement from the Chinese district. Meanwhile, civil strife between the newly minted Communist movement and the Chinese Nationalists was also boiling over into horrific violence. Deals and ceasefires were brokered between warlords and gangsters with the backing of the foreigners, particularly the British, who desperately hoped to maintain control over their respective treaty concessions—but not before many thousands of working-class Chinese were killed in the clashes. Bodies were strewn in the streets or dumped into the Huangpu River and Suzhou Creek. In some of the Chinese neighborhoods, severed heads were placed in bird cages and strung from telegraph poles. The city's loosely stitched social patchwork was coming apart at the seams. No wonder Helmi's mother continued to keep her close to home.

In an earlier photograph—most likely taken in 1925 in a photographer's studio back in Kobe—Helmi gazes out at the world with clear eyes, a plump, cherubic little girl of two in a miniature silk dress. She is seated on a child's-sized upholstered couch with her legs neatly crossed, one elbow resting on the couch's arm and the fingers of her other hand holding an artificial apple: a remarkably mature pose. Her round face tilts upward with an expression that can almost be described as bemused. She looks comfortable in this pose, her gaze radiant, open, curious. She wears the confident expression of a precocious little girl who will soon learn to read on her own before she is even sent to school and who will one day become fluent in many languages. In this setting, she could be mistaken for the pampered daughter of a wealthy foreign family—British diplomats, say, or well-heeled European or American business managers. She appears both happy and healthy, a child who has been reared, so far, in a nurturing and secure environment. This photo was taken before the death of Helmi's father, Edward Koskin, and before the great change in her mother's circumstances and the move to Shanghai. Remarkably, the traits of confidence and cheerfulness that are so evident in the photo would become permanent characteristics, despite the many hardships and trials that lay ahead.

The Garden Bridge

Shanghai, 1931

DAILY LIFE WAS not easy in the one-room flat on Congping Road for the Russian sisters, Anna and Rachel, and their daughters, Olga and Helmi. They cooked on a hotplate, stored their bedrolls folded in a corner during the day, and kept their "honey pots" on the floor behind a curtain. For teenage Olga, the cramped existence became intolerable, and in 1931, at age eighteen, she moved out to get married. She relocated with her new husband, a German Catholic named Kurt Gurski, to a better neighborhood in the French Concession—and a house with hot water and real plumbing. Not much is known about Mr. Gurski, but it seems he was prosperous enough to provide a comfortable home for Olga, at least for the time being. So by the time Helmi turned eight, in 1931, the tenement household on Congping Road was made up of just three females—Helmi and her mother, plus Auntie Anna.

The year 1931 was also when Japan began invading China in force, initially with a rapid takeover of Manchuria in the north. Harbin, where Rachel and Anna's parents remained, would soon become part of the Japanese puppet state of Manchuko. Life for both Russian Jews and White Russians was fast becoming more difficult, and the exodus south to the reputedly safer haven of Shanghai by those who could afford the rail or shipfare increased. The Russian population of Shanghai began to swell. By 1932 the city's population ballooned to well over three million, approximately the size of Chicago's, with 70,000 of the residents being foreigners. Of these, 20,000 were Russians, most of whom were concentrated in the Hongkuo neighborhoods, including Wayside—known today as Tilanqiao.

Over the next seven or eight years, as many as 20,000 Jews escaping from the ravaged, Nazi-controlled cities of Central and Eastern

Europe would arrive on the Shanghai docks, many destined to settle in this already overcrowded district. The area was made up of tile-roofed brick and wooden tenements, as well as factories and shops servicing the Huangpu River wharves. A notorious local landmark in the neighborhood was the huge prison complex known as Ward Road Gaol, occupying several city blocks in the heart of the residential district just north of Broadway, its high barbed wire-topped walls casting long shadows across the busy sidewalks of Ward Road (now Chankiang Lu). Only a block from the prison was one of Shanghai's first Ashkenazi Jewish houses of worship, the Ohel Moishe synagogue, constructed in 1927, and Anna, Rachel, and Helmi's flat on Congping Road was another three blocks away.

Throughout the 1920s and '30s Ward Road Gaol was one of the largest prisons in the world. Controlled by the British and staffed by Indian Sikhs, it housed over six thousand Chinese and foreign inmates on a seventeen-acre site. Eventually this sprawling urban detention complex, further enlarged under the Maoists after 1949, would accommodate up to 30,000 densely packed prisoners. Today known as Tilanqiao Prison, it still holds a mixture of Chinese political dissidents, peace activists, and hardened criminals.

By the 1930s Wayside was a Russian-dominated neighborhood. White Russians had been coming to Shanghai since 1918, and Russian Jews from Manchuria continued to arrive in large numbers, mostly from Harbin, Vladivostok, and other northeastern outposts. Overall the Russian population was the second largest of the foreign groups, surpassed only by the Japanese. Broadway, the main commercial boulevard that ran parallel to the river, was lined with small Russian businesses, restaurants, bakeries, and tea parlors. On the street many languages could be heard, but in that particular sector of Shanghai, well into the late 1930s, Russian was the most prevalent.

When she went out to the market in the mornings, Rachel would take Helmi along, gripping her hand tightly and admonishing her every block or so to stick very close. She kept the grocery allowance given to her by her sister in a small purse hidden deep within the folds of her coat.

By nature Rachel was chronically anxious, with a predilection for worrying out loud. Indeed, there was plenty to worry about. God only knew the evils that lurked everywhere, not to mention right in their own neighborhood. She worried about germs and disease, and about criminals and gangs on the streets. She worried about the hordes of foulmouthed, filthy sailors and dockworkers that tromped up the street day and night from the jetties and wharves at the end of the block. She worried about rumors of impending war on the streets of Shanghai, perhaps between China and Japan, or between the Chinese Communists and Nationalists or, God forbid, between the entire world and the helpless Jews. She worried about her parents in Harbin, suffering new privations because of the Japanese aggression in Manchuria, and about her younger brother, Israel, and sister Rebekah, both of whom had answered the patriotic call to return to Russia from Harbin and join the Soviet Revolution—and neither of whom had been heard from. And most of all, she worried about her daughter's future. Olga, her niece, had found a way out of the Hongkou slum by marrying. Olga's mother, Anna, did the important work of managing the building, collecting rents from the tenants, and dealing with the American property owner, the Asia Realty Corporation. Rachel and Helmi, her bright-eyed daughter with the constant cough, had moved into the tiny apartment as true refugees and were entirely dependent on Auntie Anna for their survival. Rachel helped with the shopping and with the constant work of keeping the apartment clean.

To get to the market, mother and daughter went down two flights of stairs, out the alley to the street, and a few steps north to the corner, where they turned left and crossed Congping Road. Following Broadway westward toward the center of the city, they were heading for the enormous Hongkou Market, the largest in all of Shanghai, ten blocks away. In the opposite direction, eastward, Broadway became Wayside Road, which followed the course of the river toward the heavy industrial district of Yangshepu. Frequently Rachel and Helmi would catch the double-decker bus or the electric-powered streetcar, but if the weather was pleasant and time allowed, they walked all the way to the market.

The sidewalks teemed with myriad forms of humanity—Chinese, Japanese, Russians, Poles, Portuguese, British, Americans, and Jews from practically everywhere. Halfway along Rachel and Helmi's route, Broadway crossed Hongkou Creek, part of Shanghai's network of ditches originally dug to drain the swamps, and met up with Boone Road going north and south. Hands gripped tightly, mother and daughter turned north and made their way as quickly as possible through the crowds, passing stalls and shops with every sign written in a different language. The street was filled with vehicles of all kinds, including a few automobiles and trucks, but the traffic was mostly made up of handcarts, rickshaws, pedicabs, bicycles, and other wheeled conveyances powered by human beings, virtually all of them Chinese. Many of the handcarts were piled with enormous loads, including clay pots that contained the "night soil" from the local tenements, on their way to neighborhood collection sites and finally to the outlying countryside, there to be used as fertilizer on the farms that in turn supplied produce to the city. As the carts rumbled by, the stink would mix with the other smells of the street to produce an effect Helmi would later say stayed with her more vividly than any other memory of Shanghai.

After another two blocks they would come to a large triangular plaza created by the intersection of three major streets—Boone Road, Hanbury Road, and Miller Road. Occupying the entire space of the plaza, an area the size of several city blocks, was the Hongkou Market, a sprawling five-story complex, open to the air on the street side, where farmers from the outskirts of the city would bring their meat, eggs, and produce every morning. Rachel would tighten her already viselike grip on Helmi's hand and then lean over and sternly remind her daughter to never, under any circumstances, let go. She would tell her first in English, then in Russian. She was determined that her daughter be fluent in English, this vital language of the West, the *lingua franca* of wealth and power. Some of her Russian friends in Shanghai thought she was putting on airs by insisting on speaking English so much, but it had nothing to do with appearances. It had everything to do with hard reality, with simple survival. If there was ever to be a way out of these dangerous and filthy streets, she knew that it would only come by way of speaking fluent English.

Together, hand melded to hand as if sharing the same bones, mother and daughter arrived at the corner entrance to the teeming market and made their way inside. There they encountered stall after stall piled with vegetables, live and butchered chickens, fish and eels swimming in barrels, beef, pork, burlap sacks of rice, baked goods, dry goods, fabric, medicines. This was the main market for the sprawling urban area rapidly expanding north of the Huangpu River. It served Hongkou, the northern sector of the International Settlement, plus the huge adjacent district known as Zhapei, the Chinese-governed zone spreading far out to the east and north. The hordes of people jostling and shouting reflected the polyglot population of Shanghai—Chinese, many wearing traditional long gowns, including the men; Japanese, many of whom wore western-style clothes; Russians, both White and Jewish, some ragtag and forlorn and others dressed stylishly, depending on their economic status; tall Sikhs, in colorful robes and thick beards and turbans; and occasional American or British or French women from the wealthy section of the International Settlement on the other side of the creek, accompanied by their Chinese cooks and their children with nannies called *amahs*, their chauffeured cars idling nearby, braving the chaos of the market before crossing back over the bridge and returning to their comfortable homes.

If the weather happened to be exceptionally fine, when they finished their shopping Rachel and Helmi would continue walking a few blocks west, carrying their groceries in cloth sacks, through the rapidly expanding Japanese neighborhood, to Suzhou Creek and the Garden Bridge, which crossed the narrow creek just before it emptied into the much larger Huangpu River. Crossing the creek meant entering another world. On the south side of the bridge, Shanghai immediately presented its imposing Western façade—the line of colonnaded banks, hotels, and commercial houses facing the river along the boulevard known as the Bund. As Rachel and Helmi reached the north end of the bridge, they passed the elegant Astor House on their left, China's first western-style hotel, and on their right the twenty-story sand-colored Broadway Mansions, Shanghai's first luxury apartment house.

The Garden Bridge, still in use today, is a narrow and unimposing structure—a short span, two hundred feet in length, supported by a simple double-arched metal lattice known as a camelback truss—but its modest size belies its importance to the modern history of Shanghai. Built by the British in 1907 to replace a flimsy wooden bridge, it was the first structure in the city to use high-grade steel shipped from England, and for over half a century it was the gateway into Shanghai's foreign-dominated central district. Known today as the Waibaidu Bridge, it was refurbished in advance of the 2010 Shanghai Expo, and it still functions as the main route crossing Suzhou Creek at its juncture with the river. Once a symbol of colonial control over China, the bridge is now one of Shanghai's official Architecture Heritage sites.

As they walked across the bridge, mother and daughter looked down onto a vast array of watercraft—junks, sampans, barges piled with bales and barrels of goods, water ferries crammed with passengers, and fleets of flimsy homemade rafts serving as houseboats for families. Further out in the river were ships—steamers, freighters, warships, and passenger liners—all seemingly jockeying for space at the dozens of docks that lined the shore. Shanghai was the busiest commercial port in the entire Far East through the first half of the twentieth century.

Once across the Garden Bridge, Rachel and Helmi would step a few paces to their left and enter the handsomely landscaped Public Garden, occupying a triangular plaza on a spit of land that jutted into the Huangpu River. Here there were manicured lawns and trees, carefully tended flower beds and shrubs, ornamental cast-iron benches, and a small gazebo, as well as a larger bandstand. The park was a quiet place for them to sit and look out toward the river at the ship traffic, or down along the arc of the Bund at the imposing colonnaded and copper-peaked buildings, or back the way they had come toward their own Hongkou neighborhood, with its low-lying tenements, warehouses, dockyards and—further downriver—its rows of belching smokestacks. Here in the park, at least for a few moments, a person could breathe different air and imagine another kind of life.

There were others enjoying the park, representing Shanghai's full range of nationalities, even Chinese. Prior to 1927, Chinese had been prohibited from entering the park's gates, unless acting as servants or *amahs* for foreigners. And even now, after three years under the liberalized regulations, Chinese people were still careful to keep well apart from foreigners in the city parks that were under the jurisdiction of the International Settlement. On a typical weekday afternoon, the visitors were mostly white-skinned—British, American, French, Dutch, German—plus, lately, an increasing number of well-dressed Japanese. There were women pushing prams or businessmen taking a brief break from their offices on the Bund. These were people who likely had hot water in their homes, real bedrooms, and sewer service, and who probably didn't even need to boil their drinking water. Eight-year-old Helmi would have heard mostly English, the language of privilege and comfort, spoken on the park's well-kept pathways.

This was another reason Rachel liked to bring her here, to observe and listen. And although still only a little girl, Helmi kept her eyes and ears wide open. She easily saw that another way of life existed here on the other side of the creek in Shanghai, a life entirely different from her own. She learned that there were those who experienced beautiful gardens and fountains and carefully swept walkways as their natural right, who enjoyed leisure and relaxation as a daily habit.

After sitting a while, perhaps sometimes even sharing a small treat they had purchased from the market—a sweet Chinese pastry or even an American Hershey Bar—Rachel and Helmi would gather up their groceries and leave the park the way they had come, recross the Garden Bridge, and, on the other side of the creek, catch the streetcar that would carry them down along East Broadway and back into the noisy and smelly heart of Hongkou, toward home.

Reno, Nevada

1955

WHEN I WAS A LITTLE BOY, I would accompany my grandmother Rachel—Baba, to me—on trips downtown on Saturday afternoons. Carrying a small bag of bread crumbs to feed to the ducks in the park, we rode the Arlington Avenue bus, which stopped at the corner of Mount Rose Street, three blocks from our house: a ride that took us north about fifteen blocks, across the Truckee River, and into the heart of downtown Reno. I was eager for the chocolate soda I knew Baba would buy me at the lunch counter at Woolworth's after we finished our errands, but I also remember feeling a nervous kind of anticipation, a sense of apprehension that we were embarking on a journey that, while seemingly safe and predictable, nevertheless always held out the possibility of danger. Thinking back, I know that by nature I was easily excitable, but I also believe that to a large degree my grandmother imparted that feeling of nervousness to me. Only recently settled in America, newly made a legitimate citizen for the first time in her life, Baba no doubt embarked on these afternoon expeditions into this strange new American city, this gambling mecca perched on the edge of the western desert, with a certain trepidation that was contagious to a small boy.

The Reno municipal buses of the 1950s were a beautiful color, a vivid red-orange, with cream-colored trim. They had noisy diesel engines and belched puffs of black smoke when they accelerated. We would walk the three blocks together, her hand clamped tightly over mine, and then we would sit together on the green wooden bench at the bus stop, watching for the bus. At the time, I had almost no notion of the life she had led before she became my grandmother and moved to Reno, of her experiences escaping the pogroms in Odessa as a girl, growing up stateless in Harbin, or living through war and hardship and aerial bombings in Shanghai and Kobe. She was simply Baba, my Russian grandmother, who lived with us and helped my mother cook and clean and take care of my brother and me. Terry and I were certainly aware that she came from a foreign land: she spoke Russian at home in the kitchen, Yiddish on the phone with her Jewish friends, and English with an accent exactly like Boris and Natasha on *The Rocky and Bullwinkle Show*. She baked fabulous goodies with strange names. Even when I was very small, I remember feeling proud in the knowledge that our family was different in this way, that through Baba we were connected somehow to mysteries that inhabited the larger world.

I have no doubt that my mother was happy as well about these Saturday outings. Helmi must have been excited to get us both out of the house and out of her way for a few hours. Maybe she took advantage of the time to study her lines for a play she was in; she had begun performing in amateur productions put on by the Reno Little Theater. Or maybe she just took a nap. Our dad, Bill, worked six long days a week at the hardware store and so was never home on Saturdays. Compared to my introspective and bookish brother, I was a boisterous little pest. Terry, two and a half years older than me, took after our dad; quiet and studious, he was capable of spending all Saturday afternoon sprawled on his bed with his nose in a book. Meanwhile, I prowled the house craving noisier entertainment. I liked to put on my red cowboy hat and do a stiff-legged impression of Chester from *Gunsmoke*, or act out the Saturday morning episode of *Big Jon and Sparkie* we had just listened to on the radio ("Over the Falls in an Airplane!") to get my mother laughing and my grandmother wringing her hands. The two of us, Baba and me, were the high-maintenance members of the family. By the mid-1950s Baba had already begun exhibiting signs of mental instability. Her brow was perpetually darkened by mysterious trials and tribulations that were hers alone to bear. *Oy Bozhomoi!*—her cry of alarm, meaning *Oh, my God!*—rang through the house several times a day. She worried aloud about everything: germs, criminals, unnamed perils lurking behind every bush and lamppost. To a five-year-old kid, Baba's perpetual anxiety was a source of fascination as well as a major feature of her comedic charm. I loved her, not least for her entertainment value.

Reno was a different place then, a small town made up of mostly family-run businesses, including the gambling establishments. At the corner where we caught the bus was a vast sloping lawn, dotted with evergreen trees, leading up to an elegant cupola-topped brick mansion that was home to the Mapes family, early pioneers of the hotel/casino business. The Mapes Hotel was the seat of their wealth and prestige, a twelve-story art deco edifice overlooking the north bank of the Truckee River, the city's paragon of elegance and the tallest building in town. The Sky Room, occupying the hotel's entire top floor, was considered Reno's classiest showplace, featuring the most famous entertainers of their day—the Marx Brothers, Frank Sinatra, Liberace, Judy Garland, Lena Horne, and Milton Berle.

To a small boy in the 1950s the Mapes Sky Room seemed impossibly high and far away and magnificently glamorous. I held out a fantasy that I would someday, somehow, perform on the stage there. By the time this dream came true—twenty years later, when I was a member of a rock band playing alternate sets with a strip show called the *Fun & Dames Review*—the Mapes Sky Room was a far cry from its glory days as the classiest showplace in town. Within a few more years, in 1982, the entire hotel went bankrupt and was boarded up for good. After sitting empty and derelict for nearly two decades, on Super Bowl Sunday in the year 2000 the building was finally demolished and scraped away as part of an effort to modernize and improve Reno's deteriorating downtown.

In 1955 a little boy and his Russian grandmother could catch the big red bus at the corner right in front of the Mapes family mansion and ride into downtown Reno for lunch at Woolworth's and a few shopping errands; stroll hand-in-deathgrip-hand down the sidewalks and along the river; perhaps sit for a few minutes along the riverfront in Wingfield Park feeding the ducks; and then ride home again, feeling as comfortable and safe as a world fraught with invisible dangers would allow. Baba was ever vigilant, keeping a watchful and suspicious eye out for anyone or anything that might leap out of the town's hustle and bustle to do us harm. But no harm ever came.

We strolled beneath the archway straddling Virginia Street that declared Reno to be "The Biggest Little City in the World." We ambled along Commercial Row, paralleling the railroad tracks, where my Irish grandfather's original hardware store, called Commercial Hardware Company, was tucked among the other small storefronts. Two doors down, at the corner, was another hardware store, also family-owned, called Reno Mercantile, whose owner back in 1910 had made a loan to my grandfather, his employee, allowing him to start his own business. That was the kind of town Reno was, or appeared to be, in those days: two family-owned hardware stores, almost next door to each other, could both thrive with loyal, local clientele. We stood beneath the three-story-high mural on the side of Harolds Club, depicting a silly Technicolor scene of frontier adventure: coonskin-capped pioneers camped with covered wagons and war-painted Indians lurking in the rocks above. We walked back toward the river, past the sparkling marquee of the Majestic Theater on Center Street, and then stood gazing up in wonder at my favorite downtown sign of all, mounted over the corner entrance to the Mapes Hotel: the word "Mapes" in huge cursive letters, with the capital "M" made of the adjoined, chaps-adorned legs of two gigantic and comical neon cowboys. My gaze followed the red-brick and white-tiled walls twelve stories upward to the distant floor-to-ceiling windows of the Sky Room, blazing with reflected sunlight. Then Baba once more tightened her grip on my hand and spun me around to pay attention to the next urgent task: crossing the street. Down the block was Woolworth's, our true destination.

We had probably already made several other stops—to Patterson's Men's Store for some socks for my dad, to Tony's Delicatessen for some cheese and pickles. Finally we were granted the privilege of plopping down on a couple of chrome stools at Woolworth's. I had my chocolate soda, which always managed to exceed my imagination in deliciousness. Baba simply had a cup of tea. She rarely ate anything in public, mainly because doing so would involve taking out her false teeth. For as long as I could remember, her teeth had been a frightening pair of creepy removable choppers that spent all night soaking in a glass beside the bathroom sink and for some unfathomable reason always had to be removed when she ate. What were they for, anyway? At home, her food of choice was canned baby food. Pureed vegetables and fruit and, worst of all, pureed meat. Terry and I found this profoundly disgusting, but we were required to be polite and keep quiet about it at the table during family meals.

Baba and I were a common sight downtown in those days, the wiry lady with a wrinkled brow and dark circles under her eyes, towing a five-year-old boy up to the Woolworth's soda fountain and briskly instructing him in a couple of different languages to keep his hands to himself. I perched on the stool and slurped my soda while she sipped her tea and kept a lookout for evildoers. Then she paid with silver dollars from her big black purse and we walked the two blocks to the river with our bread crumbs to spread for the ducks, then made our way another block to catch our bus. The trip never varied much, but I always returned with a satisfying sense of accomplishment. Our mettle had been tested, and the challenge had been met. We had ridden the red bus across the river and, after braving the hazards of the city, returned home unharmed. Helmi always received us with a smile of delight and open arms, grateful to have had a brief respite from us both.

Shanghai

2008

THE CORNER OF Congping Lu and Dongdamin Lu (*Lu* means street) is two blocks north of the docks that hug the bank of the Huangpu River, which snakes through the heart of Shanghai. In the autumn of 2008, I stood curbside on Congping Lu a few feet south of this corner, in front of a tall metal gatepost which marked the entrance to a large parking lot for trucks and construction vehicles. This parking lot now occupies the block where Helmi lived for most of her years growing up in Shanghai. Dongdamin Lu is a major east-west arterial in that sector of the city. In the 1930s the street was called Wayside Road east of its intersection with Congping Lu. To the west, as it meandered toward Shanghai's central business district along the river, it was called Broadway.

This neighborhood, still called Hongkou, is the northern part of what was once designated the International Settlement. In recent years the entire Shanghai riverfront has undergone drastic renovation. Huge hotels and colossal high-rise office buildings have sprung up everywhere, and the former industrial docks have been completely rebuilt to accommodate enormous modern freighters and luxury cruise ships. In the 1920s and 1930s, by contrast, the northern International Settlement was a dense neighborhood of narrow streets and tiny meandering alleys packed with hastily built two- and three-story brick tenements housing many of the city's poorer foreign immigrants.

Standing on the street, I held in my hand a photograph of Helmi standing next to that same tall gatepost. The snapshot was taken in 1987 by her second husband, Jack McCorkle. The gatepost was now a different color than it was in the twenty-one-year-old photograph, but it was unmistakably the same.

44

Helmi and Jack had traveled from their home in Reno to the Far East as part of an AARP tour, when they were both sixty-four years old. The trip had been her husband's idea. Jack had developed an intense interest in Helmi's personal history and convinced her to revisit scenes of her youth for the first time. She was extremely reluctant to make the trip, and had refused Jack's entreaties for several years. She was particularly nervous about returning to Shanghai. She always said that she had grown up in a slum and felt very lucky to have escaped, and she had no interest in going back again. But in the 1980s China had just begun to open its doors to westerners and was allowing limited tourism, and finally she allowed Jack to book the trip. She did it only for him, she said, to satisfy his curiosity. This was the only way to get him to stop nagging her to go. She put her trust in him to get her there and bring her home safely.

After a week in Japan, their first stop in China was Shanghai. The tour was tightly orchestrated, but Jack managed to secure permission for them to leave their group for a few hours in order to go to the former International District. They took a cab across the Garden Bridge, which still spanned Suzhou Creek where it meets the Huangpu River, and turned east along Dongdamin Lu, following the riverbank toward Helmi's old neighborhood. She knew exactly where to tell the cab to stop, at the corner of Congping Lu. She said later that when they stepped out onto the street, she knew immediately where she was, though not by any obvious landmarks. The familiar smell of the Shanghai waterfront hit her, a mixture of pungent odors: smoke, the river itself, sewage. She resisted a moment of panic as the cab left them standing on the curb. She managed to get out once, long ago, and now here she was again.

Congping Lu was unchanged. Brick and wooden tenement-style dwellings with crumbling tiled roofs stood packed together, facing tiny alleys barely wide enough for two bicycles to pass each other. Clotheslines packed with laundry crisscrossed overhead, tied between the buildings. There were few motorized vehicles. Pedestrians, bicycles, and handcarts were everywhere. Missing were the ubiquitous pedicabs and rickshaws of long ago. Nowadays, it seemed, human beings were used less as beasts of burden to convey other human beings. But in other ways, the scene on the street was utterly familiar. And with that familiarity came an old feeling of fear and vulnerability.

Helmi guided Jack along Congping Lu toward the waterfront. Partway down the east side of the block, she stopped in front of a narrow entrance to a large parking area marked by a tall metal post topped with a triangular-shaped cap.

She had lived just off the street in an alley tenement on this exact spot. Her old building was gone, as she well knew. It was bombed by the Japanese in 1937 and had burned to the ground. The gatepost was all that remained. Jack insisted that she pose for a photo inside the entrance next to the tall post, and then for another a few feet further inside the parking lot. She reluctantly agreed. In these photos, she is unsmiling and she clutches her purse tightly. Clearly she doesn't want to be there.

My own trip to Shanghai in 2008 was part of a family trip to China. My wife, Beth, is Chinese American, and we were visiting and touring with some of her mother's relatives. We traveled to the cities of Beijing and Tianjin, then south to Guelin and the scenic Li River region, and finally to Shanghai. I carried with me the photographs that Jack had taken in 1987 of Helmi standing on the site of her former home, along with a copy of Jack's diary of their Far East trip. For several years after Helmi's death, the photographs and diary had been missing. After Helmi died, in 2002, Jack moved from their house in Reno to a smaller apartment and disposed of a great many personal items. I had asked him to save for me the scrapbook he had put together of their journey, which included stops in Japan as well as China. When I visited Jack in Reno over the next few years, we searched together several times through his saved memorabilia for the scrapbook, without finding it. It wasn't until much later, when Jack moved for a second time—twenty years after his and Helmi's Far East trip—that the scrapbook turned up in the bottom of a box of stored photo albums. His meticulous notes, which included Helmi's careful mark on a contemporary Shanghai map showing the corner of Congping Road and Dongdamin Road plus the photographs he took of Helmi, enabled me to stand at the precise location of her former Shanghai home on a warm October afternoon.

In 2008 the city was in the midst of frenetic construction and renovation in anticipation of hosting the 2010 International Expo. Beth and I had walked from the Bund, with its historic row of former Western-style banks and hotels—now all undergoing extensive face lifts—across Suzhou Creek into the former Hongkou district and onto its main street, Dongdamin Lu. The famous Garden Bridge itself, now called the Waibaidu Bridge, had been temporarily removed for renovation, dismantled and transported further down the river to a construction dock, so we had to cross the creek on a newer four-lane bridge one block over. The bridge has since been returned to its original location, spanning Suzhou Creek where it empties into the larger Huangpu River, its graceful double span connecting the Bund with the Hongkuo district—the narrow physical link between the one-time center of colonial economic power and the poorest of the international neighborhoods.

We walked east, following a route that my mother herself had walked many times as a girl. We immediately passed a twenty-story art deco structure, a former apartment building for wealthy westerners originally called Broadway Mansions, and next to it Shanghai's first western-style hotel, the Astor House, now beautifully preserved and renovated. We followed Dongdamin Lu as it paralleled the path of the river, massive construction cranes looming on all sides. We had been told that in 2008 the two cities of Beijing and Shanghai together had more construction projects under way than all of Europe. It seemed as though we were looking at half of them right now. Looking to our right across the river, the area known as Pudong bristled with gleaming office buildings and spectacular high-rise hotels, including the hundred-story tower of the Shanghai World Financial Center, at that moment the tallest building in the world. Back in the 1930s, Pudong had been mostly a vast swampland, with only a handful of wharves and a few small factories clustered close to the river.

Walking along, we passed entire city blocks that had been bulldozed into naked expanses of bare dust, awaiting new construction projects. We also passed blocks that appeared to have remained unchanged for many decades. Tile-roofed structures, rarely more than four stories and packed tightly into narrow alleys lined with spindly trees, poured astonishing numbers of human beings, on foot or on bicycles, out onto the sidewalk of the larger street. These dense neighborhoods, known as *hutongs*, are rapidly disappearing in the Chinese urban centers to make way for modern high-rise civilization. Peering into these narrow lanes is akin to peering into Shanghai's past. As I walked along, every few blocks I felt as though I were literally glimpsing flashes of what greeted my mother's eyes as she walked along the street known as Broadway in the 1930s. One difference is that in 2008 everyone I saw flowing in and out of these ramshackle alleys was Chinese. In 1930, many of the *hutongs* in this neighborhood were occupied by families of Jewish refugees from Russia and Central Europe.

When we came to the corner of Dongdamin Lu and Congping
Road—the street signs were in both English and Chinese—we stopped,
facing east, to take stock of our quest. I looked at the map Helmi had
marked in 1987 and confirmed that we were at the right intersection. But
which corner? To the left, heading north, Congping Road was a bustling
commercial street, lined with small shops and eateries. To the right it
veered off toward the river, and on both sides of the street the block
was under imminent renovation. Closer to the river we could see several tall modern buildings, still unfinished and topped with construction
cranes. I decided to look to the left first. We walked up the block and
immediately noticed the tiny alleys of the *hutong* connecting from both
sides perpendicular to the street, lined with crumbling brick tenements,
here and there a few scraggly shrubs, and dense masses of people of all
sizes and shapes. Certainly here was a block that had stayed much as it
had once been. I took several photos down the alleys, imagining that I
was photographing my mother's front stoop. But when I pulled out the
snapshot of her standing where she had lived, I was reminded that this
block was wrong. Even in 1987, over twenty years before, she had been
standing in front of a large vacant area that had been cleared of dense
housing. I recalled again that she had always said her home had been
destroyed by Japanese bombs in 1937.

We decided to look in the other direction, south of the corner, toward
the waterfront. I walked along holding in my hand the photo of Helmi
posing nervously on the sidewalk, standing near a dusty driveway beside
a tall gray gatepost with its peculiar triangular top. About twenty feet
from the corner, I looked up from the photo and there, directly in front
of me, to the right of an opening that led into a large area filled with
trucks and construction equipment, was that gatepost. It was part of a
pair, spaced fifteen or so feet apart, marking the entrance to an industrial parking lot. They had been painted yellow sometime in the last
twenty years. Faded remnants of handbills were stuck to their sides. But
as my eyes darted from the photo to the post and back again, I realized
there was no mistake to be made: this was where she had posed. Here
is where she had lived.

It was a nondescript spot on an ordinary block in a drab waterfront
neighborhood of Shanghai, one of thousands of similar blocks that were
in a state of rapid transition. In the photo of Helmi, the parking area
behind her held a small cluster of dilapidated vehicles—trucks and small

Helmi in 1987, on the Shanghai street corner where her home (bombed in 1937) once stood; the author, on the same corner, 2008.

buses—perhaps out of service, or in need of repair. Behind the buses was a single house, the remnant of a brick tenement building that probably dated from the 1920s or '30s. Before me now, the parking lot held several monstrous bulldozers, parked in a state of readiness. Further back, the brick building was gone and had been replaced by a colossal high rise, perhaps thirty stories tall, either very recently completed or about to be. That the parking lot was still accessed from the street through the same entrance marked by the same pair of metal posts seemed astonishing to me, given the changes that had occurred nearly everywhere else I looked. At that moment, I was struck by a feeling I had never before experienced. All my life I had held a vague image in my mind, a murky impression of a place I had heard of only in passing. It had been described to me with a minimum of words: a Shanghai slum. My mental picture was made up of images from books, unspecific, monochromatic. A crowded urban district, that was all I knew. Now here I stood on the exact spot, breathing the air, smelling the smells, hearing the sounds. I felt both thrilled and humbled, plus something else—strangely liberated. There was no need to imagine it any longer.

Of course, this street corner of Shanghai had changed since the 1930s. But it had remained similar enough that when Helmi returned in 1987 it had sent a jolt of fearful recognition through her. And now, in 2008, a resonating spark of connection went through me as well. Standing in this alien place halfway around the world from where I came from, I felt for a moment peculiarly centered, as if I had arrived at a destination I hadn't even understood I had been seeking.

The Thomas Hanbury
School for Girls

Shanghai, 1932

A T THE AGE OF NINE, Helmi was finally allowed to go to school. In the fall of 1932 Rachel enrolled her at an elementary school for foreign children that was close to home, only three blocks east of the Hongkou Market, at the intersection of Boone Road and Chapoo Road. Called the Thomas Hanbury School for Girls, it was staffed by British teachers and administrators and was one of several public schools in the International District under the jurisdiction of the multinational Shanghai Municipal Council.

Although students at Thomas Hanbury represented many different nationalities and widely varying economic backgrounds, the common denominator was that all classes were taught in English, and in this respect Helmi was very well prepared. Rachel's insistence on speaking to her daughter in English would pay a dividend. Although she had never yet set foot in a classroom, Helmi had already read many books in English by age nine—*The Wind in the Willows, Doctor Doolittle, The Wizard of Oz, Winnie the Pooh*—and she was bursting with eagerness to read and learn more. On the first day of school, each girl was asked to stand up and announce her nationality. There were girls from England, America, Russia, and several European countries. When her turn came, Helmi proudly announced that she was Russian, as did several other girls. A few declared themselves to be "White Russians." Helmi obeyed her mother's edict to avoid identifying herself as Jewish, although she didn't yet fully understand why this should be necessary. She did have an inkling, from being told and also from her own observations on outings to the parks or to the market, that Shanghai was full of people who wore masks in one way or another. Many of the foreign residents carried no passports and were free to declare themselves to be whatever they wished, at least temporarily. Jews pretended to be Gentiles. Russians pretended to be Germans or Frenchmen. Gangsters pretended to be bankers and business leaders. Everyone seemed to want to be American. It was a place where new identities were forged every day.

The year 1932 was also when open war broke out in the streets of Shanghai for the first time, mainly in the neighborhoods north of Suzhou Creek, including Hongkou. In the previous year Japan had invaded Manchuria, in the north of China, taking control of Harbin and other northern cities and establishing the puppet state of Manchuko. Rumors abounded that the Japanese were preparing incursions against the Chinese in southern cities, including Shanghai. The Japanese population of Shanghai had swelled in recent years to become the largest foreign presence in the city, outnumbering the Russians, British, French, and Americans. Blocks adjacent to the Hongkou Market had become heavily populated by Japanese and were now known as Little Tokyo.

The Japanese Imperial Navy had sailed a fleet of warships up the Huangpu River and anchored them prominently off the Bund, supposedly as protection for the increased number of Japanese residents. In January 1932, responding to Chinese protests against Japan's recent invasion of Manchuria, which included organized boycotts against Japanese businesses and shipping companies in Shanghai, Japanese imperial troops and warplanes launched a military attack on the Zhapei district, the sprawling Chinese area north of Hongkou, with the intention of punishing the citizenry for the boycotts and gaining full control of the Chinese neighborhoods. The Japanese expected little resistance. Floatplanes attached to the Japanese warship *Idzumo* took off from anchorage in the nearby river and repeatedly strafed and bombed the Zhapei neighborhoods. This attack was one of the first aerial military actions ever deliberately targeting a civilian urban population. It marked a change in the way future wars would be fought. Within a few years, increasingly sophisticated air forces belonging to a host of different nations would be systematically bombing the cities of their enemies. If history were to designate a single incident as the birth of modern aerial warfare, the Shanghai Incident of 1932—as it came to be known—would be a strong candidate.

The Japanese were surprised by the strength and tenacity of the Chinese defense forces in Zhapei, made up of ragtag groups of independent street fighters. Calling themselves the 19th Route Army, the defenders operated without official support from the local Chinese government, which favored acquiescing to Japanese demands for increased economic and political control in Shanghai in the interest of maintaining a semblance of civil order. Along with fighter planes, the initial Japanese attack included 3,000 Japanese ground troops moving into the streets, but as Chinese resistance increased, the operation became a major invasion involving 90,000 Japanese troops, 80 ships, and an air force of over 300 planes. The fighting went on for two months, and what the Japanese expected to be a minor military disciplinary action eventually attracted the eyes of the world.

By the time the Chinese fighters surrendered in June 1932, approximately 20,000 Chinese civilians had been killed and at least 100,000 more had been driven from their ravaged neighborhoods, mere blocks from the safety and comfort of the foreign zones. In fact, this "incident" had been treated as an entertaining spectacle by many of Shanghai's wealthy foreign residents; they gathered in large numbers night after night on the south bank of Suzhou Creek, taking a break from the busy nightlife of Shanghai's famous cabarets and dance halls, to gawk at the sight of low-flying Japanese planes lighting up the sky with their loads of bombs less than a mile away, as if it were only a spectacular fireworks display and not the reason thousands of people were dying. The short route flown by the Japanese warplanes from the aircraft carrier in the river passed over the Wayside neighborhood of Hongkou. The planes would have flown very low directly above Rachel and Helmi's own rooftop on their way to drop their bombs.

It was in this tense atmosphere of September 1932, just a few months after the official cessation of the street war, that nine-year-old Helmi finally began school. The route between her home and the Thomas Hanbury School, approximately twenty blocks, crossed directly through Little Tokyo, the now Japanese-dominated neighborhood just north of the Garden Bridge. It isn't hard to understand why Rachel—who herself, at age nine, had witnessed the horrifying street violence of the Odessa pogrom—was fearful of sending her daughter out the door. And no doubt she could have come up with more reasons to keep Helmi at home under her watchful eye every second of the day. But her daughter was bright, exuberant, and growing up rapidly. For Helmi to have any chance of surviving, let alone thriving, in the nightmare atmosphere

Helmi's former school, the Thomas Hanbury School for Girls, currently a Shanghai municipal government building, photographed by the author in 2013.

of fear and poverty that defined life for stateless refugees in this chaotic part of the world, she absolutely had to go to school. It couldn't be put off any longer.

Helmi said, many years later, that this was when she felt her life truly began. From the first day, she adored school. She was already an avid reader. Now she was given the opportunity to truly immerse herself in the world of books. She eagerly devoured the English novels of Jane Austen and Charles Dickens. She acquired the slightly modified English accent that was common among British Shanghailanders, retaining it for most of the rest of her life. She loved participating in school plays, and she excelled at languages. Though all classes were taught in English, the girls attending the Thomas Hanbury School also studied French and German, both of which came easily to Helmi. From early on the students were also given instruction in typing and stenography—necessary skills for office and secretarial work, which were the main fields of employment, along with teaching, that women of the era could expect to enter. Helmi learned these secretarial skills easily. To her they were simply new and interesting ways to manipulate language.

Naturally outgoing and gregarious, Helmi began to make friends, some of whom lived in relatively comfortable circumstances. One girl, whose family was British Shanghailander, traveled to England to visit relatives for Christmas, and when she returned to school after the holidays she told Helmi all about her trip. Helmi was fascinated by her friend's firsthand account—traveling by steamship, staying with her family near London, playing in the snow, celebrating Christmas. It was all magical, like something out of a beloved English novel. A year later, the Municipal Council sponsored a citywide essay contest, open to all non-Chinese residents, on the subject "My Favorite Vacation." All the girls in her class were required to write an essay, and the best ones would be entered in the contest. Helmi had never been on a vacation of any kind, but this did not deter her from sitting down to write an essay. She simply borrowed details that she remembered from her friend's trip the year before, disguising and inventing both people and incidents, and wrote it up as her own. Her teacher was delighted with the result and entered it in the contest, where it won first prize.

Helmi had already seen how various Shanghailanders forged new identities for themselves. This was her first chance to put such a skill to use for herself. It would not be her last.

The French Concession

Shanghai, 1935

T HOUGH SHE GOT A LATE START on her education, Helmi moved rapidly through the curriculum and soon was placed in a grade above her age level. She also learned, along with the other girls who attended the Thomas Hanbury School, that factors such as race, religious background, and economic status do not define a person's character. In this respect, Shanghai was not a bad place to grow up. The school was much like a microcosm of the International Settlement. Under the watchful auspices of their British teachers, girls of many nationalities and backgrounds, rich and poor, sat together, studied together, and made friends with one another.

By the mid-1930s, Shanghai's population had swelled to over three million, making it the fifth largest city in the world. Most of its residents were Chinese, of course, but all official control was shared by the various foreign powers. The Japanese were the largest foreign contingent, followed by the White Russians, refugees from the newly created Soviet Union. If any city on the globe could be called a polyglot metropolis, it was this uniquely structured treaty port on the banks of the Huangpu River. Unfortunately, the city was the primary flashpoint for the trouble that continued to brew between the Japanese and Chinese, as well as between the Chinese Nationalists and Communists. More Russian Jews were pouring south from Manchuria, where the Japanese had solidified their occupation and control. Jewish refugees from Germany and elsewhere in Europe were also beginning to arrive, desperately poor and lacking the skills—knowledge of English, primarily—needed to navigate the complex workings of the city. War was on the horizon in every direction and could be seen coming by nearly everyone except those, such as the well-to-do foreign Shanghailanders, whose view of contemporary events was clouded by a nostalgic faith in the colonial system that was on the verge of crumbling around them.

For girls attending a British-run school, Shanghai, while growing ever more dangerous for foreigners and Chinese natives alike, could still seem an exciting and even glamorous city. One of Helmi's school friends was Anne Bernstram, also a Russian Jew born in the Far East but one who lived in the French Concession with her family in much more comfortable circumstances than Helmi and her mother. The two girls shared many similarities. Anne's father, Solomon Bernstram, traveled between China and Japan on business, just as Helmi's father had, and the family had also lived for a time in Japan. Anne's mother, like Helmi's, had lived in the Manchurian city of Harbin in her younger years. And, much like Rachel, Anne's mother was high-strung and prone to emotional histrionics.

There were also important differences in their lives. Anne had been born in China, in the coastal city of Tsingtao, whereas Helmi had been born in Japan. Much later, at the end of the Second World War, this would prove to be key in determining their respective U.S. immigration statuses, the critical factor being the country of birth. Anne's father was alive and, while something of an aloof figure, was nevertheless still a presence in her life. The family lived in a comfortable apartment in Shanghai's French Concession, a district of tree-shaded boulevards, well-kept parks, large homes, and modern plumbing—drinking water that didn't need to be boiled, taps that ran both cold and hot, and indoor flushable toilets.

Anne's apartment was in a terrace-style building on the corner of Avenue Joffre and Rue de Soeurs. The Concession functioned as a nearly autonomous municipality controlled by local French authorities, its principal street names having been bestowed during the early days of colonial partition of the city. The neighborhood was home to Shanghai's most prosperous citizens, whether Chinese, American, British, French, Japanese, or Russian. Business figures, government officials, and gangsters of varying nationalities and conflicting loyalties lived and raised their families close by one another behind tidy hedges and gated driveways. Anne's windows looked out across the street at Grosvenor House, one of the largest and most modern of Shanghai's apartment buildings, newly built by Sir Victor Sassoon's Cathay Land Company.

The Grosvenor House featured an eighteen-story central tower flanked by twin curved thirteen-story wings, as well as a broad expanse of manicured gardens and grounds. One block further west, on Rue Cardinal Mercier, was an exclusive private French club known as Cercle Sportif Francais, featuring an elegant clubhouse with broad white verandas, twenty lawn tennis courts, an indoor swimming pool, a bowling alley, an ornate roof-garden ballroom, and a large private park with broad, manicured lawns. Throughout the 1930s, this was considered Shanghai's most glamorous club, with a glittering international clientele.

For teenage Helmi, the opportunity to make afternoon and weekend visits to Anne's neighborhood was an invitation to step into, or at least get close to, another world. She only possessed one party dress, and until now it had been worn solely for school functions—such as the day she was given her essay contest prize. Now, carrying her dress carefully wrapped in a cardboard box, she would venture to Anne's by taking three streetcars: down Broadway in her own Hongkou neighborhood, then over the Garden Bridge and along the Bund through the International District, and finally east on Avenue Edward VII, the wide meandering boulevard that formed the northern border of the adjacent French Concession. The north side of this street fell under the authority of the British- and American-dominated Municipal Council, while the south side was fully under the jurisdiction of the Shanghai French Authority. Since traffic drove on the left, this meant that once on board the last streetcar, Helmi was fully on French soil. Or so she could tell herself.

Frenchtown, spreading out to the south and east for several miles, was Shanghai's upper-class district. One could imagine it being just like Paris—with street names like Avenue Joffre, Rue Vallon, Rue LaFayette, Rue Admiral Corbet, and Avenue Du Roi Albert. Behind high walls and hedges, protected by big trees and deep curving driveways, were the mansions and stately homes of the wealthy. Where back in Hongkou the streets were jammed with buses, streetcars, rickshaws, and handcarts and teeming with barefoot pedestrians loaded like beasts of burden, here there were mostly private automobiles, often driven by chauffeurs, sometimes carrying only one or two people in the back seat. Interspersed among the houses were neat rows of apartment buildings with colonnaded entryways and facades, fronted by sidewalks. Even the blocks made up of more modest rows of flats, known as terraces—outwardly resembling the building where Helmi and her mother lived—were clean and well maintained and looked as though, inside, one might encounter spacious apartments with drawing rooms, living rooms, dining rooms, separate bedrooms, and, best of all, real bathrooms.

After climbing down from the streetcar on Avenue Joffre and before walking toward Anne's building, Helmi would first stop and inhale a breath of fresh air, blissfully free of the stink of raw sewage that pervaded her own neighborhood. To be invited here on a Saturday, to sit in the living room of Anne's apartment in her white party dress with a cup of tea and some sweet biscuits, gazing out across the street at the magnificent Grosvenor House and its adjacent private grounds, was to enter a world she had barely imagined. It was like stepping into a dream, or better yet, a novel.

Anne Bernstram was raised in a household with a Chinese *amah*, or nanny, and other servants, and considered herself quite sophisticated. She had learned Chinese from her *amah*, spoke Russian at home with her parents, and, like Helmi, had attended British-run schools for foreigners where she had learned to speak English. But Anne learned English at an older age than Helmi; her mother had not pressed English upon her beginning in her toddler years, as Rachel had with her daughter, and consequently Anne's English remained tinged with a Russian accent.

After tea, if weather permitted, the girls would be allowed to venture outside, as long as they obeyed the edict to stay within one block of Anne's building in any direction. There was plenty to see and do within this radius. To the immediate west was the imposing Grosvenor House, and although signs were posted indicating that its verdant grounds were for private use, it was easy enough to stroll through them quickly, as a shortcut across the block.

One block to the north was the Cercle Sportif Francais, with its magnificent white veranda, its lawn bowling courts, and its Sunday afternoon tea dances held in the first-floor ballroom, which the girls could stare at in wonder through the tall windows. The veranda, reached by a long set of curving steps from the lawn below, was ringed by an ornate concrete railing with massive shrubbery pots mounted at the corners. Once, the girls borrowed a camera from Anne's mother and took turns photographing each other seated on the railing. In her photograph, the young Helmi smiles nervously as, perched in her white dress, white

The only known photo taken of Helmi in Shanghai, about 1934.

shoes, and white socks, she leans back against a potted plant, legs dangling from the railing and crossed at the ankles. Her brunette bangs have been freshly trimmed across her forehead. A jaunty white hat, probably borrowed from Anne, rests on the railing beside her, no doubt removed so as not to cast a shadow across her face. It is a striking image of a happy young girl enjoying a beautiful spring day. And it is striking for another reason: this is the only photograph Helmi kept from all her years in Shanghai.

There were also two beautiful movie houses in the immediate neighborhood, both of which showed first-run Hollywood films. Across the street from Cercle Sportif, at the corner of Rue Bourgeat and Route Cardinal Mercier, was the Lyceum Theatre, and at the south end of the same block, at the corner of Avenue Joffre, was the even more imposing Cathay Theatre. On any given week, there might be posters of Errol Flynn, Charlie Chaplin, Fred Astaire and Ginger Rogers, or the Marx Brothers. The Lyceum was also the headquarters of Shanghai's amateur British theatrical troupe, which frequently put on stage plays and musicals there. On Saturdays, Anne's mother would sometimes treat both Anne and Helmi to a movie or play and then lunch at a nearby café, where the girls would pour over American fan magazines procured at the corner newsstand right outside the theater. Helmi, in particular, became an expert on the lives of American and British movie stars. She memorized their vital statistics and diligently kept up with news of their romances. By now she had read enough novels and seen enough movies about America to have formed a clear vision of the place for herself. She fell in love with the notion of America as it was presented in books and movies.

The girls became steadfast friends. On a sunny Saturday afternoon during the summer of 1936, when they were both thirteen, they strolled out onto the street with no particular aim and cut across the Grosvenor House's private grounds, as they had several times before, stopping briefly to admire some freshly blooming roses. They chatted casually in English, as they always did once they had left the apartment. Russian was reserved for communication with Anne's parents, who never learned English well. Anne, well aware of the advantages she had grown up with, was envious of her friend on only one score: Helmi's perfect English. She spoke with no trace of an accent to give her away as a Russian, or even worse, a Russian Jew. As the girls laughed together and leaned over to sniff the beautiful roses, behind them a deep voice spoke suddenly.

"Excuse me."

The girls whirled around to face a tall, slender, mustachioed man, dressed in a stylish summer suit. He smiled at them.

"Pardon me, young ladies, but I must ask you—do you live here?"

Anne, who was taller and more physically developed, and who consequently thought of herself as more worldly than Helmi, replied, cheekily, for the two of them: "Oh, yes, sir. We live on the eighteenth floor." Of course it was a blatant lie.

The gentleman, who was perhaps in his mid-thirties, smiled again and gave Anne a quick look up and down. When he next spoke, it was in Russian.

"I don't think so. You see, I am the manager of this property. My name is Mr. Bashkiroff. Who are you?"

Anne blushed and looked down at her saddle shoes. She felt ashamed and embarrassed. He obviously had recognized her accent. Then she replied to him in Russian, as if speaking to her mother. *"I am very sorry. I am Anne Bernstram."*

The man then turned to Helmi, who met his eyes with a steady gaze of her own. He spoke again in English. He himself had a faint, but noticeable, Russian accent. "And who is your British friend?"

"My name is Helmi," she replied in her own perfect English. "How nice to meet you, sir." She realized that he had mistaken her for a British Shanghailander. She was aware that in the international atmosphere of Shanghai many foreigners engaged in a subtle game of evaluation, constantly comparing their status to that of others, and that a person's accent was a crucial piece of information in that game. This man, seemingly polished and elegant, had revealed himself to be Russian and was having fun making Anne uncomfortable. But he had mistaken Helmi for a British girl, several rungs higher up the social ladder than she was. She saw that she could easily reinforce this mistake. It would be a bit like her trick in winning the essay contest at school. Yet, in the same instant, she saw that she could turn the tables and enjoy her own bit of irony.

"*Ya Rooskye, gavoryo Angleeskey byez aktzyenta,*" she said. (I am Russian also, but I speak English without an accent.)

He raised an eyebrow in surprise. For a moment he simply stared at her. Then he smiled even more broadly, as if to appreciate the joke. He made a slight bow of his head. "*Pazhalsta, I zvi neetye.*" (Please excuse me.)

Then it was back to English. "I am indeed sorry to inconvenience you both," he said. "But these are private grounds. I'm sure you understand." He gestured with his arm to the gate where they had entered.

Once back on the sidewalk, Anne said to Helmi, "Why in the world did you do that? You had him completely fooled. We probably could have stayed there all day. You could have told him that you lived there, and he would have believed you."

Helmi shrugged as the girls continued their stroll along the sidewalk. "I suppose it seemed better to tell the truth." She laughed out loud then. "Besides, he was lording it over us so much. It was fun to give him a little shock."

Sometime later, as it happened, Anne would renew her acquaintance with this same older gentleman, Mr. Bashkiroff, after seeing him many more times in the neighborhood. Eventually she would marry him and move to San Francisco. Helmi, long after beginning her new life in Reno, remained good friends with them both for many years.

The War at the End of the Street

Shanghai, 1937

THE SUMMER OF 1937 was particularly hot and humid along the Chinese coast. As the thermometer climbed upward in the months of June and July, so did the political tension. By now it was widely understood that the Japanese intended to initiate a full-scale takeover of China. The puppet Manchuko regime, with the Emperor Pu-Yi on the throne but under the control of Japan, was in place in Manchuria and Japanese troops were rumored to be on the verge of a massive invasion southward.

Shanghai being the most important shipping port for international trade on the Asian coast, and consequently the seat of economic power for all of China, it became more clear every day that conflict would return to the city, probably on an even larger scale than the fighting of 1932. The Chinese Nationalists and Communists, who had been ferociously attacking each other in an ongoing civil war since the early 1930s, had temporarily agreed to create what they called the United Front in order to face up to the Japanese threat. A large Chinese army was assembled outside Shanghai preparing for a fight. In recent years the neighborhood just north of the Garden Bridge near the Hongkou Market, although still technically under the jurisdiction of the International Settlement, had filled with Japanese residents and, known locally as Little Tokyo, was under de facto Japanese control.

Helmi had finished her first year of high school at the Thomas Hanbury School for Girls. Attending high school was not free, and Rachel could not afford the tuition, but Helmi had been awarded a Henry Lester Scholarship, named in honor of an early British benefactor of the International District and given annually to a small number of exceptional students from poor families. She loved going to school—for the opportunity to learn, for the friendships she was making, and for the chance to spend the day away from her home neighborhood, in a clean room in a well-appointed building with real bathrooms and honest-to-goodness plumbing. Her mother, however, was not one hundred percent pleased. For one thing, Helmi had to travel every day through Little Tokyo to get to school. Rumors were flying that, when the fighting began, it would be concentrated in the district of Zhapei, immediately north of Hongkou and not far from their home. Moreover, the street where they lived, Congping Road, was only a single long block up from the riverfront wharf owned by the Nippon Yusen Kaisha Steamship Company, known as the NYK, a Japanese-controlled enterprise. Japanese soldiers already were being ferried over from the ships anchored in the river, landing near the NYK warehouse, and parading right by their door. Their neighborhood of Wayside stood directly between the Japanese warships and the Chinese districts likely to be attacked. This time Rachel was not imagining danger. Danger was right outside the doorstep.

Helmi's cousin Olga and her German husband, Kurt Gurski, now had a young daughter, Ursula, born in 1934 and now three years old. They lived near the southern border of the French Concession, considered one of the safest parts of the city, on Rue Stanislaus Chevalier, across the street from a large French police station. Rachel and Helmi were still living in the Wayside tenement along with Rachel's sister Anna, plus Helmi's grandparents—Solomon and Feiga Cooper—who had come from Harbin to join their daughters in Shanghai to escape the Japanese aggression in Manchuria. With summer coming, the idea was discussed that, for the sake of safety, perhaps they all might move in with Olga and her family. Some of the district's foreign residents had begun evacuating to other parts of the city, if they had a place to go. However, Olga's apartment, although in a much better part of town and considerably bigger than the Wayside flat, would be very crowded with eight of them living all together. So it was decided to keep this plan in reserve as an emergency measure.

Sometime in the spring of that year, 1937, Rachel had begun a relationship with a German man, who claimed to have the patent on a new process for improving the quality of cotton fabric and wanted to take his idea across the water to Japan. He asked Rachel to accompany him there. Rachel had maintained some friendships in Kobe from her brief time of contentment there, as the paramour of Edward Koskin and then as a young mother—a time which now seemed very distant. To the surprise of her family, she decided to accept the German man's offer. In their eyes, it was another rash and impetuous act. Rachel's parents, as well as her older sister, felt that Helmi should not have to accompany her mother to Japan. They believed it was likely that this venture would fail and that Rachel would soon return. They knew very little about the German man, or how serious Rachel's relationship with him was. The family knew him only by a Russian nickname, Dudchke. It counted very little that he was Jewish, unlike Olga's husband. The relevant fact was that Olga was *married*, and Rachel was not. Once again Rachel was planning to commit a suspect act, running off with a man who was not her husband.

After much discussion, Rachel was persuaded to let Helmi stay behind in Shanghai for the time being and continue high school on her scholarship. She was thriving at school, with many friends, and she very much wanted to remain in Shanghai. As summer arrived, the general hope across the city was that, despite the escalating tensions between the Chinese and Japanese, the International District would remain relatively safe, and so far both the Wayside neighborhood and the Hongkou Market district near Helmi's school, including the blocks that had come to be called Little Tokyo, seemed calm and unaffected. No one wanted to believe that full-scale war might be fought in the streets of the foreign-controlled districts. Helmi was also quietly thrilled at the prospect of stepping out from under the wing of her protective mother for the first time in her life. For Rachel, already nervous and fearful by nature, and seeing more reasons than ever to worry for her daughter's safety, leaving Helmi behind in Shanghai was a painful prospect. Nevertheless, against her own better judgment, she relented. So in mid-July, shortly after Helmi's fourteenth birthday on the 15th, Rachel sailed to Japan with the man they called Dudchke, leaving Helmi in the care of her parents and her sister Anna.

Almost from the very moment Rachel set sail, the undeclared war in China escalated rapidly. By the third week of July, serious fighting had broken out in the northern Chinese provinces, and by the end of the month the Japanese had taken control of the major city of Tianjin, near Beijing, and Chinese troops had responded with a massacre of Japanese civilians in the city of Tongzhou. Japanese naval and air forces moved into new positions up and down the Chinese coast, and troops continued to gather in large numbers north of Shanghai. Now, suddenly, the Japanese militia evicted the International Settlement police from the northern neighborhoods and declared Japanese authority over the entire Hongkou district. More Japanese soldiers and sailors could be seen every day congregating in the streets. In late July, a fleet of twenty-six Japanese warships sailed into the mouth of the Yangtze River and up the Huangpu into the heart of Shanghai, anchoring just off the wharves in front of the Bund. Among these was once again the *Idzumo*, one of the biggest flagship cruisers of the Japanese fleet.

By August 5, word had spread throughout Shanghai's northern Zhapei district that a large-scale Japanese attack could be imminent, prompting a mass exodus southward of several thousand panicked Chinese residents hoping to find safety in the International Settlement. In the next two days many more Japanese marines were deployed into the city and Japanese residents were advised by authorities to evacuate. On August 12, Chinese fears were realized when the northern Shanghai districts were attacked on three separate fronts. The street war had begun.

In addition to supplying troops for street fighting, the *Idzumo* made use of its attached floating fighter planes. The next day, Saturday, August 14, several Japanese planes took off from the river and flew north over the Wayside streets to drop bombs on the Zhapei railroad station and bordering neighborhoods, causing hundreds of civilian casualties. A new flood of Chinese refugees immediately began pouring toward Suzhou Creek and the Garden Bridge. At the bridge the panicked families became a virtual stampede; met by Japanese guards with bayonets, many were killed as they tried to cross to safety. Later that same afternoon a Chinese warplane, based outside the city at the Lungwha airfield, attempted to bomb the *Idzumo* but prematurely dropped its two bombs after being damaged by Japanese anti-aircraft fire. One landed in the street directly in front of the glamorous Cathay Hotel, and the other penetrated the roof of the Palace Hotel, on the opposite corner. Over seven hundred people were killed, including scores of foreigners. Minutes later a similar incident occurred when another Chinese warplane accidentally dropped its load on the intersection of Avenue Eduard VII and Tibbets Road, in the heart of the International District and right in front of the Great World Amusement Center, where rations and tea were being distributed to a huge crowd of refugees from Zhapei. This time over a thousand people were killed, almost all of them Chinese. This was the worst single-day carnage of civilians anywhere in the world up to that moment, and it became known as "Bloody Saturday." War was now at the doorstep of the foreign concession. Across the creek in Zhapei the bombing and destruction continued unabated for many more weeks, killing thousands of Chinese and destroying hundreds of square blocks of residential neighborhoods.

And so Helmi began the school year of 1937 in early September, at age fourteen, in a city under siege. Yet while war raged in the streets, the city, or at least the foreign-controlled areas—the International District and French Concession—still managed somehow to function. The Thomas Hanbury School for Girls kept its doors open, along with several other British or American-controlled schools. The streetcar still ran along Broadway as it always had, stopping in front of the building at the corner of Congping Road. Helmi could ride it all the way down to Boone Road by the Hongkou Market, and then walk the two familiar blocks to school.

It might have seemed like madness to send an adolescent girl off to school each day into such an atmosphere. For much of that summer the residents of the foreign districts of the city, in both the French Concession and the International Settlement closer to the fighting, had consoled themselves with the delusion that they were safe from the bombs and shells, believing that the conflict was strictly between the Chinese and the Japanese. The errant bombs of mid-August, which had fallen into the heart of the business district, killing foreigners as well as Chinese, had provided graphic proof that no one in the city was truly safe. Still, the civilian casualties continued to occur almost exclusively in the Chinese population. In the International District many shops stayed open, most foreign businesses continued to prosper, restaurants and bars and nightclubs still buzzed with activity, and young students of many nationalities continued to ride the buses and streetcars to and from school. A feeling of detachment was shared by many of the foreign residents, rich and poor alike: a feeling that this was not their war.

This feeling finally ended for Helmi and her family in late September. On the night of Saturday, September 18, Chinese planes launched extensive air raids against Japanese troop positions in the southern portion

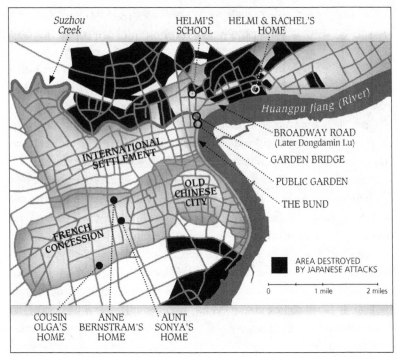

Shanghai, 1937. Map by Kirk Johnson.

of the International Settlement. The raids lasted from seven p.m. until after midnight, destroying numerous buildings along the riverfront and in some cases killing civilians trapped in their homes. Several incendiary bombs fell into the Wayside district, including one right on the corner of Broadway and Congping Road. There were so many planes in the air conducting dogfights that it was never entirely clear whose bomb it was, but in any event, the bomb made a direct hit on Helmi's building, the block-long tenement called Congping Terrace where she and Rachel had lived with Anna since 1927.

The fire began in the upper stories, and Helmi and her family were awakened by the sound of panicked residents fleeing the building. In their small apartment on the third floor, the four of them took only what they could hastily grab of their clothes and possessions and joined the crowd on the sidewalk. Soon the building was engulfed in flames, and no help was forthcoming. The Shanghai firefighters had long since given up responding to calls this far from the city center. The building was totally destroyed. The burned block remained vacant for the next seven decades, eventually becoming a paved parking lot, with the only remnants of the original structure being the twin metal gateposts that still stood next to the sidewalk in 2008.

With the aide of two late-night Chinese rickshaw drivers, the four of them—Helmi, Anna, and the grandparents, Feiga and Solomon Cooper, both now in their seventies—made their way down Broadway, across the river, down along the Bund, and through the French Concession to Olga's apartment. Here they were taken in and given shelter. They had lost almost everything of the little they owned, but they were alive.

The apartment was small, but it had running hot water and a real bathroom. The fire had been a terrifying experience, but they knew how lucky they were to have a safe haven in what appeared to be the safest part of the city. Helmi went right back to school the following Monday, taking a much longer route to get there. She would board the streetcar at the corner of Rue Stanislaus Chevalier and ride north along the leafy boulevard Route Pere Robert, past several of Shanghai's most sumptuous mansions, including the sprawling Morris estate, home to the wealthy British publisher of the *Shanghai Daily News*, the city's main English-language newspaper. The streetcar continued on to the corner of Avenue Joffrey, near both the Cathay Theatre and Anne Bernstram's apartment and in the shadow of the massive Grosvenor House, where the year before the girls had encountered the elegant Mr. Bashkiroff. Helmi would get off the streetcar and wait for her friend, and the two girls would then catch the eastbound Avenue Joffre bus, which skirted the northern boundary of the walled Old Chinese City and continued to the corner of Szechuan Road. Here they changed again to a northbound streetcar, which traveled through the heart of the International Settlement's business district and finally crossed Suzhou Creek—the water more crowded than ever now with a floating Chinese population living on rafts and junks and sampans, refugees from the fighting in the northern part of the city—then headed up to the corner of Boone Road. Here the girls got off and only had to walk one block east to their school at the corner of Boone and Chapoo Roads.

By crossing the creek on the Suzhou bridge into Hongkou, they had moved much closer to the city's war zone. Only a few blocks further north was the boundary of the International Settlement. Another dozen blocks away was the North Shanghai Railroad Station, which remained under heavy siege, with pitched battles between Japanese and Chinese troops under way on a daily basis in the nearby streets and alleys. Japanese shells were launched into the district from ships anchored in the river, and planes engaging in dogfights swooped overhead, delivering bombs with less-than-pinpoint accuracy. Chinese civilians, including families with children, were dying in their homes by the hundreds. Droves of desperate refugees from the northern districts of the city were making their way on foot into the International District every day, driven out by the destruction. Stacks of bodies were being carted regularly to the outskirts of the city to be hastily buried or cremated.

When word of the bombing and fire reached Rachel in Japan, she wasted no time in rethinking the decision she had made reluctantly a few weeks before. She wrote immediately and insisted that Helmi be put on a boat, as soon as travel to Japan was allowed again, and sent to join her. She would no longer have her daughter dodging bombs on her way to school.

Meanwhile, the fighting was subsiding as the Chinese began to acquiesce and lay down their arms. By November the city was relatively quiet again as the Japanese took full control of the Chinese districts. There were once again rumors of civil war ramping up among the Chinese, but for now it was deemed safe to travel, and ships were again using the docks. Money was pooled, and at the end of the school term in early December a ticket was purchased. Helmi, now fourteen, didn't want to leave. Shanghai was the only place she had ever known. Moreover, she was enjoying life away from the fretful vigilance of her mother. She had sensed that everyone else—her aunt, her cousin, even her grandparents—had been somewhat relieved when Rachel left for Japan, despite their outward disapproval of her reason for doing so. Helmi, young as she was, had understood for some time that she was not the only one who considered her mother difficult to live with. She couldn't help feeling some resentment that now, with the street war seemingly at an end, she was offered no choice in the matter.

Rachel had sent half the money for the ticket, and Auntie Anna and Helmi's grandparents split the other half. On a rainy December morning soon after the school term ended, Helmi was taken by her grandparents to a dock off the Bund and put on a steamer, which sailed first ten miles down the Huangpu River, where it met the mouth of the mighty Yangtze, and from there out into the open China Sea and across to Kobe, Japan, the place where she was born.

Mrs. Blacksill's School

Kobe, 1937

H ELMI REMEMBERED NOTHING of her birthplace, having been taken to China when she was a toddler. Her mother had written to assure her that she had secured decent living quarters and that Kobe was a clean and safe city. Moreover, there was a school nearby for foreign students, staffed by British teachers, called Mrs. Blacksill's, reported to be similar to her school in Shanghai. A transfer scholarship had been arranged, and she could continue her education in Japan.

In some ways, life in Kobe was an improvement. The city was cleaner than Shanghai. The entire municipality seemed to have modern plumbing. Situated on a protected coastal bay and backed by steep green hills, Kobe was regularly served by fresh ocean breezes and had none of Shanghai's signature stench of raw sewage, factory smoke, and the odors from open-air cooking pots. The air in Kobe smelled only of the sea.

It was another bustling port city, although considerably smaller than Shanghai. Kobe's harbor was Japan's main gateway for global trade, and as a result the city had a substantial international population. Japan had not been exploited by the Western powers as much as China had in the first decades of the century, so the Japanese saw their foreign residents— Europeans, Americans, Russians, and others—more as guests than colonial overlords. Within the foreign population of Kobe was a small contingent of Jews, primarily Russians. Most of the foreigners lived on the steep hillsides rising above the downtown district.

By the time Helmi arrived, Rachel had situated herself somewhat comfortably. She had followed her older sister's example and rented a small six-bedroom apartment building in the Kitano residential district, high up the hill from the businesses and the seaport. It was on

Ikuta Suji Street, only two blocks from where she had lived in the previous decade with Edward Koskin, Helmi's father. The neighborhood had many other foreign residents, including several other Russian Jewish families whom she had known in her girlhood in Harbin. Just as her sister Anna had done in Shanghai, Rachel rented out five of the units and kept one for herself and her daughter. The German gentleman called Dudchke, with whom she had traveled to Japan six months earlier, occupied one of the rooms. He had helped her secure the rental of the building and even cosigned the lease. However, his plan to sell a technique for improving cotton fabric to the Japanese had not proved successful, probably due to the fact that the Japanese had amassed hundreds of years of experience refining cotton and already produced the finest fabric in the world. It was never entirely clear to Helmi what Rachel's relationship was to this gentleman. He behaved like a friendly uncle to her. Nothing else is known of Dudchke. Within another couple of years he was gone, never to be heard from again. Still, he had served an important purpose in Rachel's life, providing her with an opportunity to return to Japan.

Kobe was where Rachel had once been happy, if only for a brief time. The places where she had lived as a child—first Odessa, then Harbin— were lost to her now. Kobe was much the same as it had been fifteen years before. Her daughter had been born here. Helmi's father had died here. It was as near to a home as she could claim. Moreover, after the destruction of the rented tenement building back in Shanghai, she saw now that her sister Anna was completely dependent on her own daughter's husband for support. There was nothing to return to in Shanghai, even if she had wanted to go back.

Helmi enrolled in Mrs. Blacksill's School as a high school student, but it was clear from the start that it was not a good fit for her. The school was run and staffed by the British for the children of foreign residents, but unlike the school in Shanghai there were not many impoverished scholarship students like Helmi there. There were also not many Jews. Most of the students were American or British or European, living temporarily in Japan because their fathers were doing business there. Despite her British-sounding Shanghailander accent, in Japan Helmi felt she was looked upon by some of the teachers and the students as a refugee, an identity that conferred a kind of second-class status. In Shanghai nearly everyone seemed to be a refugee from somewhere, and the social boundaries were far more porous: with the proper language skills, plus careful attention to outward appearances, a Jewish teenager could freely mingle, at school and elsewhere, with children of the well-heeled and the blue of blood. Here in Japan, distinctions of status among the children of foreigners were more self-consciously observed. The wealthier British and Americans kept to themselves, and the poorer Russians and Europeans and Jews did likewise. The Japanese themselves were unconcerned with such social issues among the foreign population. As the military escalated its strategy of aggression around the Pacific region, the only factor that ultimately mattered to the Japanese authorities was a person's official nationality. This would mean that, in a few years—once the Second World War was under way—the British and American citizens in Kobe and other Japanese cities, as well as in Shanghai and the other Japanese-controlled areas of China, would be interned in prison camps, while stateless refugees for the most part would be left alone.

Despite the relative safety of Kobe, the winter term of 1938 was not a happy one for Helmi. For the first time in her life, she knew what it meant to be lonely. Rachel felt much more at home in Japan than her daughter. She was reunited with a small coterie of friends from her time there twelve years before, and she enjoyed a measure of newfound autonomy as the sub-landlord in charge of her small rooming house. She had never experienced being in charge of her own destiny, even in a small way. Kobe had a very small but tightly knit Jewish community of about thirty Jewish families, many of them Russian exiles like herself, which gave her a true feeling of belonging. In some cases they shared remarkably similar histories. One of these families, Boris and Fania Sidline and their two small sons, for a time rented a room under her roof. Boris and Fania had also come to Kobe by way of Shanghai. Boris was a Belgian Jew and Fania, originally Lithuanian, had, like Rachel, grown up in the Manchurian city of Harbin, where they had known each other. The Sidlines, who ran a small import shop, had lost their home near the Kobe waterfront in the typhoon that had struck the city in 1934 and were struggling to rebuild their lives. Rachel felt proud to be able to provide them with a temporary home. Whatever her relationship with the mysterious Mr. Dudchke, Rachel now retained a sense of independence. She had seen that living under the protection and support of her sister Anna had been a strain for everyone involved. Despite being separated from her sister and her parents, she did not even consider returning to Shanghai.

Japan was considerably colder than Shanghai, and for Helmi the winter weeks seemed to drag on. She continued to do her best to fit in at school, but she never shook off the feeling of being an outsider. Moreover, Mrs. Blacksill's School seemed to be more like a finishing school than a place to study and learn. Most of the other girls couldn't wait to return to their true homes in America or England. In Shanghai it had been different—the foreigners, including their children, shared a certain pride in being Shanghailanders. Helmi didn't know it yet, but this strong sense of identity with Shanghai would soon prove an illusion, part of an era of Western domination in the Far East that was about to come to an end.

When spring arrived in Kobe, bringing with it the end of the school year, Helmi began to lobby her mother to let her return to Shanghai. Her argument was simple: the fighting there was over, and peace had returned to the streets. This was being reported in the Japanese press. At first Rachel would hear none of it. She was adamant about staying in Japan herself, and she wanted her daughter to stay with her. However, Helmi soon hatched a plan, with the help of her cousin Olga back in Shanghai, who sympathized with her plight.

There were now more of their relatives gathered in Shanghai. Rachel's aunt, her mother's older sister, had joined the Russian-Jewish exodus from Manchuria in the early 1930s and had moved in with her daughter Sonya—Rachel and Anna's first cousin—who had recently married a Shanghai-based American businessman named Mr. Jensen. Sonya Jensen had distanced herself from her impoverished cousins, at first wanting very little to do with them, less because of her new wealthy status than because she sought to hide the fact that she was Jewish. This was not uncommon among those who married across religious or cultural lines. But with her mother now living with her, Sonya couldn't help being in closer contact with her other relatives in the city.

Olga met discreetly with Sonya over tea at the Palace Hotel on the Bund, a favorite haunt of Sonya's, and proposed that Helmi be allowed to come back from Japan and stay with Sonya long enough to finish high school. After all, she argued, Sonya's house was a large villa-style mansion with plenty of room. She had servants, a cook, even a chauffeur. Surely one more person in the household for the school year would make very little difference. Helmi's life had been marked by one difficulty after another. She deserved the chance to finish her education in Shanghai, away from the tight grip of her mother.

Perhaps partly out of guilt for not previously offering help to her poorer relatives who had lost their home in the bombing, and perhaps also out of an understanding that her young cousin Helmi was indeed a worthy cause, Sonya agreed to this idea. Helmi was thrilled beyond belief to receive word from Olga that she had been offered a new temporary home in Shanghai, and she brought the proposal to her mother. She passionately made the case that the school was better in Shanghai, particularly in practical subjects. She promised to return to Japan once she graduated, when she would be certified in many areas, including shorthand and typing, and would be able to find a job. More letters were exchanged, and Rachel was at last persuaded to let her daughter go, though she remained displeased and fearful.

So, in midsummer 1938, Helmi sailed alone back to Shanghai.

The Fourth Floor

Shanghai, 1938

S HORTLY AFTER HER FIFTEENTH BIRTHDAY, Helmi moved into the attic of Sonya Jensen's spacious home in Shanghai's French Concession. She had never before even set foot in a house like this, though she had walked passed a great many stately houses and villas on her strolls with her friend Anne, admiring them from the outside. The girls had peered through hedges and wrought-iron fences, past curved driveways filled with elegant automobiles, at columned porches and ivy-covered walls, imagining who might live inside. It was widely understood that, in such neighborhoods, a powerful politician or business potentate might share a backyard fence with a notorious Chinese gangster. If a pair of curious teenage girls lingered too long on the sidewalk, admiring the fountains or statuary or trying to catch a glimpse of the residents, soon enough a uniformed butler or chauffeur would step out to gruffly shoo them away. And now here she was, living in such a place.

The home's servants were Chinese, all of whom spoke pidgin English, the standard mode of communication with westerners. Besides the butler and chauffeur, there were groundskeepers, kitchen staff, and several household maids. The house was enormous—two full stories of lavishly furnished rooms, including a formal dining room and a large library with floor-to-ceiling bookshelves, plus a third-floor attic with servants' quarters and a few extra bedrooms. Upon her arrival, the butler, an elderly Chinese man with a calm demeanor, escorted Helmi up to the attic and showed her to her small bedroom. Down the hall was a bathroom she would share with the maids and another attic resident: an old lady, who dressed every day in a black dress with a high white lace collar. It took several days for Helmi to learn that this lady was Sonya's widowed mother, the sister of Helmi's grandmother. She had come to Shanghai from Harbin, in the same exodus of Jews that included Helmi's grandparents, to live with her daughter because she had nowhere else to go. There seemed to be something shameful about the way she was lodged with the servants on the fourth floor. Clearly she had not been welcomed into her daughter's home the way Helmi's grandparents had been received into theirs.

Helmi was instructed that she would live under the same rules as the old lady. The main strictures were that they must eat their meals, which were always on the skimpy side, away from the family, and that they must keep well out of sight and sound whenever company was invited into the house. It didn't take Helmi long to figure out that, since Sonya had married an American with money, for certain social purposes she hoped to conceal from the public the fact that her mother was Jewish and consequently she herself was. This was a new phenomenon for Helmi, and indeed it was something of a laughing matter among the women back at Olga's apartment, when Helmi would pay a visit and fill them in regarding goings-on at Sonya's. Poor as they were, the women in Helmi's immediate family were proud of their Russian-Jewish heritage and rarely saw a need to conceal it. To them, everything about cousin Sonya, from her prominent nose to her heavily accented English to her love of gaudy jewelry, proclaimed her Jewishness to the world and therefore this masquerade of hers was comical. She could parade around as much as she liked at fancy tea parties at the Palace Hotel on the Bund with other wives of wealthy *goyim*, or host elaborate dinner parties for the Shanghai social set, but she wasn't fooling anybody. As Helmi's grandmother liked to say, the only one in the family who could ever pass as a non-Jew would be Helmi, with her beautiful British diction and her status as a star student at the international Thomas Hanbury School.

Helmi was told to address Sonya as Auntie Sonya and her husband as Mr. Jensen. She didn't meet him face-to-face for several weeks, and he seemed surprised to learn that she had been living in the house. She was given a small allowance of spending money, which she saved up for outings with Anne, who now lived much closer. In that late summer and fall of 1938, they spent many hours watching American and British movies in the air-conditioned Cathay Theater, just around the corner from Anne's home. They never missed a Marx Brothers movie if they could help it, or a musical with Fred Astaire and Ginger Rogers. The girls devoured every bit of information about Hollywood stars that they could find in newspapers and fan magazines. They also attended amateur plays put on at the Lyceum Theater by the British Amateur Dramatics Club or the American Players of Shanghai, and fantasized together that they could do as well as or better than some of the actresses they saw.

In the aftermath of their invasion, the Japanese had partly taken control from the foreign powers of the Shanghai Municipal Council. Life in the wealthier foreign communities continued for the time being as if there had been no significant change. Shops and nightclubs thrived, and international business continued on at the usual brisk pace. Yet the Chinese districts were now policed by the Japanese, and a great many more Japanese had taken up residence in Zhapei, Hongkou, and other neighborhoods. Meanwhile, the simmering civil strife between the Nationalist and Communist Chinese factions was approaching a boiling point. The opposing groups had been temporarily united in their struggle against the Japanese invasion, but deep and passionate divisions now overshadowed their common cause. In this rapidly evolving atmosphere, the foreigners—mainly the British, Americans, and French— clung to their still considerable economic power, but their collective hold was weakening. Alongside the continued frenetic activity of this once wide-open city there was now plenty of evidence, visible to those who cared to notice, that the era of unchecked colonial control by Western powers was over.

The Jensens' butler informed Helmi that, as long as she kept out of the way, she was free to make use of the home's extensive private library. This was far and away the best thing about living in the house. With all her wealth, Auntie Sonya was strangely stingy about providing food, but the supply of books was beyond ample. Helmi was already a voracious reader, and she considered the use of the library on the second floor of the house to be a great gift. She made her way through book after book, strengthening a habit that would remain throughout her life. A light sleeper since childhood, Helmi would oftentimes stay awake most of the night to finish a book. With hundreds of volumes on the shelves, the world of literature opened up to her. For this reason, together with the comforts of the house and the freedom of living apart from her mother, Helmi would later call the time spent living in Auntie Sonya's house the happiest year of her life in the Far East.

In the fall of 1938, Helmi returned to the Thomas Hanbury School for Girls, still on her scholarship. On the first day of class she was informed by the headmistress, Miss Hodgson, that she had been accelerated into the final form, meaning she would be ready to graduate the following spring, before her sixteenth birthday. This would be her last year of high school, and she made up her mind to make the most of it.

Simply getting to school each day was now more complicated. Needless to say, the house's chauffeur service was not available to her. Sonya's home in the French Concession was even farther away than cousin Olga's apartment had been, and the trip required several more bus and trolley transfers. With the Japanese now controlling all the neighborhoods north of Suzhou Creek, including the Boone Road area where her school was located, she had to carry a special pass with her every day on the bus that crossed the bridge out of the International District. The bus was stopped every morning and boarded by Japanese military sentries posted on the bridge, who checked the identities of all the Chinese passengers and made them bow in supplication. Once across the bridge, the bus simply stopped, and everyone had to get out. The Japanese had suspended all bus and trolley traffic north of the creek until further notice, forcing everyone without their own vehicle to walk. Helmi needed to allow extra time to walk the three long blocks up Chapoo Road to her school.

Helmi found it ironic that in Auntie Sonya's house she was under strict orders to keep out of sight of guests and to eat all of her meals in the kitchen with her elderly great-aunt, her dormitory-mate from the attic, yet when no one else was around she was free to wander the house, carrying around an armload of books, and to sit and read wherever she pleased. At their private mealtimes in the kitchen, she and the old lady conversed, mostly in Russian, and Helmi learned more about the peculiar workings of the family. The old lady, the sister of Helmi's grandmother Feiga, talked of growing up in Odessa and then making the long journey with her family to Harbin in search of a better life, just as Rachel's family had done. She would drop her voice to a whisper when speaking of her daughter's great success in marrying such a wealthy American as Mr. Jensen. He was an *important* businessman, she would say, leaning closer to Helmi, although she seemed to have no clear idea what he actually did.

The Chesterfield Girl, Phyllis Crudgington, from a magazine advertisement, 1941. Original copyright 1941 Liggett & Myers Tobacco Company. Current copyright holder unknown.

Mr. Jensen, the benefactor to them both, was a distant figure, usually only seen in the hallways when passing from room to room. Now and then he would appear in the library, cigarette in hand, when Helmi was there, and he might inquire bemusedly about her reading. No one else seemed to make much use of the library. She was tempted to tell him that being under his roof sometimes felt like living inside a novel by Jane Austen or Charles Dickens or one of the Brontë sisters, but of course she never did, always making sure to greet him politely but to say very little. At her relatives' behest, and for her own interest, Helmi kept her ears open, and by paying attention to snippets of overhead conversations she eventually was able to deduce that Mr. Jensen's main business was importing American goods to China. In time she learned that, among other enterprises, he was involved with selling American arms and munitions to the Chinese Nationalists. *Important businessman*, indeed.

American products were advertised widely in Shanghai, in news-papers and on the streets, and the picture that began to form in Helmi's mind of the US was of a magical place where freedom and prosper-ity reigned—where all the men were suntanned and handsome and the women slim and glamorous and impeccably dressed, and where the streets of the cities were always clean and bright and sweet-smelling. One day a new billboard appeared, high in the air at the intersection of Avenue Edward VII and Szechuan Road, on Helmi's daily bus route to school. It depicted a smiling, blonde, rosy-cheeked, young woman, close to Helmi's age or perhaps only a bit older, strikingly dressed as an archer, in a bright-green close-fitting Robin Hood outfit complete with a jaunty peaked cap, a bow tucked in her arm, and a quiver of arrows slung over her shoulder. Leaning forward over a heart-shaped target, she held a package of cigarettes enticingly in one hand and a lit cigarette elegantly in the other. "Aim For the Best—Chesterfield!" proclaimed the slogan beneath her picture. Something about the image captivated her. For Helmi, the billboard came to represent something essential and seductive about the United States, a spirit bold and bright and wonder-ful. Helmi found herself gazing longingly at it every day when the bus passed beneath. She wanted to feel as carefree and fanciful as that girl on the billboard, glamorously puffing on a Chesterfield. She wanted to be that American girl.

The Next World

Shanghai, 1939

S HANGHAI WAS CHANGING, and even the most willfully blind foreigners couldn't deny it any longer: not even schoolgirls who rode the bus every day through the armed Japanese checkpoints, and who otherwise spent their Saturdays curled up reading Jane Austen novels or watching Marx Brothers films in the cool darkness of the Cathay Grand Theater. Nervous conversations could be overheard everywhere, on the streetcars along the Bund, on the sidewalks and in the cafes of the French Concession, in the hallways of the Thomas Hanbury School for Girls, and in the kitchen and servants' rooms of Sonya Jensen's mansion. The Japanese had brutally seized greater control of the country, murdering tens of thousands of innocent people in Nanjing and other Chinese cities and exerting ever-tighter control in Shanghai, where they demanded obeisance from the Chinese and more concessions from the foreign residents. In addition, the civil conflict between the Communists and Chiang Kai-shek's Nationalists was becoming more open and dangerous. In the shadows, meanwhile, racketeers and gangsters were continuing to collude with politicians and bankers to rake in the last of the old-style profits before the existing order collapsed altogether.

Along with these tensions, another problem had arisen in the city. With a suddenness that caught everyone unprepared, new shiploads of desperate and impoverished refugees were beginning to arrive on the Shanghai docks. Coming from Germany, Poland, and Austria by way of Suez, as well as via the much longer route around the Horn of Africa, they were Jews, in many cases entire families. They were escapees from yet another wave of mass persecutions, this time pogroms perpetrated by Hitler's German regime on its march through Central Europe.

Boatload after boatload of families disembarked at the Shanghai piers with little more than the clothes on their backs. They poured into the International District, straining the capacity of the city to house and feed them. Within a short time the number of new refugees grew to twenty thousand people. It seemed that the Nazis were bent on expelling every last Jew from their conquered territories. The refugees came to Shanghai simply because it was one of the only places that would take them. Most ended up crowding into the blocks of poorer tenements north of the Huangpu River, in the Hongkou and Wayside neighborhoods near Helmi's former bombed-out home—areas still trying to rebuild from the devastating Japanese shelling of two years before. The refugees brought horrible stories with them, which circulated rapidly through the Shanghai Jewish community: stories of massacres, entire communities emptied and deported, homes confiscated, property taken away. Many families were unable to escape. No one knew what would become of them.

It was in this atmosphere of ever-escalating tension that Helmi continued with her studies in her last year of high school at the Thomas Hanbury School for Girls. The tuition was expensive, but in addition to being given a comfortable place to live, with her relatives, she continued to receive a stipend overseen by the Shanghai Municipal Council that covered her school expenses. Despite being younger than most of the girls in her form, she had been promoted to school prefect, or student monitor. In June of 1939, a month before her sixteenth birthday, she would be ready to graduate.

One day in mid-May, at the end of the school day, Helmi was called into the office of the headmistress, Miss Hodgson, where she assumed she was to be given her final written report. The headmistress beckoned her to sit down in the chair facing her desk, an invitation Helmi had never received before.

"Well, Helmi," said Miss Hodgson, "or perhaps I should now call you Miss Koskin." She gave a hint of a smile. Helmi couldn't suppress a slight giggle. What in the world was Miss Hodgson getting up to?

The headmistress's smile vanished in an instant.

"This is nothing to laugh at. I meant that very seriously, young lady. Because that is what you are now, a young lady. You may be young, but in a few weeks' time this school will graduate you into the adult world. What will you do next?"

Helmi adjusted her demeanor. "Pardon me, Miss Hodgson. Do you mean what *should* I do next? Or what would I *like* to do?"

Miss Hodgson was familiar with this girl's boldness. Yet there was no impertinence now in Helmi's tone. She was asking a reasonable question.

"I appreciate the point you make. So, first off—what would you like to do next?"

Helmi pondered for a moment. She decided to be candid. "I would like to stay in Shanghai and find a job. I would like to keep on living with my Aunt Sonya, so that I could earn enough money eventually to attend college. I believe I have acquired the skills to be successfully employed." She paused. "But I don't know if this can happen. My mother has gone to Japan and wants me to join her there."

Miss Hodgson tapped the small stack of papers before her on the desk. "I have been looking over your final form report," she said. She lifted her glasses to her nose and looked down at the report. "You have done well here. Particularly in the English subjects—grammar, composition, literature, and dictation—you have been outstanding. Miss Adlam, your Form Mistress, indicates that you have imagination and express yourself with ease and accuracy. You read carefully, critically, and with great appreciation. In dramatics, your characterization is distinctly good." She had been reading from the report, but now she lifted her gaze. "Do you imagine yourself, perhaps, as an actress?"

Helmi saw this for what it was—a trick question. Of course every girl imagined becoming an actress. If she answered yes, she would be revealing herself to be like any other frivolous schoolgirl. This was a moment to demonstrate maturity.

"I hardly think so, Miss Hodgson. I believe I am better equipped for clerical work."

Miss Hodgson seemed pleased with the response. She looked down again at the report. "Yes, I should think so. You have earned top marks in both shorthand and bookkeeping. But for your deficiency in age, I certainly would consider you highly employable." She scanned the report further. "In art, the Mistress only rates your work as 'fairly good.' She also indicates that you are inclined to waste time, and that you talk too much."

These points were easy to concede. "Yes, Miss Hodgson," Helmi replied. She was beginning to suspect there was a larger purpose to this interview, but she knew very well not to ask what it was, at least not yet.

Miss Hodgson removed her glasses and sat back.

"If you were someday to attend college, Miss Koskin, what do you think you would like to study?"

This question sounded less loaded, more like a sincere query. "I'm not entirely sure," Helmi replied. "I have dreamed at times of becoming a journalist. That is, if I had the opportunity."

Now Miss Hodgson allowed herself a larger smile. "I don't know if you are aware that from time to time we are able to recommend certain outstanding girls for college scholarships."

Helmi sat up very straight. She felt her breath suddenly coming shorter. "I have heard of this, yes, Miss Hodgson."

"Well, there is a very fine women's college in America, called Mills College—in California, near the city of San Francisco—which has a scholarship available. Miss Koskin, I am pleased to say we have recommended you for the scholarship. You are not yet even sixteen. We have never before recommended someone so young. We realize it may not be possible for you to go to America. Moreover, time is of the essence. You will have to decide quite soon whether you can accept this offer."

Miss Hodgson drew a breath and then added, in a kinder tone, "I understand very well that there may be serious difficulties for you. The future is uncertain for all of us."

Helmi stared back at her. What had she just heard? College in America? Could this be possible, and if so, how on earth could such a thing be arranged? What would her mother say? For once, she was at a complete loss for words. After a long moment, she heard herself thank the headmistress feebly and promise to meet with her again within a week, and then, still in a daze, she walked slowly out of the office and out to Boone Road. She turned eastward, past the big triangular Hongkou Market where she had shopped so many times with her mother, and then went right on Woosung Road toward the creek and the Garden Bridge. At the bridge, she dutifully showed her identification to the Japanese sentry, but instead of waiting for the streetcar, she decided to walk across. On the Bund side of the bridge, the south side, the Public Garden remained what it had always been for her—a quiet refuge. She followed the path into the garden and found an unoccupied bench facing the wide river. She sat down and pondered the questions she had asked herself, and more. How far was America? Was she ready to go there alone? What about her mother in Japan? Rachel had written only days ago to say that she missed her daughter terribly and expected her to come to Kobe as soon as school was finished. She could hear her mother's anxious voice in the letter, her pressing and imploring tone.

Rafts and junks and sampans passed back and forth in front of Helmi, sometimes shrouded by mist. She watched for a long time, but no answers came. Finally she got up and walked to the bus stop on the Bund to make her way back to Auntie Sonya's—her home for now, or the closest thing to it.

Helmi had seen for herself that her mother felt at home in Japan. In Shanghai Rachel had not been able to provide for herself or her daughter. She had been entirely dependent on her relatives. Across the water in Kobe, Rachel was supporting herself, or so it seemed. There she had been welcomed back into the tiny, tightly knit community of Russian Jews, some of whom had known her family in Harbin when she was young and, later, when she had lived in Kobe as a young mother. With these people she had a sense of belonging, rather than a feeling of being judged or pitied or beholden. It was kinship without the emotional weight of family. The Japanese treated the foreigners on their own soil, even Jews, with tolerance and even a certain measure of respect.

And yet there were always new reasons to be afraid. Word had reached Japan, as it had Shanghai, of the new horrors being inflicted on Jews in Central Europe. A few escapees, those with enough money to pay for passage and the necessary bribes, had even begun to pass through Japanese ports. The terrors they described, in places like Poland and Czechoslovakia, were beyond belief. It was well known that, in 1936, a year before it launched its invasion of China, Japan had entered into an alliance with Nazi Germany, supposedly as protection from the expanding Soviet empire. What did the future hold for Jews anywhere? The only thing for a mother and daughter to do was live together and protect each other. Rachel had written to Helmi in Shanghai, telling her precisely this.

Helmi decided to discuss the offer of the American scholarship with Auntie Sonya, as well as with her Auntie Anna. Her relatives all agreed on one thing—whatever Helmi decided to do, she should not remain in Shanghai. Even Mr. Jensen, who had rarely taken the time to speak to her, invited her into his study and declared gravely that Shanghai was not safe and that he saw things only getting worse. As a matter of fact, he added, he and his wife had themselves begun preparations to move to

America. Life for everyone in the Far East was about to change. "In the next world," he said to her from his armchair, his pipe held aloft, "few of us will remain what we are today." Helmi sensed that Mr. Jensen spoke with authority. She thought of the gossip among the servants that he had been involved in the Chinese arms trade. Perhaps he knew better than anyone what lay beyond the horizon. Across the room, Aunt Sonya sat stiffly upright, holding a cup of tea, and stared out the window at her garden, saying nothing to contradict her husband's words.

Auntie Anna, her mother's sister, spoke of America as if it were a place out of a storybook, somewhere not quite real. "You would be so very far away from us all," she said. And she added, with a sigh, "And of course we must take your mother into account."

This last message was reiterated by her grandparents with great seriousness. Rachel was alone in Japan. They seemed to imply that they she was destined to be alone forever. No one expected the relationship with the German man to last. Helmi also understood that they meant something else. Her mother was emotionally unstable. Rachel's life had certainly not been easy, but circumstances alone could not fully explain her constant and intense anxieties. She was more than a mere worrier, and Helmi had seen the negative affects her instability could have on others. Though only fifteen years old, Helmi could see that responsibility for her mother's welfare would soon rest partly on her own shoulders. She had not asked for this responsibility. Nevertheless, it was her inheritance.

Helmi wanted more than anything in the world to accept the scholarship offer from California. It was a dream come true, like something out of a movie. She was certain that passage to America could be arranged somehow, money could be borrowed, guarantees provided. She felt fully confident that she could make the trip alone and, young as she was, enroll in college and thrive as a student. The fantasy of becoming an actress, or more realistically of studying journalism, suddenly were real possibilities. All she had to do was say yes. Her mother, across the water in Japan, for all her imploring, for all her neediness, could not stop her. Helmi already knew more about America, from books and movies and magazines, than any of her family or friends. She was confident that she would fit in there. Here in China she was just another stateless, faceless foreigner: not truly Russian, although Russian was one of her native languages, and not at all British, although she spoke English like a Brit. She felt that her identity up to now had only been a faint shadow cast upon the Shanghai sidewalks.

The implications of this decision were not lost upon her. She was being offered a chance that would not likely come again. Here, in the spring of 1939, the fabric of society seemed on the verge of coming apart. In two short months, shortly before her sixteenth birthday, Helmi would finish school in war-torn Shanghai. Until now she had led a sheltered life, protected by her mother and her relatives from trials and difficulty. She had never before faced a choice that would determine the direction of the rest of her life.

Making up her mind would require more time in the Public Garden, sitting on her favorite quiet bench facing the river. She took the streetcar, by herself, on the next Saturday afternoon. There, in the garden beside the water, where she had sat so many times in the past with her hawkeyed mother keeping close watch, she again pondered the matter. She recognized that many people in similar situations would probably pray for guidance. This was not her inclination. Although she had been raised with the clear understanding that she was a Jew, she had formed no particular devotion to the Jewish faith. To her, the idea of God represented all that could not be understood, all that was mystery. When she sought actual clarity, her limited experience had taught her to simply look within herself for the answer. It was a matter of carefully weighing and considering all the factors, and making the right choice.

In due time, she would do so.

Reno, Nevada

1956

IN LATE MAY OF 1956 the Reno Little Theater presented a seven-day run of a comedy by Howard Teichmann and George S. Kaufman titled *The Solid Gold Cadillac*, a broad satire of business and politics. The play had been a hit on Broadway beginning in 1953, where it ran for 536 performances. In the amateur Reno production, the role of Amelia Shotgraven, a secretary in the offices of the fictional General Products Corporation of America, was played by Helmi Horgan, age thirty-two.

Helmi had already appeared in a number of Reno Little Theater productions. Her first role was seven years earlier, in a play called *The Women*, by Claire Booth. When *The Solid Gold Cadillac* was presented, I was five years old and my brother Terry was six and a half. Our dad, against his better judgment, decided to bring us both to a Sunday matinee performance, right after church. Other than the familiar costume drama of Mass every Sunday, this was my first exposure to the concept of live theater.

I remember: the big darkened room, the soft seats, everyone around us paying rapt attention to the swift comings and goings up there on the brightly lit stage, the sudden eruptions of laughter at odd intervals. I peered forward, kneeling on the seat, trying to see between two large heads blocking my view. We had been told that we would see our mother performing, though I had no clear idea what she would be doing. Suddenly there she was, stepping out from the darkness and strolling rapidly across the stage. Her hair was pinned up in a peculiar shape and she was wearing big, funny-looking glasses. I had been told to keep quiet and managed to suppress the urge to wave. She stopped mid-stage, and there was a burst of rapid-fire dialogue. The voices grew louder. Then an astonishing thing happened, something I had never before witnessed or even imagined: my mother burst into tears. With several years' experience playing a variety of roles, Helmi had earned a reputation as a good amateur actress. At age five, I certainly found her performance convincing. Horrified, I did the natural thing. I also burst into tears.

Our dad was a person who labored to present a dignified face to the world, but underneath he was someone who was easily stressed. We always knew he found public displays of emotion—anger or tears—hard to take. I wondered later if his quick reaction in the theater wasn't in some way akin to my own—if, in fact, he found it just as unbearable to see my mother weeping up there on the stage as to have me wailing in the seat beside him. At any rate, he did the smart thing. Whispering to my brother to stay put, he scooped me up and hustled me out of there, to the front steps of the theater, where he held me in his lap until the play was over. He made a good effort to explain that my mother's tears were only pretend tears, that a play was like a movie. It wasn't real life. And after the play was over my big brother, himself deeply embarrassed by my display of immaturity, helped to hammer home this point.

When my mother finally came out the stage door, she hugged me close, laughed her wonderful big laugh, and told me how sorry she was that she had given me a scare. She was no longer wearing those ugly stage-prop glasses, and her hair looked normal again. And so I learned a lesson that day. My mother liked to pretend. She was an actress. She had the power to radically alter the persona she presented to the world. This in itself was impressive, but to me the real magic was that she could so easily reverse the process. She could turn back into herself.

Stateless—Shanghai to Kobe

Incendiary bombs falling on Kobe harbor from an American B-29 bomber, 1945. United States Army Air Forces military records.

The Thomas Cook and Son
Travel Service

Kobe, 1939

O N A JUNE AFTERNOON, a week after graduation from high school
and a month short of her sixteenth birthday, Helmi Koskin
boarded a Japanese steamer docked at the end of Avenue Edward VII,
after being seen off by her Auntie Anna, her cousin Olga, and Olga's
four-year-old daughter Ursula. Helmi went up on the deck of the ship
as it pulled away and waved at the group standing on the shore as they
shrank into the distance, with the row of stately copper-domed and
colonnaded buildings of the Bund rising behind them. Watching the
receding figures on the dock, she was made keenly aware that her family
was almost entirely composed of women: strong women, all of them,
sturdy Russian Jews who had forged lives for themselves in the Orient
with only passing assistance from men. Even her mother, though volatile and emotionally fragile, nevertheless had demonstrated a powerful
instinct for survival.

As the ship followed the sharp eastward bend of the river, passing
first the Garden Bridge where Suzhou Creek came in, then the Russian
and Japanese consulates on the north bank, followed by the docks and
low warehouses of Hongkou, Helmi had a good view of her old Wayside neighborhood close to the shore. She could see that the row of
tenements where they had lived had been scraped cleanly away after the
bombings and fires, the entire block now just a flat expanse of empty
rough pavement. Rubble from other destroyed buildings still lay heaped
on some of the street corners. Shanghai was crumbling before everyone's
eyes, and more war was expected. The boat continued on, and the city
slowly faded into the summer mist.

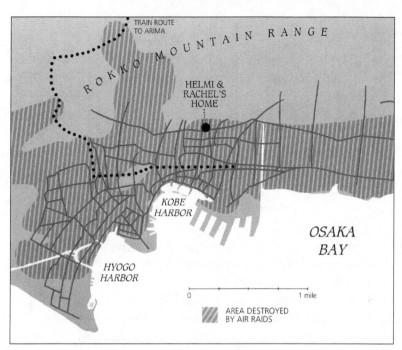

Kobe, 1945. Map by Kirk Johnson.

In the end, the decision had been clear. Of course she had desperately wanted to escape completely, to America and to college. She had realized, however, that she was not free to do what she wanted. When she tried to picture going to America and leaving her mother behind in the Far East, with war clouds looming on all horizons, she saw that there was no such thing as a true escape. The fear and the worry would travel with her wherever she went. Her mother had made it abundantly clear that she wanted and needed her daughter with her in Japan. Rachel, for all her efforts to make an independent move and strike out on her own, had said in her letters that survival continued to be a struggle. Helmi had always done what her mother had asked of her, and now was not the time to do the opposite. She was sailing to Japan, to the city of Kobe, where her mother awaited her, and where a part-time job had been secured for her. She was to be a teacher's assistant at Mrs. Blacksill's School, the same school she had attended briefly only a year before and had hated. None of this was what Helmi wanted to do. But it was what she had to do, and she accepted it—not, however, without lingering regret.

Rachel's only marketable skill was operating a boardinghouse, which she had learned from the example of her older sister Anna, and it provided only a meager living. Helmi's language skills would be useful in communicating with her mother's foreign tenants, but this was not a job that would bring in income, so with the help of friends the position at Mrs. Blacksill's had been arranged. But once again Helmi found the school rigid and stifling, with nothing like the nurturing atmosphere of her former school in Shanghai. She still felt hints of disrespect from those she dealt with there, and it didn't help that she was actually younger than many of the students she was charged with overseeing. She soon began to look around for other opportunities.

Helmi heard of a full-time opening at the Kobe office of Thomas Cook and Son, the large British-owned international travel service. She was well below the minimum age for such a position, but a new friend named Ada, one of her mother's borders, assured her that this would not matter at all as long as she dressed properly, used the right amount of makeup, and was very careful not to admit how young she was. So Helmi interviewed for the job, and after demonstrating her shorthand and typing skills as well as her fluency in Russian and several other languages, including German and French, she was hired on the spot. She was now working full-time, at age sixteen. The job was a boon to her mother. Rachel no longer had to keep every room rented in order to make ends meet. As the principal breadwinner, Helmi was given one of the larger rooms in the boardinghouse to stay in and was able to buy some of her own clothes, instead of having to wear the hand-me-downs of relatives. Rachel was able to shop for groceries regularly and cook fresh meals every day for the two of them.

Beginning in 1938 and continuing until the start of the war in the Pacific three years later, a stream of Jewish refugees came through Asian ports from Eastern and Central Europe as Nazi Germany overran country after country. The numbers were very small compared to the millions who could not get away. They escaped by any means and any route, as long as they could afford the price of passage, disembarking at any port that would take them. Shanghai was one such place. Kobe was another. The Jewish community in Kobe up to that time had been made up of fewer than fifty families. Under the leadership of two dedicated Russian Jewish businessmen, Anatole Ponevejsky and his brother-in-law, Moise Moiseeff, the Jews of Kobe worked with the Japanese authorities to secure aid for several thousand European Jewish refugees who passed through Kobe up until mid-1941. They came mostly from Russian-controlled areas of Lithuania and Poland, which had been partitioned in an agreement between Germany and the Soviet Union; the route eastward through Siberia and across the China Sea to Japan was one of the last possible means of escape for Jews trapped in Europe. The communal organization they created, known by its Western Union telegraphic acronym, JEWCOM, also acted as a conduit for financial aid from the Jewish Defense Council in the United States, which helped secure passage for Jews to final destinations in South America, Australia, Canada, and other nations that would accept them. The U.S., ironically, was not one of these. Although financial aid came from private Jewish U.S. aid organizations, America's strict immigration laws had made entrance visas extremely difficult, if not impossible, to obtain.

Helmi, as both a member of the Jewish community and an employee of Thomas Cook, found herself in the midst of this aid effort. Though still only a teenager, she was able to bridge language barriers and assist with complex travel arrangements for individuals and families, and in some cases groups of unrelated people posing as families. Many had been issued hasty transit visas by a sympathetic Japanese vice-consul stationed in Lithuania named Chiune Sugihara, who single-handedly provided them a way out. They had traveled by train all the way across Asia on the Trans-Siberian Railway to the Russian port of Vladivostok and then to Japan. Once in Kobe, many of these refugees were provided with food and temporary housing for several weeks, some of them in Rachel's rooming house, while waiting for travel clearance to their ultimate destination. Since many spoke German or Russian, or perhaps only Yiddish, Helmi's language skills were very useful. She helped to arrange their passage out of Japan to places like Brazil, Argentina, or the Dutch colony of Curaçao. She found that she had an instinctive understanding of their difficulties and an ability to empathize, and with a combination of good humor and tenderness she could help them stay calm. She believed that this skill or talent or whatever it was had to do with growing up in Shanghai, among so many different kinds of people. It also seemed to her to be a matter of simply being Jewish and thus connecting with the tribulations of other Jews, no matter where they came from or whether they had been rich or poor. In wartime, it seemed, these differences mattered very little.

From these desperate travelers, Helmi and Rachel, along with their other Jewish friends in Kobe, heard firsthand accounts of the terrors being inflicted on Jews in Europe. In many cases, the refugees coming to Kobe were the only survivors from their towns. Some were the only survivors from their families. Sometimes they went to great lengths to express their gratitude. One elegant Polish gentleman came to the Thomas Cook office shortly before his boat was set to embark for South America and formally presented Helmi with a bouquet of roses, then bowed to her, kissed her hand, and made a speech of thanks in her honor. This period of exodus and rescue, however, would be short-lived. The Siberia-Japan escape route from Europe would be cut off by mid-1941, when Germany invaded the Soviet Union. By the end of that year, when the Pacific War officially began, Japan would shut its doors entirely to refugees.

Helmi had another new Jewish friend in Japan, named Eda Wiznitzer, who seemed to have a marvelous stroke of good luck—an opportunity to go to America. Eda's young husband, Sol, had applied for and received a highly prized student visa to study in the United States and bring his family along. The Wiznitzers, who had been boarders in Rachel's rooming house, had a three-year-old daughter and were pregnant with another child when the travel arrangements were made late in 1941. Tickets in hand, they were particularly thrilled that their second child would be born in the United States and would therefore be an American citizen. At the end of November, Helmi saw them off at the dock and couldn't help feeling envious, since she had missed her own opportunity to make such a journey, perhaps forever. A week later, midway across the Pacific, on the morning of December 8 (December 7 in the U.S.), the young Wiznitzer family woke up and went to the ship's dining room for breakfast as usual. Another passenger turned to gaze out the window and wondered out loud why the sun that morning was rising behind the ship rather than in front of it. Apparently they had turned around during the night, with no explanation. And for another week no explanation was given, until they arrived back in Kobe and were ordered to disembark.

On that same morning, December 8, Helmi, now eighteen years of age, stepped off the streetcar in downtown Kobe and walked to the offices of Thomas Cook only to find the door barred by a Japanese soldier. One of the agency's clerks, an English-speaking Japanese man, was standing outside smoking a cigarette. He informed her brusquely that all the British employees had just been arrested and taken away, including the manager, Mr. Edgar, who had lived in Japan for over forty years. The office was closed permanently, the Japanese clerk told her, and she should turn around and leave immediately.

"Haven't you heard?" he said. "Japan's air forces have bombed the American naval base in Hawaii. The war is on. Go home."

Stateless

Kobe, 1941–1943

WITH NO CITIZENSHIP in any country, Rachel and Helmi found themselves marooned in wartime Japan, entirely at the mercy of whatever fearsome global forces had been unleashed. Yet despite the many privations they would experience during wartime, they considered themselves lucky. Their stateless status meant they would not be subject to internment, unlike their British or American friends, who were immediately arrested. They remained part of a tightly knit, albeit tiny, community of foreigners in similar circumstances.

Having lost her job, Helmi was provided part-time employment by Mr. Moiseeff and Mr. Ponevejsky, the leaders of JEWCOM, which was reorganized under the name Foreign Food Distribution Service to provide food rations to the small number of foreigners who remained trapped in Japan. The group's work for European refugees was finished, because no more were passing through the country. Japan had entered into a Tripartite Pact with Nazi Germany and Italy. The last escape route for Jews from Europe was closed.

As the war progressed, Japan's ally Germany put pressure on Japanese authorities to round up its Jewish population, but through most of the war this request was ignored. Though Japan's cruelty to fellow Asians, particularly the Chinese, was vicious and unyielding, and though the Japanese were likewise cruel to their Western enemies, they never subscribed to the Nazi's anti-Jewish fanaticism. There was no pogrom in Japan. The Japanese government actually provided a small amount of free food to its stateless residents. As part of a campaign for a healthier wartime population, early in the war Japan adopted an official policy of promoting the consumption of brown rice by its native citizens. Consequently, there remained, throughout the war, a surplus supply of white rice for the foreigners. Helmi and Rachel ate little else for four years. A typical week's official allotment distributed to the fifty Kobe families would be a truckload of white rice, perhaps a dozen eggs, and several bundles of moldy celery.

Later in the war, giving in to Germany's insistence, the Japanese did finally institute a halfhearted policy of identifying and containing Jews in Japan and their occupied territories. A so-called "quarantine zone" was established, curiously enough, in Shanghai—which the Japanese now fully controlled—and many of the Jews living in Kobe and other Japanese cities were deported there, particularly those who had arrived as refugees from Nazi-occupied countries. The Wayside district of Hongkou, Rachel and Helmi's old Shanghai neighborhood, ironically became a quasi-ghetto (the Japanese officially called it the "Designated Area for Stateless Refugees," deliberately leaving out any specific reference to Jews), and nearly twenty thousand people were ultimately confined there, almost all of them Jewish refugees from Europe, in strained and overcrowded conditions. The relatively small number of Jews who had come to China or Japan before 1937, including Rachel and Helmi, were exempt from this policy and were not required to relocate. Conditions in this Shanghai "quarantine" never became comparable to the horrors of the European ghettos and concentration camps created by the Germans. Although confined to their district and required to carry IDs, the residents were nevertheless allowed to keep their families intact and to live with a certain measure of freedom. Rachel was not allowed contact with her sister and parents back in Shanghai, but it could be assumed they also had not been forced to relocate. When it came to the Jews, the Japanese remained indifferent to the Nazi policy of persecution and extermination. Helmi would declare, decades later, "It's crazy to say, but we were in luck, I suppose. The Japanese didn't really care if we were Jews. They merely pretended to."

At the beginning of the war, in 1941, Helmi was eighteen years old. She and her mother belonged to a group of foreign families who did their best to look after each other. They shared what was available on the black market—extra food items, fuel oil, medicine—in a determined effort to survive. When asked later about the war years, she would say one of her most acute memories was of the intense cold in winter. Fuel oil was in short supply and there was never enough to keep the house warm. Despite bundling up in every layer of warm clothing she possessed, she endured several winters where she contracted painful chilblains on her arms and legs. There were many times when she longed to return to the comfort of her attic room in Auntie Sonya's Shanghai mansion. Then again, she knew that Sonya would have been lucky to escape from Shanghai before the war began. It was to be assumed that the Japanese had arrested Americans and British in Shanghai, just as they had in Kobe. For all she knew, Sonya and her American husband had been sent to a prison camp. There was no way now to find out.

Early in the war, Helmi eagerly took up smoking cigarettes. In Shanghai, under the influence of British and American movies, she had come to think of cigarettes as a symbol of high glamour. Every Hollywood heroine and femme fatale seemed to light up a cigarette and puff her way through the most important scenes. Helmi couldn't wait to be old enough to do the same. During the war Japanese cigarettes, though harsh and foul-tasting, were cheap and easy to come by on the black market. Rachel also smoked, as did most other adults, and she made little effort to prevent her daughter from taking up the habit. After all, there were few other pleasures to be had. Before the war began, vastly superior American cigarettes had been available. Riding the streetcar on her way to work at the travel agency, Helmi had looked up and seen the same billboard for Chesterfields that she had admired in Shanghai, with the enticing image of a young blonde woman in a Peter Pan costume, holding a lit Chesterfield in her fingers. After Pearl Harbor the billboard had come down and American cigarettes were banned. Chesterfields remained the brand that she craved.

She never gave up the smoking habit, although late in life she pretended to. While visiting her in Reno when she was in her mid-seventies, I got up in the middle of the night to use the bathroom. I found the door to the guest bathroom locked, and I could hear the fan whirring inside. I stood for a moment wondering who might be in there, since Helmi and her second husband, Jack McCorkle, had their own bathroom at the other end of the house. Suddenly the door opened, and out she stepped. Despite the fan, the bathroom reeked of smoke. After a split second of surprise, she looked me in the eyes and said matter-of-factly, "Well, now you know." She and Jack had vowed to quit together several years before, under doctors' orders. While Jack had valiantly upheld his end of the deal, she had continued to sneak smokes at night while he was asleep.

Before bidding me good night, she swore me to secrecy. They are both dead now, so I consider myself released from my vow.

In the summer of 1942 Helmi made contact with actual Americans, strangely enough. A group of about forty American construction workers who had been employed in Guam, which was controlled by Japan at the time Pearl Harbor was bombed, were brought to Kobe as civilian detainees. The Japanese had commandeered a large house known as the Marks Mansion, previously owned by a British banker named Marks, in the foreign community's neighborhood and had converted it into a detention center for the American workers. The men would exercise in the yard and would sometimes try to engage people in conversation on the street outside the fence, looking for anyone who spoke English. Helmi had recently turned nineteen. She hadn't had much personal exposure to Americans, other than Mr. Jensen back in Shanghai, whom she had barely known, and in movies. She and her friends would walk by out of curiosity, and they were surprised by the brashness and boldness of these fellows. It didn't take long for a certain rapport to be established. The Americans occasionally received Red Cross packages with highly desirable items, including chocolate and the prized Chesterfield cigarettes. Their regular prisoner rations from the Japanese were meager and inadequate, so Helmi and her friends devised a barter system, bringing them black-market food items like butter to exchange through the fence for cigarettes. Helmi kept an empty coffee can at home where she stored her precious Chesterfield butts, which she would smoke down to the last quarter-inch through a cigarette holder. Eventually, more than just butter and cigarettes were being bartered: the Americans found ways to sneak out in the dark for forays down the hill to sample what there was of Kobe's wartime nightlife. After the war, three of her girlfriends, two Turkish sisters named Naila and Aisha and one of their cousins called Effie, ended up marrying three of these American construction workers.

Helmi wasn't looking for a husband. She was content enough, for now, with the American cigarettes.

On a Saturday afternoon in April 1942, just four months after the Pearl Harbor attack that began the war, Helmi was at home with her mother. She had spent the previous week helping with the weekly distribution of rice to the foreign families. Today was wash day, and because the weather was clear and warm—a much-welcomed spring day—she and Rachel were outside just before 2:00, hanging sheets on the line strung in the alley behind their rooming house. Suddenly they heard a roar overhead, from a large plane of some sort, but a sound much louder and deeper than that produced by the small Japanese fighters that periodically passed over Kobe. They looked up and saw a bulky-looking twin-engine plane come in very low directly overhead, then turn sharply toward the harbor district. The plane passed close enough for them to see a face in the cockpit window and then another in the glassed-in gun turret underneath. As it leveled out, the wing markings on the underside were easy to see. The symbol painted was clearly not Japanese—it was a five-pointed white star on a large blue circle. "Americans!" Rachel shrieked over the plane's roar. "Bombs!" She dropped her laundry and ran for the house, assuming her daughter would follow. Helmi stayed where she stood and watched in amazement.

The white star symbol was indeed familiar. Japanese propaganda had been relentless, describing to the populace in vivid terms—including in the English-language newspaper the *Japan Times & Advertiser*, published expressly for the foreign community—the vicious inhumanity of Americans. The star was declared an emblem of evil. The U.S. barbarians would stop at nothing to pursue their bloody ends, including indiscriminate slaughter of civilians. All reports were that the Pacific War was going spectacularly well for Japan, island after island taken, the Empire broadening its reach on a daily basis, winning huge victories over the weak-willed U.S. forces on land, in the air, and on the sea. No one dreamed that American planes had the technical capacity to reach the mainland. There had been a couple of test air-raid drills in Kobe; since the city was a major transportation and industrial center, they were mostly to make certain that the sirens would function correctly in the unlikely event they were ever needed. Yet here, unchallenged, with no warning whatsoever, was an American plane.

Helmi kept her eyes on the plane as it swooped away toward the harbor below, the sun glinting off its silver surface. It leveled off again very low, engines roaring, seeming almost to graze the tops of buildings. As if watching a movie, she saw several objects drop from the airplane's belly, followed by a succession of explosions amid the factory buildings and then columns of black smoke. The plane rose, turned sharply left, and flew away from the city and out toward the China Sea. She heard a few sharp pops and saw some white puffs of smoke where the plane had been a few seconds ago, but now it was gone, untouched. The sirens started up. Several fires were blazing in the harbor district. Her mother had been right: bombs.

Helmi knew she should feel fear—bombs had fallen on the city right before her eyes. Yet what she felt was a strange thrill. The few Americans she had encountered in Shanghai and Kobe were not the monsters portrayed in the Japanese press. There were not many in Kobe who would agree, but she was almost glad that they had come.

The American plane was not alone. It was one of sixteen B-25 bombers, each with a crew of five, that had taken off early that morning from the U.S. aircraft carrier *Hornet*, stationed at sea 600 miles east of Tokyo. Carrying small loads of bombs and tanks of extra fuel, the bombers' daring mission was to strike at a handful of targets in several coastal Japanese cities and then quickly cut across to China, intending to land and refuel at airstrips in friendly Chinese territory. Lt. Col. James Doolittle, a former champion air-race pilot from Alameda, California, was the mission commander and pilot of plane #1. The mission thereafter became known as the Doolittle Raid. Most of the planes, including Doolitle's, targeted the Tokyo/Yokohama area. Plane #15, piloted by Lt. Donald Smith of San Antonio, Texas, was the single bomber sent over the city of Kobe. Its engineer/gunner, seated at the machine gun station in the plane's nose, was a 23-year-old sergeant, Edward J. Saylor of Brusett, Montana. His main job during the bombing run was to defend against Japanese fighter planes, but no planes appeared so he never had to fire a shot. Three months later, in an account of the raid that appeared in *Yank*, the U.S. Army newspaper, Sgt. Saylor wrote:

HIROHITO, THE YANKS ARE COMING PAL!

It's 1:40 p.m. and a clear day. Below me the country is rugged, but through the valleys the land is streaked with green, with trees and terraces. Maybe I got a little catch in my throat, but I don't notice it much. The skies are empty and clear. We've left the other planes in our squadron, and here we are all alone sitting over several million Japs. I used to live out west, and I've never been to Japan before, thank God, but I've heard stories about how they plant stuff on these terraced hillsides in the Far East, and I keep wondering how they work it, having once been a farmer myself.

We just sighted the outskirts of Kobe. The skies are still vacant, and that scares you a little. 1:52 and we're over the edge of the city. We're coming in at 2,000 feet. We roar across the city, raising such an almighty racket the noise kind of bounces back, it seems like, and the Japs down there are running back and forth in the streets like so many ants in an ant hill. There's our target. She's an aircraft factory, a mess of buildings down there, scattered over a block or better. There are the docks. All we got to do now is let go. Hirohito, the Yanks have arrived.

The white puffs of smoke had been some ineffectual anti-aircraft fire. The plane was gone as quickly as it had arrived. The only sound now was of sirens down near the harbor where the fires burned.

Helmi ran into the house to check on her mother and found her standing at the sink with her hands over her ears, staring up at the ceiling.

"It's fine, Mama," Helmi said. "It's gone now."

"Bombs," cried Rachel, hands still over her ears. "They dropped bombs."

"Yes, but only a few. They were Americans."

"I don't care who they were. Bombs are bombs." She put her hands down and looked her daughter square in the eye. Her voice was calmer now. "And you can be sure, they will be back with more."

None of the sixteen planes were able to land in China as planned. Darkness, bad weather, and lack of fuel made this impossible. One plane veered off to the north and crash-landed in Russian territory, where the crew was captured and interned, since the Soviet Union was not yet an ally of the U.S. The other fifteen planes either ditched in the ocean off the China coast or crashed after their crews bailed out over Japanese-controlled Chinese territory. With the help of sympathetic Chinese residents, most of the crew members escaped. Eight were captured by the Japanese, and of these three died in captivity and five were interned for the duration of the war. Plane #15 ditched in the water, and its crew of five was rescued and eventually led to safety by the Chinese.

The damage done by the bombers to Japanese targets was minimal, but the raid had powerful repercussions both in Japan and the U.S. Though they put out propaganda that played down and ridiculed the mission, the Japanese were shocked that planes from an American carrier could reach the mainland without detection, and plans were instituted to redirect the Pacific war effort to take on the U.S. carrier fleet, a strategy that would backfire and contribute to their eventual defeat in the decisive Battle of Midway. American morale, meanwhile, both in the military and on the home front, would receive a tremendous boost at a critical moment in the war when some good news was sorely needed from the Pacific theater. The raiders were treated as heroes, and Doolittle himself would be promoted to brigadier general and receive the Congressional Medal of Honor. In the short term, however, the Chinese felt the greatest repercussions. The Japanese took revenge for the rescue and protection of the downed American airmen by burning hundreds of villages in the coastal districts where the planes went down and killing upwards of two hundred thousand Chinese civilians.

And within three years, my grandmother would be proven correct. The Americans would indeed come back with more bombs.

Fire From the Sky

Kobe, 1943–1945

TENANTS FOR Rachel's six rented rooms continued to come and go throughout the war, including some Germans, who were the main international travelers still passing through the port of Kobe. One couple arrived, Germans from the Dutch East Indies, who needed housing for a period of weeks while the husband saw to some business affairs. His wife sat home in the rooming house during the day and spent much of her time complaining—about the wartime conditions, the strict rationing, and the poor inventory of goods in the stores. She was also a strong believer in Nazi propaganda, and when she realized that her landlady, Rachel, was Jewish, she was horrified. At first the women avoided each other, but Rachel eventually made a concerted effort to be friendly, mostly in order to stop the woman's complaining. She finally won her over by way of food: she showed the woman how to make use of the ample supply of cash provided by her husband to shop on Kobe's underground black market, which most residents knew about but few could afford. Together, using the German woman's money, they procured vegetables and chickens and cuts of beef. For a period of one month, everyone ate well. Rachel made chicken soup for the household and taught the woman how to make Russian borscht. When it was time for the couple to finally leave Japan, Rachel and the German *frau* tearfully hugged goodbye.

Late in the war, other kinds of Germans passed through. Rumors circulated that German U-boats had made it past American-laid minefields and into Kobe harbor. One day Rachel answered the door to a pair of Japanese soldiers, who informed her that she was required to provide housing for several weeks to a pair of German officers. That evening, two men arrived, outfitted in the black uniforms of the German SS. Rachel was not asked to provide them with any meals, and she did not offer to do so. The officers were gone during the day, presumably attending to military business, and during the rest of the time Rachel, Helmi, and their few other tenants were careful to steer clear of them as much as they could. Helmi was designated as the communicator when necessary, because of her ability to speak fluent German. The officers were polite to her, and never showed any awareness that they were being housed by Jews.

Helmi had another acquaintance, a young woman of Russian-Japanese descent with no family, whose method of survival was to take up prostitution. This friend, named Maria, latched onto one of the most senior German officers in Kobe, becoming his paramour and hostess for the soirees held at his large commandeered residence at the top of the hill. But the Germans didn't stay long, and soon Maria was left alone again, once more out of luck and on her own. She gave Helmi a souvenir of her brief time as a society hostess, a luxurious pair of nylon stockings, the first pair Helmi had ever owned.

In early 1945 the war came directly to Kobe, in the form of massive American bombing raids. In the previous year, the Americans had retaken many Pacific islands and had established a major air base in the Marianas, within easy striking distance of Japan with the new, larger B-29 bombers. High-altitude raids had been conducted over several cities without much success: the Japanese weather made for poor accuracy. In 1945 a new Pacific bombing policy was put in place, on the heels of great success in Europe—low altitude carpet-bombing, using incendiary bombs designed to ignite firestorms in both industrial and residential neighborhoods. The first of these raids was conducted over Kobe, in February 1945, targeting the area near the downtown waterfront and resulting in tremendous destruction of factories and shipyards. On March 9, the effectiveness of this tactic was further proven by a much larger bombing raid conducted over the capital city of Tokyo, creating a massive firestorm that destroyed sixteen square miles of the city and left over eighty thousand people dead. A week later, on March 17, Kobe was again bombed, this time with a force of 330 B-29s in low-altitude formation. The resulting fires destroyed several square miles of the city and killed tens of thousands of people.

Damage from American bombing in downtown Kobe, 1945. From Helmi's personal collection.

Air-raid sirens would go off in the center of the city to warn the population in advance of attacks. Rachel and Helmi lived far up the hill from the downtown docks and factories, but they knew no neighborhood was truly safe. When they heard the sirens, they would grab heavy pots from the kitchen and hold them over their heads as they ran from the house and followed their neighbors up the hill and into the dense woods at the end of the street. The woods were much closer than one of the dugout air-raid shelters. From the protection of the trees they sat and watched as the planes rained bombs onto the city and smoke from the fires rose high into the sky.

Kobe was the target of seven American bombing raids in the first six months of 1945. The largest was on June 5, when nearly five hundred bombers swooped in low over the city in the middle of the day. The wingtip-to-wingtip formation of planes covered the sky from horizon to horizon, blocking out much of the daylight. When it was over, five more square miles of the city had been incinerated and approximately seventy thousand people had been killed. This time, after making their way back down the hill, Rachel and Helmi saw that even their own neighborhood had been severely damaged. The homes on both sides of Rachel's small boardinghouse were destroyed and still smoldering. Many other buildings on the block had been hit, but their own house remained untouched—miraculously, or so it seemed. One of Rachel's boarders, an elderly British man whom the Japanese had not bothered to intern because of his advanced age, steadfastly refused to leave the house during air raids. There he sat once again, at his perch beside his upstairs window, waving at them below. When they went back into the house, Rachel found an unexploded incendiary bomb, the size of a baseball bat, resting on the kitchen counter next to a shattered window.

Many of their friends lost their homes in these bombing raids, and Rachel made an effort to accommodate whomever she could, making extra space in the dining room and kitchen of her boardinghouse. The Sidlines, Boris and Fania and their two sons Alex and George, moved in with Rachel for the second time, after losing their home with everything they owned as well as their dry-goods business located down the hill.

Rachel also rented two extra rooms in a house on the other side of the Rokko mountain ridge, in a suburb twenty miles inland from Kobe called Arima. This neighborhood featured a small hot springs and served as a cheap vacation spot close by the city. Most of the time she sublet these rooms for extra income, but now she formulated a plan to get herself, her daughter, and as many of their unfortunate friends as possible out of the fire zone. She gathered together everyone who had crammed into the boardinghouse, a collection of war-weary adults and terrified children, and announced that she and Helmi were going over the hill to Arima and anyone who wished to join them was welcome. They would have to pack themselves into only two rooms, but she believed they would be safer there. She was tired of hiding from the bombs with a cooking pot over her head, and she knew that next time they might not be so lucky. The four Sidlines accepted her offer, along with half a dozen others. And so this motley crew, led by Rachel, trooped down the hill into the obliterated center of the city to see if the train to Arima was still running. To their amazement, the central train station was still intact, and after a long wait the train actually arrived; they got on board and rode around the mountain.

So it was that Rachel, diminutive and temperamental, took charge of a small group of war refugees and led them to a place of relative safety for those final terrible weeks of the war. This story comes from the recollections of George Sidline, part of the group who followed her to Arima in June 1945, when he was only ten years old. Rachel was not able to do much, but she had the presence of mind and generosity of spirit to do what she could. No one who knew Rachel later, in Reno—Baba, as everyone called her then—would have identified her as leadership material. To us, she was a ridiculous character, shuffling around in a state of perpetual anxiety, wringing her hands and muttering to herself in Russian, easily sent into paroxysms of fear by the smallest trifle. Yet at this harrowing moment in the last months of the Second World War, she tapped into a hidden reserve of fortitude and resourcefulness. There were four more aerial attacks on the city of Kobe in June and July of 1945, conducted by squadrons of both B-29 bombers and smaller fighter planes. By late summer, much of the city had been eradicated. Just over the hill in Arima, no bombs ever fell. Crowded and uncomfortable as they were, everyone remained safe.

By the first week of August, the attacks seemed to have come to a halt. Rachel and Helmi made a trip back over from Arima and found that their home was one of the few left intact on their street. The skies had been quiet since the last American raid on July 30, which had targeted mostly airfields, factories, and railroads. The crowded conditions in Arima, coupled with the intense summer heat, were becoming difficult to endure, so Rachel decided to move back home.

By now it was widely understood that the nation of Japan had been brought to its knees. Throughout the war the local newspapers, some printed in English for the benefit of foreigners, had published an unbroken string of reports touting great victories over the Allied Forces. With the horrific evidence of their own eyes, everyone realized that the continuing propaganda was false and defeat was all but certain. In recent months relentless bombing raids had decimated Tokyo and most other urban centers. Hundreds of thousands had been killed and millions more had lost their homes. If the strategy of the U.S. was to terrorize the entire country, it had worked well. Curiously, a small number of Japanese cities had been spared any attacks while others, Kobe included, had been firebombed repeatedly. Then, on August 8, word quickly circulated that a single plane had dropped a single bomb on the city of Hiroshima, just 300 kilometers southeast of Kobe, reportedly causing enough damage to equal, or perhaps surpass, the heaviest carpet bombings. Then a similar attack came against Nagasaki, another previously undamaged city at the southern tip of Japan. Again, unbelievably, one plane dropped only one bomb, but it wiped out much of the city in a single blast. The newspapers called it an "atomic" attack. The next day more American planes flew low over Kobe, this time dropping not bombs but leaflets, printed in both Japanese and English, warning that more such attacks were imminent if Japan did not declare an immediate surrender.

Against such a weapon, it seemed pointless for Helmi and Rachel to hold pots and pans over their heads, or even to run back to Arima. There was no safe haven from this new horror. The Americans could easily eradicate the entire country from end to end with a few more of these bombs. In Kobe, and no doubt everywhere else in Japan, a heavy resignation settled over the remaining populace, Japanese and foreigners alike. There was nothing to do but wait and see what would befall them next.

A week passed, with no news of any new attacks. Wednesday, August 15, was particularly hot and humid. At midday Helmi journeyed into the center of Kobe to search for extra fresh food in the remaining illegal markets. After walking down the steep hill in the stifling heat, she boarded one of the few electric-powered streetcars still in operation and rode for several blocks through the rubble of the market area. When the conductor stopped the streetcar and ordered everybody into the street, and when she heard the speakers crackle to life and begin broadcasting the tinny and incomprehensible voice, supposedly that of the emperor himself, she felt both curious and annoyed. If he was giving a pep talk to his disheartened countrymen, it wasn't accomplishing its purpose. Around her everyone seemed more miserable than ever. The broadcast was short, no more than a couple of minutes. Only after she returned home with a few provisions and told her mother what she had seen and heard did they learn, from a neighbor, the momentous news: the emperor had surrendered. The war was over.

They walked back from the neighbor's home in a daze. Once in their house, Rachel went straight to the cupboard and took out something she had been saving since the war began. She had kept it hidden away until now, at times doubting that this moment would ever come. It was a can of sweetened condensed milk, something no one had seen in Japan for a long time, not even on the black market. They had lived for four years on mostly rice and beans. Their main indulgence had been cheap Japanese cigarettes. Rachel opened the can and handed it to her daughter. Helmi began to drink and didn't stop until the can was empty. For the rest of her life, she would say it was the best thing she ever tasted.

Immigrant—Kobe to America

Bill Horgan in his US Army uniform, about 1942.

Sentimental Journey

Baguio, Philippines, 1945

I N MIDSUMMER 1945, Sgt. William Patrick Horgan of the U.S. Army Counter Intelligence Corps, a native of Reno, Nevada, was feeling fed up. He had been confined for two months to a hospital bed in a sweltering Philippine military hospital, recovering from jaundice. Not quite sick enough to be sent home to the States but not yet well enough to be discharged from the sick ward, he had been languishing there week after week, gradually recovering his strength, making a meager contribution to the war effort by spending a tedious couple of hours a day summarizing field reports from fellow CIC operatives in the Pacific theater. Information was coming in daily as Allied forces secured additional islands and moved ever closer to mainland Japan. He longed to be back in action, though his experience hardly merited the term: he had not seen any combat.

Sgt. Horgan considered himself lucky to be in the military at all. When he had originally tried to enlist, back home in Reno after law school, he had been summarily rejected. They told him he was so severely nearsighted he could be declared legally blind. But his two brothers had both enlisted, and he felt compelled to serve if he could. What good was a Harvard Law degree in a world ripped apart by war? His older brother, Jack, was a skilled pilot who had spent the war stateside training other pilots, and his younger brother, Tom, had been in command of a B-24 in Europe that was shot down over Germany and spent a year in prison camp. His brothers were married to a pair of sisters, local Nevada girls. Jack already had two young sons, and Tom was now the father of a little boy, too. Since they were both serving, it seemed wrong for him, the only bachelor among the three, not to join up, too. Bill—or Pat, as school chums knew him—made up his mind to contribute to the military in some way. Midway through the war he tried again, traveling to Texas, where the CIC was signing up potential operatives with special skills, and there he convinced the army recruiters that his Harvard law degree and analytic ability should outweigh his blindness. Bill spent a hasty two weeks in boot camp, then was given the rank of corporal and sent first to Australia for more training and then to New Guinea, where after a short time he contracted dengue fever and was sent to bed for a month. And now, here in the Philippines, having been promoted from corporal to staff sergeant for no reason that he could discern, he was completing his second tour of duty as a hospital patient.

The war in the Pacific was finally going well after many months of protracted battles and tremendous loss of life. The Japanese mainland had been pummeled by huge squadrons of B-29 bombers based mainly on the island of Guam. The talk was that a land invasion of the mainland, the plans for which had been in the works for many months, perhaps would not now be necessary. Just a week ago, a new type of atomic weapon had been used with devastating effect on two Japanese cities. Two bombs had done more damage and killed more people than hundreds of B-29s dropping thousands of conventional bombs. Sgt. Horgan had taken physics courses in college, and he had followed what he could about this astonishing new weapon, whose power derived from the fission of atomic nuclei. Einstein was right after all—mass could be converted directly into energy. But Einstein might not be altogether happy about this method of proving it.

On the afternoon of August 15, Bill lay in his Philippine hospital bed, dozing with the radio tuned to a daytime music program. A song began that he had heard many times before and that had become a favorite— Doris Day's sultry rendition of "Sentimental Journey." He kept his eyes closed and let Doris's voice wash over him.

Over the course of the last year and a half, first in New Guinea and now in the Philippines, Bill had struggled to maintain his sense of purpose as a soldier. Supposedly he was a member of an elite intelligence unit, made up of supposedly smart people like him, lawyers and college professors, charged with uncovering dope about spies and saboteurs— but in New Guinea what they had mostly done was sit far behind the lines of combat, holed up on the beach for weeks on end in sweltering pup tents, fending off mosquitoes. Once the battles had finished raging and territory had been secured, he and his cohorts were called in to inspect the aftermath of combat, take photographs, and file reports, finding mostly burned villages, destroyed cropland, and terrified people eager to be friends with the new American occupiers. In the Philippines he had been busier, because the Japanese had recruited many civilian agents among the populace, ordering them to set fires and cut power lines, and it would turn out that these "agents" were easy to interrogate and ultimately win over simply by treating them decently. As in New Guinea, the CIC patrols were called in only after combat operations had ceased, so Bill never faced any real danger. With the CIC he had been given perks and privileges but not nearly enough in the way of a serious military mission.

And now for a second time he was sweating his time away in a hospital bed. Between illnesses, while working out of an improvised office in Manila in a commandeered mansion, he had developed a friendship with a fetching young Spanish-Filipino woman named Lulu (short for Lourdes), who had begun hinting boldly that she would like nothing better than to follow him back to the United States. Bill had been preparing to tell her that this would be impossible when he found himself back in the hospital. Lulu had since come to see him often, bringing him magazines to read and cold drinks to stave off the heat. He was grateful for her attention, though it made the prospect of telling her that he could not be her ticket to America all the more difficult. What kind of brave soldier was he, anyhow?

Doris Day had come to the bridge of the song ("*Seven, that's the time I leave, at seven…*") when the music abruptly cut off. After a few seconds of silence, a scratchy voice from Armed Services Radio broke in with a bulletin from Pacific High Command: the Japanese emperor had officially issued a proclamation declaring his country's unconditional surrender to Allied Forces. The war was over.

The announcer signed off, and after another few seconds of silence Doris Day was back, right where she had left off. Wide awake now, Bill took a deep breath, knowing that he would remember this moment, and this song, for the rest of his life.

He had already been told that when he recovered sufficiently he would at some point be part of post-combat intelligence operations in Japan, following either a protracted land invasion or a quick surrender. So here it was—the second option. He had no idea precisely where he might be deployed, but he knew the overall plan was to send CIC units into all the major Japanese cities. There were unconfirmed intelligence reports that since VE Day, in June, some German military personnel, including possibly high-ranking officers, had made their way to Japan in U-boats, hoping to escape American retribution. And there were reputedly small pockets of non-Asian refugees, including Jews from various countries, hidden in the shadows of the Japanese port cities. These were things worth investigating. And with the war over, eventually he would earn enough army "points" to be able to finally return home to Reno— a sentimental journey, indeed.

Staff Sgt. Horgan sat up in bed with renewed energy. He had been out of commission for a long stretch, but things were going to be different now. Lulu would need to hitch a ride to America with someone else, and he would let her know that straightaway. He was going to Japan. It was time to get out of the hospital and back into the world.

The Counter Intelligence Corps

Kobe, 1945

O N AN AFTERNOON in early September, Helmi and her mother met their first American soldiers. She and Rachel were walking up the hill from the streetcar stop toward their house, returning from a birthday party for the young child of a Jewish friend—the same friend, Eda Wiznitzer, whose ship had turned around in the middle of the night after Pearl Harbor. The party had been for Eda's four-year-old daughter, born in Japan instead of the U.S. and therefore stateless like her parents. Suddenly a vehicle came whizzing up behind them, seemingly out of nowhere, and stopped alongside. It was a U.S. Army jeep, and in it were two men in uniform.

All through the war the Japanese authorities had publicized warnings to the populace that Americans were savages and that a land invasion of Japan would bring mayhem and mass murder on a horrible scale. The Jewish community, of course, knew otherwise. Together with their other Russian friends, ever since the surrender Helmi and Rachel had looked forward eagerly to the arrival of the American occupiers.

The driver asked the women who they were and where they lived. He spoke with a peculiar drawl they had never heard before, and even though they recognized he was speaking English he was difficult to understand. Rachel replied that she and her daughter were Russian refugees who lived just up the street, and then, without hesitation, she invited the soldiers to visit their home. After all, these were the first representatives of the conquering forces that they had encountered, and it might be useful to make a good impression. Rachel was not shy by nature, and if she had learned anything in all her years of hardship and deprivation it was to make the most of any chance opportunity.

The soldiers were glad to accept the invitation, partly out of duty, since they were in fact charged with identifying non-Asians in the city of Kobe, of which there appeared to be a substantial number. No doubt these American soldiers also took keen notice of the pretty, dark-eyed daughter of this eager little Russian lady. Helmi, now in her twenties, had learned to present herself as a sophisticated young woman, despite her impoverished background. This was a skill she had acquired from observation, growing up in the cosmopolitan atmosphere of 1930s Shanghai, and it would serve her well for the rest of her life. She was well aware, for instance, that her clear English and British-flavored accent set her apart from many of the other foreigners in Kobe, including in her own circle of Russians. The soldiers made room in the jeep, offering seats to the two ladies, and they all rode up the hill together.

Once inside the house, Rachel offered to make the soldiers tea and something to eat. Probably thinking they might get more interesting fare than their standard military rations, the men accepted eagerly, only to be disappointed by the plain rice and beans offered. One of them ran out to the jeep and brought back some of their own K and C rations—canned beef, canned fruit—to augment the meal. The men apologized for their meager contribution, but both Rachel and Helmi were downright thrilled by what seemed to them a gourmet feast.

The soldiers conducted an interview during the meal, dutifully determining how long the women had lived in Japan and ascertaining something of their prior history. One introduced himself as George, from Chicago. He explained that they were with a branch of the army called the Counter Intelligence Corps, and one of their jobs was to collect information about non-Asian residents of the city. The soldier who had driven the jeep was much harder to understand because of his odd accent. He managed to convey that he was from Mobile, Alabama, and that everybody he knew back home sounded just like him. Not even in American movies had Helmi ever heard such a thick Southern drawl, and she found it comical. There was another strange feature to these soldiers—a sickly complexion, an odd greenish tinge to their skin.

Before leaving, the men asked if they could return the next day with their unit sergeant, whom they believed would wish to conduct a more extensive interview. They may have been motivated to come back out of purely professional concerns, or perhaps they simply wanted to continue enjoying themselves. Likely both. At any rate, the women agreed, and the date was made.

The following afternoon the same jeep presented itself at Rachel's house with the same two soldiers plus their unit leader, a skinny and bespectacled staff sergeant sporting the same peculiar green complexion as the other two. He seemed shyer than the other men, even though he was their superior, and spoke softly, with no discernible accent. He introduced himself as Sgt. Horgan, from Reno, Nevada. They had heard of this place, Reno—the divorce capital of the world. Helmi always said that her first impression of him was nothing special, other than that she found him more serious in demeanor than most of the other American soldiers she got to know during that time.

Sgt. Horgan's questions for the women were more detailed, delving into their background and their reasons for being in Japan. He was particularly curious about other non-Asians of their acquaintance. He interrogated them, politely but thoroughly, about the other Russian and Jewish residents of Kobe and about the various tenants who currently or formerly rented rooms from Rachel. He took detailed notes about the German officers they had housed, saying that this might well require a follow-up interview. He also wanted information about how the food distribution network had functioned and who had done the communicating with the Japanese authorities. Like the soldiers the day before, he found this dark-eyed young woman particularly interesting. She may have been Russian, but her English was perfect, with a slight British accent, even though she had spent her entire life in China and Japan. She was poised and articulate in a way that belied her apparent refugee status. When he learned that Helmi's language abilities had enabled her, before the war, to serve as a liaison between people of varied nationalities, he mentioned that despite her stateless status she might well qualify to be a contract employee for the American military occupation force. The positions might be short term, but the pay would be decent. Would she be interested?

Interested? Indeed, she told him, she would be very interested.

Before he departed with his fellow soldiers, Sgt. Horgan left several more boxes of army rations with the two women and promised to bring more, including some fresh fruit, vegetables, and even meat, that would be arriving soon. He also suggested that Helmi present herself at the office of the commander of the U.S. Army's Thirty-Third Infantry Division, Brigadier General W. G. Skelton, at her convenience, to be interviewed for possible employment. On his way out, Sgt. Horgan asked if the women had any questions for him.

"Only one," Helmi said. "Why do you all have such pale and sickly complexions? Are you ill? The color of your uniforms is called 'olive drab.' Your faces seem to match."

Rachel clutched her daughter's arm and hissed at her to not be so rude.

Sgt. Horgan smiled for the first time. "No," he said. "We aren't sick. Some of us were. We take a drug to prevent us from getting sick again, an anti-malarial medicine called Atabrine. This," he said, touching the side of his face, "is called the 'Atabrine Tan.' You'll get used to seeing it on a lot of guys." He thanked the women for their time, and the soldiers drove away in their jeep.

Over the next weeks, Helmi would indeed meet many more pale Americans. The day after meeting the staff sergeant from Nevada, she put on her best clothes and presented herself down the hill at the American army headquarters, as he had suggested. After an interview and an opportunity to demonstrate her typing and shorthand skills, she was hired. Within a week, she was serving as secretary to Col. A. T. McNash, the head of the Personnel and Administration Division of the Thirty-Third Infantry Division, the occupying force based in Kobe. She was soon promoted to the Chief of Staff's Office because of her secretarial skills, her language abilities, and her apparent knack for connecting with people and making them feel comfortable and less intimidated by the military setting. The American army personnel were charged with conducting numerous interviews with Japanese and non-Japanese residents of the city, and Helmi's fluency in Russian, French, and German, as well as her more than passing familiarity with both Japanese and Yiddish, made her extremely valuable to the U.S. military as an interpreter and translator.

In one instance, a report came through the office that one of the Counter Intelligence unit leaders, the same Sgt. Horgan who had interviewed her at home with her mother, was trying to locate a young Russian woman who had reportedly been the paramour of a German officer. Sgt. Horgan requested a meeting with Miss Koskin and came to her home again. Over lunch, she informed him that the woman he sought was her friend Maria, who had turned to prostitution in order to survive during the war.

"I doubt you'll get much from her," Helmi said. "She's on tough times since the Germans sailed away in their submarines. You should leave her alone." Then she added, "If you want to know more about the Germans, you ought to ask my mother. She kept her eyes open when they were around. She worried every minute that we would be shipped to a concentration camp." The sergeant thanked her for the suggestion and said he would indeed follow up on it. The rest of the lunch was taken up with lighter conversation. The sergeant asked Helmi more about her life in a way that seemed less related to his professional duties.

Staff Sgt. Horgan from Reno was not the only American soldier to find Helmi interesting. A number of other soldiers, both enlisted men and officers, took notice of this petite young woman who had been recruited from the local population to work for the Americans and who would eventually become the personal secretary to General Skelton, the initial commanding officer. She socialized with some of them. One, a thirty-seven-year-old lieutenant colonel from Caruthersville, Missouri, named Peter Scott, took her to dinner several times. He told her he had until recently been engaged to a woman back in the States, where he had been based prior to coming to Japan, but that was all over now. He seemed lonely, and clearly he enjoyed Helmi's company. To her, he had an appealing sense of humor. There was an informal atmosphere in the office, set up by the army in one of Kobe's few undamaged buildings. Levity was allowed, even encouraged, including clowning around for silly pictures, even though outside the city still lay in ruins. Col. Scott asked Helmi what future she saw for herself now that the war was truly finished. She explained to him that she had missed the opportunity to go to the United States five years earlier, and admitted that now she couldn't help reviving her dream to somehow get there. He assured her that he would be glad to help in any way he could.

As 1945 came to a close, the Counter Intelligence Corps was wrapping up its postwar mission and many of its military staff members were to be discharged and sent home by Christmas, including Sgt. Horgan from Reno. He had not taken Helmi on any formal dates, but he took her to lunch several more times before he sailed, in his own way making an effort to strengthen the acquaintance. He took Rachel to lunch

Helmi clowning around with one of her US Army supervisors, in Kobe, 1946.

separately, treating her with great courtesy and respect, partly in order to finish interviewing her about the German officers. She provided what names she could and also told him that, according to rumors she had heard, some other Germans, in anticipation of Axis defeat, had stayed on in Japan in order to hide and try to blend in, masquerading as refugees from the very countries whose populations they had slaughtered—even pretending to be Jewish. To Rachel this attempt at subterfuge was an obscenity that could easily be exposed: her advice was to simply say a few words in Yiddish to them. If they could understand them, fine, they were Jews. If they could not, arrest them and make them pay for their crimes, or at least send them back where they came from. This was better than an I.D. card.

It was true that a number of Germans had indeed hidden in Japan at the end of the war, military personnel and civilians alike, hoping to pass as refugees. The mountain town of Karuizawa, north of Tokyo—where Rachel's friends the Sidlines spent the last year of the war—had been a favorite getaway for German tourists and soldiers. Ironically, a considerable number of Japan's Jewish families, particularly those with passports to neutral countries, had also been relocated to Karuizawa, as another way of partially satisfying Germany's demand to keep an eye on them. In Karuizawa the Sidlines witnessed firsthand the forced depor- tation of several trainloads of German nationals, including some former Nazis—not loaded into boxcars, as European Jews had been, but onto ordinary passenger trains, and eventually onto ships bound for German ports—in an eerie reversal of history.

Before departing Japan, Sgt. Horgan made a point of providing both Rachel and Helmi with extra gifts from the army commissary, including more cigarettes by the carton and boxes of Hershey's chocolate bars. By the time he left to go home to America, he hoped that a friendship had been well established, one that he had every intention of maintaining from across the ocean. When he stopped at their home to say goodbye, he made a careful note of their address and said they would be hearing from him again.

The Quota System

Kobe, 1946

HELMI KOSKIN WAS EMPLOYED in various capacities by the U.S. Army in Kobe for a little over a year. Through her work in assisting people of various nationalities with repatriation to their native countries or with seeking visas to third countries, she became familiar with the complexities of United States immigration quota policy. The quotas were based on country of birth and racial status. Prior to the war, all persons of Asian descent had been barred entirely from immigration. China, a wartime ally of the U.S., in 1943 was rewarded with a token annual quota of 105 immigrants of Chinese descent. Japan, however, having been an enemy state, remained under the most severe restrictions. Absolutely no one of Japanese descent was eligible.

Helmi realized that her unusual status, having been born in Japan but being both stateless and non-Japanese, might actually provide an advantage. With the help of some of the other army clerical staff, in the spring of 1946 she began applying for a visa, assuming that it would be a long and complicated process. She told her mother that the outcome would not be known for some time and was doubtful, in any case. Rachel made no objection. In fact, she seemed encouraging. The proper paperwork was assembled and filed, including a duplicate birth certificate obtained from the International Hospital of Kobe, establishing that Helmi had been born there on July 15, 1923, and was of Russian descent. She continued her work, expecting a long wait. However, within a month she received word from the U.S. consulate that quota numbers for 1946 were forthcoming and that, as long as she met certain stringent requirements for additional documentation, including letters of support and sponsorship, she would be given a quota number for immigration from Japan:

number *two*. She carried the letter around to several of her co-workers and superiors. Did it mean what she thought it meant? Yes, of course, they all told her. She was second in line to receive an immediate visa to emigrate from Japan to the United States.

Helmi took this astonishing news straight to her mother. Life had improved dramatically for them both since the American occupation began. Helmi was being paid a good deal more by the U.S. Army than she ever had by the British travel agency before the war. Thanks to the Americans, food and heating oil were now plentiful and affordable. The winter of 1945–1946 was the first time in years they had been able to eat decently and stay warm. And now this.

Helmi expected her mother to show some resistance. After all they had been through together—so many years of poverty and war—to arrive now at this moment of peace and comfort only to have Helmi proclaim that she was moving to America might be too much for her. Rachel was now fifty years of age, and for all the strength she had shown in the last months of the war in helping shelter their friends, she was as fragile as ever in many ways and still capable of dark moods. It was widely understood how much she depended on her daughter for all manner of support, both material and emotional. Yet this time, Helmi did not want to be denied. She meant to go to America.

To her amazement, Rachel was supportive of the idea. "Yes, yes, by all means, go!" she proclaimed, with what appeared to be genuine enthusiasm. "You are a grown woman. You must not lose this chance!" There were tears in her eyes, but she declared emphatically that they were tears of joy. For all her obvious desire to keep her daughter close, Rachel could see a different future opening up, one she had never dared imagine: a life for Helmi in America. Her words echoed exactly how Helmi felt. She was now twenty-three years old. If there was ever a time to seize an opportunity and step forward toward a new life, this was it.

Passage on a Freighter

Kobe, 1946

AS SUMMER MOVED INTO FALL, Helmi's life began to accelerate. She had given notice to her army employers, but they asked her to stay on the job until the end of October. Meanwhile, she began making plans to sail to America. She needed a ticket, of course, which was a more complicated matter than she had realized. And she needed the required documentation, including at least two letters of support from U.S. citizens, as well as a formal affidavit of financial support from someone with demonstrated assets in a U.S. bank account. This was required, since Helmi had no assets of her own and no guarantee of employment in the United States, to insure she would not become a burden to the government. This is where her army supervisor, Col. Peter Scott from Missouri, stepped in to help.

In the second half of 1946, Col. Scott had moved up to assume command of the military government team for the city of Kobe, the highest level of local authority. When Helmi approached him, he not only provided her with a detailed letter of recommendation for future employment, extolling her clerical and language skills in addition to her exceptional personal qualities, he also signed a legally binding affidavit of support for her, in which he voluntarily incurred an obligation to provide for her support in the United States, if necessary. Attached to the affidavit was a copy of Col. Scott's personal bank record from the First State Bank of Caruthersville, Missouri, showing his total assets of $5,556.87, offered as proof of support and collateral. She also had personal letters of support from a distant cousin in New Jersey and a couple named the Blooms, who had emigrated from Kobe to San Francisco before the war. All she needed now was a boat ticket.

This was not a simple matter. Civilian travel was severely restricted between Japan and the U.S. in 1946. Again, the U.S. Army stepped in to help. By this time commercial freighters were being utilized to transport goods and supplies into Japanese ports, which were rapidly being rebuilt under American supervision. Their incoming cargo was virtually all under military contract. However, for their return trips to the U.S., the freighters were mostly empty. As a way to defray costs, the military therefore tolerated, if it didn't actively encourage, a policy allowing these freighters to take on a very limited number of civilian passengers as long as they possessed all proper documentation needed at the U.S. end. To circumvent bureaucratic red tape, a simple system was utilized. A berth would be booked, but paid for in cash directly to the ship's captain, handed over once the ship was out of port and officially in international waters. It was an efficient system, if not fully compliant with maritime regulations. The fare was five hundred U.S. dollars—a sum neither she nor her mother possessed.

Helmi was never sure where the money came from: possibly from some of her mother's friends, or possibly even from Aunt Sonya, who reportedly before the war had made it out of Shanghai to somewhere in the U.S. just in time, with her husband and her money. If Rachel herself were somehow responsible, she never did own up to it. One day in early November, she simply handed Helmi an envelope with five hundred dollars cash, along with a voucher good for a berth on an American freighter sailing to San Francisco in two weeks. "Don't worry about who is paying," Rachel told her daughter. "Just take it."

During the months leading up to this turn of events, Helmi had exchanged letters with several of the American soldiers she had met during their time of duty in Kobe, including the shy Sgt. Horgan, now back in Reno, Nevada, discharged from the army and launching a law practice. In his letters he had expressed a hope that that the two of them might cross paths again once she made it to the U.S. He had also sent more gifts, including one that she cherished greatly—a makeup kit, with lipstick, facial powder, mascara, and perfume, all top American brands that had been unavailable in Japan. She was impressed by his thoughtfulness, and showed the makeup kit to her mother. Rachel was also impressed. "I'm not surprised," she said, with a smile. "I could see this was a good person from the very first. Quite smart, too. I remember him well."

"Is that so?" Helmi didn't fully realize that her mother had paid such close attention to the American soldiers. "Well, he has certainly sent me a nice gift." She tried to picture this American now, but she found that in her mind they all looked much the same, with their drab uniforms and sickly complexions. She did recall that he had been an interesting person to talk to, in a quiet sort of way. They had read many of the same books. And of course there were the cigarettes and chocolate, too. No doubt these also partly accounted for her mother's positive opinion now.

On a morning in November 1946, Helmi boarded an American freighter in Kobe harbor along with sixteen other passengers, and was given a small room with a small round window. She had a berth and a sink, with a bathroom down the hall. Her clothes and belongings were packed into a sturdy five-piece set of luggage purchased in downtown Kobe, made out of salvaged aluminum from shot-down American bombers. She hugged and kissed her mother, who remained surprisingly calm throughout, as if this were all part of some plan she had foreseen—although there was no way that could be true. An hour into the voyage Helmi handed her envelope of cash to the captain, as she had been instructed.

The voyage was scheduled to last seventeen days, though it turned out to be two days longer because of heavy weather halfway across. She saw very little of the other passengers for the entire trip. Most of them stayed in their rooms, and she learned from the crew that the main reason was seasickness. There were also complaints about the food provided, but she found it abundant and delicious. She had brought a stack of books and did a great deal of reading.

When the ship finally docked in San Francisco two weeks later, she had gained several pounds. She felt rested and relaxed. This, she thought to herself, must be what a vacation feels like.

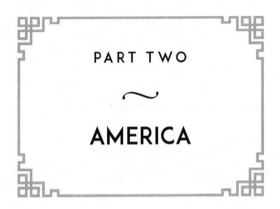

PART TWO

AMERICA

Family—San Francisco to Reno

Helmi photographed by a stranger on the street, San
Francisco, December 1946.

The Evangeline Hotel
for Women

San Francisco, 1946

A T FIRST IMPRESSION San Francisco bore a certain resemblance to
Kobe: the huge protected bay, the harbor bustling with industrial
docks, the city streets climbing up steep hills. The freighter docked on
the Oakland side of the bay. After presenting her papers at the customs
desk, Helmi stepped forward into the lobby to look for the person who
was to meet her, a woman named Anita Matthews. Almost immediately
a young woman walked up who looked to be about her own age, and
with a broad smile put out her hand and immediately told Helmi that
her name would not be Matthews for long. She was married, but only
technically, and it would all be over soon. She had received word from
another gentleman friend in the army, Pete Scott—"Okay, *Colonel* Scott,
he would want me to call him," she said, with a laugh—to help out this
nice Russian girl he was sending over, in any way she could. "So, are you
going with him now? I suppose that's why he's helping you out."

It was Helmi's turn to laugh. "No, nothing like that. But he has been
very kind to me."

"Oh, he's a good enough guy, I guess. We get along better as friends
than we ever did as sweethearts." She laughed again. "Then again, I'm
about to get a divorce, so I don't seem to get along with anybody, do I?
Anyway, I'm glad to hear you're not engaged to him, or anything."

"Nothing of the sort," Helmi assured her. "I'm totally unattached."

"Well, okay. You know, you sure don't sound very Russian. And you
look pretty healthy for a supposedly miserable little refugee. Pete—
pardon me, I mean Colonel Scott—gave me a different impression."

Helmi found that she rather liked this brash American girl. Maybe they could be friends. "Well, I'm not the least bit miserable, now that I'm here. And I am Russian, but that's a long story."

"Well, you can fill me in later. You'd better come along. After all, I'm under orders from the U.S. Army to take good care of you."

Anita immediately delivered Helmi to the apartment of the Blooms, the couple who had known Rachel in Kobe before the war, who had agreed to house her until she found a place of her own. There were a few others Helmi had known in Kobe who had made their way to San Francisco, including the Moiseeffs, Moise and Esther, and the Ponevejskys, Anatole and Gita. Moise and Anatole had established a successful import-export business in Japan prior to the war and had revived it from a new base in the U.S. They also stepped in to provide assistance to Helmi.

Within a few days she was told to report to the downtown office of something called the American Asiatic Corporation, where she found a job waiting for her in the secretarial pool. She was given a desk and a typewriter, but not much in the way of responsibility. She spent much of her work time reading novels and smoking cigarettes. After a week, Anita stopped by the office. She worked nearby as a secretary in the offices of the San Francisco district attorney, Edmund G. Brown (who would later became governor of California).

Lighting cigarettes for them both, she asked, "How are you getting along?"

"Just fine, I suppose," Helmi replied. "I hardly have anything to do. We seem to be in the packaged food business." She reached under her desk. "Here, have a sample. They give us all the cookies and candy we want. Soon I'm going to be fat as a pig."

"Thanks," said Anita, putting a candy bar in her purse. "Count your blessings, that's what I say. So listen, I have some more good news for you. We've got you a swell apartment, all arranged. Pulled a few strings. I'll come by again after work and take you to see it."

It was true. Using her boss's connections, Anita had put Helmi at the top of the list for the Evangeline Residence Hotel for Women, owned and managed by the Salvation Army. A furnished room was available. That very evening, Anita helped her carry her few possessions and clothes on the streetcar, and she moved right in.

The Evangeline, an eight-story building at the corner of McAllister and Market Streets named after the daughter of the Salvation Army's founder, was built in 1924 expressly to house "young working girls employed at a small wage." Most of the rooms were doubles, but there were a few singles and Helmi was given one of those. (The Evangeline was taken over in the 1980s by the Tenderloin Neighborhood Development Corporation, a charitable nonprofit, and today, under the name of the Civic Center Residence, it provides subsidized housing for over one hundred formerly homeless individuals.)

At work, with plenty of time on her hands, Helmi typed letters to her mother back in Japan.

~

December 1, 1946

Dear Mama: I hope you are well and much warmer and more comfortable than last winter. San Francisco in December is not at all cold, most days quite sunny and pleasant in fact. They say that in summer here when the fog settles in for many days it can be colder than the dead of winter. I don't quite believe this, but we shall see.

The Evangeline Residence is just the place for me. We get two meals a day, breakfast and dinner. I find the meals wonderful. Many of the other girls here stick their tongues out at it. I suppose it depends on what one is used to. They are almost all American girls, mostly from here in California. They all think I'm British at first when they hear my accent, and when I say I came from Japan they laugh and tell me to come off it.

They served us up a big dinner for their Thanksgiving holiday, roast turkey with "all the trimmings," meaning potatoes and vegetables and some odd condiments like jellied cranberry. Also pie, which the girls say is either made from sweet potatoes or pumpkins. I ate it all like a starving sailor, and fear that I shall become hugely plump by the time I see you again. The Americans do love their holidays. Christmas is next, and you can begin to see the preparations already in some of the store windows. We are told we will have a tall tree to decorate in our dining room. In America, being Jewish has nothing to do with it—everyone loves Christmas!

I am attending night school not far away from the Evangeline. I walk most of the time, and it seems quite safe even at night. I take a literature course plus American-style bookkeeping, which I have already learned from the U.S. Army. But I am told it will help my prospects to show a diploma in the course. A bit boring actually, but the other girls in the class are all very nice.

My good friend Anita, who got me the apartment, is quite a pistol. It seems she is ending her marriage. She has a very cute daughter, two years old or so. No sign whatsoever of the husband, soon to be the ex-husband. I think she was also once a sweetheart of Col. Scott, which is why he put me in touch with her. She is my one true friend so far.

I enclose a snapshot of me on the sidewalk in front of my building. A strange fellow took it and later left it in my mailbox. I never even got his name. Don't I look quite sophisticated? The outfit is from my first shopping spree. Anita took me to Macy's, her favorite store, which had a sale, because she said I needed a sharper outfit. No need to worry, I only bought the one suit at great discount. Your daughter is no spendthrift! Enclosed is another money order for you, in fact. I will keep sending what I can.

Anita tells me Americans are great ones for giving and receiving Christmas cards. I am planning to send some out, to all the addresses here that I brought with me, including to Col. Scott who I believe has gone home to Missouri, and to some of the other American soldiers we met. It seems a good way to let them all know that I have at last come across the Pacific Ocean. I must tell Col. Scott that I am gainfully employed and have no need to drain his bank account.

I am happy to say that all is well so far! And I miss you, of course.

Love, Helmi

An Invitation

San Francisco, 1947

Helmi did indeed send out a dozen or so Christmas cards in December 1946 to various people she had met in Japan who had provided their addresses, some of whom she had corresponded with, including a few of the American soldiers she had met in Kobe.

On a quiet Saturday morning in early January, one of the house matrons knocked on her door and summoned her downstairs to the Evangeline's telephone desk in the lobby, where she was told she had a call. When she answered, on the other end of the line was the former sergeant, Bill Horgan, from Reno, Nevada. He wanted to thank her for the nice Christmas card that she had sent. And, after a hesitation, he said he had called with an idea. He wanted to invite her to pay a visit to Reno.

"Where is Reno?" she asked, with total sincerity. She had no idea where it was.

The voice on the line laughed nervously. "It's where I live. In Nevada."

"Is it a long way from San Francisco?"

"It's not far at all," he told her. "Just over the mountain. If you'd like to come, I'll send you a plane ticket. The flight is less than an hour."

"My, it's as close as that?" She had no idea what else to say. She was having some trouble forming a clear picture of this fellow. She remembered who he was, of course. He had been on her Christmas card list. He was one of the Americans with a very bad complexion, caused by the army drugs. He had sent her a number of thoughtful gifts, including her cherished makeup kit. And she recognized his soft voice. Hadn't he seemed quite shy, in Japan? Now here he was, out of the blue, inviting her to visit.

"Well, can you come? Should I put a ticket in the mail?"

She felt oddly self-conscious standing there in the Evangeline lobby with the heavy black receiver held to her ear. She had to say something. This must be how Americans went about things. They simply called up and invited one another to visit. Probably she should say no, absolutely not. Then again, she was equally self-conscious about hurting his feelings. What was so wrong with paying someone a visit?

Too much time had gone by in silence.

"Okay," she heard herself say. "Sure. Why not?" She tried to sound like a happy-go-lucky American, but to herself she sounded a bit ridiculous.

"That's great! When can you come? Can you stay a weekend?"

She gathered herself. From what she remembered of him in Japan, and now over the phone as well, he did not seem at all to be the type of person one ought to be wary of. He sounded very nice and quite sincere. It suddenly occurred to her that making this call might well have been difficult for him. She got the feeling it was not the kind of thing he did every day.

"Well, I suppose so. I could come on a Friday, and go home on a Sunday."

"That's perfect!" he said, louder than before. She could almost hear a sigh of relief. "I'll send you the ticket for next weekend. The flight arrives late in the afternoon, around five o'clock. I'll pick you up at the Reno airport."

And so it was done, just like that. She was going to visit this man, whoever he was, in a town called Reno, wherever that was. Her first trip on an airplane.

The ticket did indeed arrive in the mail on the following Wednesday, and on Friday afternoon she took a bus to the airport and climbed on board a United Airlines DC-3 in the rain. The flight to Reno hardly seemed like a journey at all—up, then almost immediately down again. When she stepped off the plane, it was much colder and a light snow was falling. She entered the terminal, and a man walked up to her, smiling, carrying a small bouquet of flowers. She didn't recognize him at all. The person she remembered from Japan a year earlier had been thin and sickly looking, with a very short military haircut. This man, pink-cheeked with neatly combed dark hair, dressed in a suit and tie, seemed like someone else entirely. The difference was startling.

They greeted each other politely and a bit awkwardly, shaking hands. He called himself Bill. In Japan, the other soldiers had sometimes called him Pat, and he explained now that Patrick was his middle name. There had been too many other Bills in his unit. It ran through Helmi's mind once more how odd it was to be visiting someone—someone who was now carrying her suitcase with her things for two nights—yet knowing practically nothing about him. Would she stay in a hotel? That certainly had been her assumption.

He seemed to read her thoughts. "I'll take you to meet my parents," he said. "That's where you'll be staying."

Parents? This was useful information. He didn't say anything about a wife or family. She now knew significantly more about him than she had just a few minutes ago.

"But first," he said, with sudden eagerness, "I'll show you a little of Reno. We'll make a stop downtown, if you like."

"Sure. What is there to see?"

"You've heard that we have gambling here, haven't you?"

"Yes, of course. There were such things in Shanghai, too. Card parlors. And opium dens, of course." She grinned, to make sure he knew she was making a joke.

"Well, we have more than card parlors, but no opium dens. I'll show you one of our famous Nevada casinos."

Bill Horgan then took Helmi to Harolds Club, on Virginia Street in the heart of downtown Reno, where a childhood friend of his named Tuffy Ward worked as a bartender. After Bill briefly introduced her to Tuffy, they continued on through to the casino, where he escorted her to a blackjack table. He took a five-dollar bill from his wallet, put it on the table, and exchanged it for silver dollars. A few cards were dealt, there were some quick exchanges of more cards, and the next thing she knew the five dollars were gone. She was horrified. She couldn't believe people did this for fun. For the next fifty years, she claimed she never got over it. Bill took her to Harolds Club thinking she would be impressed, as a supposedly sophisticated woman of the world, but she was appalled that money could simply vanish like that, in the blink of an eye, under the pretense of recreation. For the rest of her life she avoided the casinos like the plague.

The remainder of the visit went much better. Bill, as promised, delivered her to his parents' house, where he had grown up along with his two brothers, and the four of them sat down to a pot of tea. Bill's father, John E. Horgan, was an Irish immigrant who had established himself in the hardware business, working his way up from stock boy to owner of his own small store. His mother, Veronica, also Irish, had grown up in the mining camps of rural Nevada. As a young woman she had taught in a one-room schoolhouse where she had to ride a horse to work five miles every morning and then stoke a wood fire before her students arrived. Helmi learned these facts about Jack and Von, as they were known, while sitting at the parlor table, sipping her tea, and taking deep drags on her unfiltered Chesterfields. She, in turn, readily answered their questions about her own unusual background. Bill also chain-smoked through the conversation, while his father puffed leisurely on an aromatic pipe.

A neutral observer, eavesdropping on this meeting, might have assumed that this young Russian woman from the Far East and this older Irish couple had very little in common. From all the crucifixes and various images of the blessed Virgin mounted on the walls, it was plain to see that they were devout Catholics. Yet she would always say that she got on famously with them from the very beginning. It wasn't clear if they were primed in advance by their son to be on their friendliest behavior, or if they actually liked her right away. At first she assumed the former, but in the months and years to come, as they all grew to know each other better, she came to believe the latter. Helmi had formed her own belief that all staunch Catholics were rigid and intolerant people, a notion that Bill and his family by their example would ultimately convince her to discard.

The next day she was given a more extensive tour of the town. Bill seemed intent on showing her all the sites of his own upbringing: his neighborhood elementary and high schools; his parish church (they only drove by, without going in); the hardware store, called simply Commercial Hardware Company, owned by his father; and the small building where his law office with two other partners was housed. And she found herself truly interested in these things, in ways that surprised her. Here was a man who was more than merely proud of his hometown, his family, his life. He wanted to show them all off, and not just to anyone, but to her specifically—as if knowing that she would appreciate them in a special way exactly because she had never experienced anything remotely similar. And he was right. She never had. And she found it wonderful.

That evening, over dinner at his parents' house, Helmi would meet Bill's two brothers, Jack and Tom, along with their wives. The brothers had married a pair of sisters, Mary Margaret and Grace Cantlon, who had grown up nearby on a ranch along the banks of the Truckee River, east of Reno. Two brothers married to two sisters—she had never heard of such a thing! And all together they seemed such a warm and close family. This was an atmosphere utterly foreign to her. In her experience, the men of the family for the most part had been invisible—dead or ignored—and the women had taken charge of life. Here marriages remained intact, and seemed to be equal partnerships. Over dinner, a great deal of attention was paid to Helmi, and she began to grasp that this meeting had been a highly anticipated event. Everyone was prepared to be charmed by her, and she did her best to meet their expectations.

By the time the weekend was over, Helmi was aware that the invitation to visit Reno had been far more than a mere courtesy. In the same shy yet earnest manner he had displayed back in Japan during the brief time she had known him there, Bill Horgan was pursuing her. When he took her back to the airport on Sunday evening, before seeing her off he took her hand and asked how soon they could see each other again. She took another good look at this young man, whom she hadn't even recognized two days before. He was not especially handsome or glamorous, but he had an openness and honesty about him that was something new to her. She felt happy sensing that he liked her so much. He was smart, but he did not flaunt his intelligence. He had a serious demeanor, but not so much that it stopped him from enjoying himself. Up until this moment, she had never really considered what sort of general qualities she would look for in a person she might get close to.

She told him she hoped to see him again very soon.

Over the Mountains

San Francisco and Reno, 1947

As Helmi would say decades later, the next few weeks moved along quickly. Throughout the spring she made several more excursions over the Sierra Nevada to Reno, and Bill in turn made several to San Francisco. The two of them found that they shared many interests—books, movies, music. Books, above all. Bill prided himself on being well educated, with a bachelor's degree from Santa Clara University and both a law degree and MBA from Harvard, but he nevertheless was impressed that Helmi, having only a high school diploma from Shanghai, was far better read than he was, especially in literature. She had read much of the British and American canons in her youth, and in San Francisco she had immediately become a passionate patron of the public library, eagerly catching up on contemporary novels. She was an avid movie buff as well, and had seen more films and seemed to know more about the lives of her favorite stars than almost any of his American friends.

Bill's taste in books ran more toward history as well as science—he had developed side interests in physics and astronomy while in college and law school—and in their conversations he made no effort to disguise how seriously he took his Catholic beliefs. He told her that his father, an Irish immigrant with almost no formal education, was the person in his life he admired most, in part because of the purity of his religious faith and the way it permeated, in a very natural way, every aspect of his life. His father didn't need to study his religion. He simply lived it. He had never read the great theologians such as St. Paul or Thomas Aquinas, or struggled with himself over matters of doctrine or liturgy, as Bill had. Bill told her he wished he had that kind of simple belief, but he did not. Unlike his father, he told Helmi, he was forever questioning his own faith.

Helmi found herself strangely touched by this open discussion, all the more so since she herself had no interest in religion and was quite sure she never would. She stated this position clearly to him, and he just as clearly replied to her that it would never be a problem. He would never ask her to believe. And at a certain point she realized that they were both looking ahead into the future, a future together.

It was on one of her subsequent visits to Reno, in March 1947, that they announced their engagement to Bill's parents over dinner. They had spent the afternoon on an outing together, just the two of them, taking a short drive through the foothills southeast of Reno to Virginia City, the small mining town well known for the discovery there of the Comstock Lode silver bonanza. On their way back to Reno, they had stopped at a turnout beside the road that wound up the steep pass, known as Geiger Grade, where they ate the hot dogs they had bought in a small restaurant—she later said it was the first hot dog she had ever tried, and she swore she would never eat another. Bill had his camera along, using slide film, and he took several photos of Helmi. It was a warm spring day, but there was still snow on the ground between the pine trees and on top of the rock retaining wall overlooking the Washoe Valley below. In one of the photos Helmi is seated right in the snow, holding her hot dog and laughing. She had slipped and fallen straight down on her rump, and had been a good sport in allowing Bill to snap a photo. Her hair is tightly curled in the style of the day, and she is dressed in wool slacks and a tailored blue jacket with wide white lapels. Despite the half-eaten hot dog, her lipstick is undisturbed. In another photo, taken a few minutes later, she is posing next to the retaining wall with her hands on her hips, the snow-dusted desert hills descending behind her. She has taken off the jacket, revealing a bright red western-style shirt with pearl snaps on the sleeves, along with a silver-buckled cowgirl belt looped through her slacks. Her face is confident and clear-eyed. These photos reveal a young woman proud to look her stylish best, yet not so proud that she can't have a good laugh at herself after falling on her fanny in the snow. It is remarkable how comfortable she appears, how convincingly she appears to *belong* there, in her natty western outfit, on that road winding through the snowy Nevada foothills: a place completely foreign

Helmi visiting Reno, March 1947.

to anything in her experience, a place that until very recently she had barely even heard of.

On the drive back to town, with Helmi sitting on her jacket because of her wet slacks, they decided together that this was the day to make their announcement. They had already agreed, in private, that they would marry soon, and they could see no impediments to moving ahead with their plans.

Over dinner with Bill's parents they delivered the news of their engagement, or rather Bill did, in a somewhat formal manner. Jack and Von made no attempt to hide that they were old-fashioned people in many ways. Helmi was charmed by the way Bill showed deference to them, and she could see how proud they were of him. In his lovely Irish brogue, and with a sweet smile, Jack said that this was happy news indeed. Then he stood up, stepped over to a cabinet, and came back to the table with a bottle of whiskey. Von went wide-eyed at this. Jack poured out small amounts into tiny shot glasses and passed them around.

"A toast," he said, "to the handsome couple." He held out his glass to clink with Helmi's. "*Slainte*," he said. "An Irish toast, my dear. It means the best of luck to you."

Bill later told her that he almost never saw the whiskey come out, except on Sunday evenings for his father's regular poker game with his

Irish pals, including the local parish priest, Monsignor Patrick Connors. She should take it as a great honor. When Helmi returned to San Francisco the next day, she assumed, happily, that there was nothing more to discuss except setting the date.

Midway through the following week, she was called from her desk at ten in the morning to the front office of the American Asiatic Corporation to take a telephone call. She had been in the process of typing out a letter to her mother in Japan with the exciting news. On the phone was Bill's father, saying that he and Von had driven to the city that morning and would like to take her out to lunch. Bill was at work in Reno, and was not with them. She agreed, naturally, as she wondered what in the world was going on.

Over lunch in downtown San Francisco, Jack Horgan now seemed like a different person. He had trouble meeting Helmi's gaze, as he awkwardly explained that there were some serious things for her to hear, serious things that she may not have understood fully. Von sat stiffly, saying almost nothing, looking miserable. They were clearly so far out of their comfort zone that Helmi immediately felt sorry for them, even though she had no idea what might be causing them to act this way.

Jack went on, haltingly. Marrying into the Catholic Church was not a light commitment. There were many promises she would need to make, and she ought to consider that she may not be prepared to keep them. She should think very carefully before entering into such a marriage. It might not be for the best, in the long run. After a pause, he added that Bill did not know they had made this trip.

She replied that in her view no marriage should be taken as a light commitment. She told them that Bill had already explained many things to her. Their children would need to be baptized into the Catholic faith and raised as Catholics. She had no problem with this. She herself was not religious, as they already knew, but she fully respected Bill's beliefs and those of the rest of his family, and she would not stand in the way of any of the requirements of the Church.

As she said these things, she considered that she ought to be outraged at this encounter—Bill's parents appearing like this without their son's knowledge and attempting to dissuade her from marrying him. She ought to be furious. She had a perfect right to stand up and walk out. Yet there was something about their clear discomfort that told her they were not acting solely on their own behalf. Something, or somebody, must have put them up to this. She had gotten to know them in Reno, and here today, delivering their attempt at a stern warning from the all-powerful Catholic Church, they didn't quite seem to be themselves. So Helmi remained polite in the face of this intrusion. She thanked them for coming, and for buying lunch, and before they parted she told them she would take their words into consideration. What she didn't say was that she felt more determined than ever to marry their son.

A few days later, on the weekend, Bill himself visited, and by then he knew all about his parents' visit to San Francisco. He also didn't seem to be himself. He was very agitated and said only that he was in a great state of confusion. They took a walk through the Market Street neighborhood, saying very little, and when they returned to her building, nothing seemed any better. Helmi began to think that he was working up the courage to break off the engagement. Suddenly he suggested that they take in the afternoon movie at the President Theater next door. And so they entered the empty theater and sat down in the middle of a row of seats. There was no sign of a movie starting up. She found herself beginning to cry, and when she looked over at Bill he also had tears running down his cheeks. Perhaps this was the moment when their relationship would end.

Instead of saying anything, he took her hand and held it tightly for a long moment. She squeezed back. She would always say that they communicated very well in the theater that day, even though they hardly spoke. In a little while, the lights went dark and a newsreel began, preceding the film. Normally she would have been eager to see almost any movie. This time, however, they got up together and went back out in the daylight before the feature even began. She hadn't even paid attention to what was playing. Outside, they finally agreed that nothing had changed for either of them. Bill seemed suddenly much calmer. He took her arm and led her off again for another turn around the block. Maybe it was time, he said, to set a date, and she replied that indeed it was high time.

She didn't press him that day to tell her what had transpired in Reno with his parents, or perhaps with someone else in the family. If he had broken off the engagement, then certainly she would have wanted immediate answers to some questions. But, under the circumstances, there would be time to discuss all of this later.

Outside the Rail

Reno, 1947

HELMI KOSKIN AND BILL HORGAN were married on Sunday, June 15, 1947, at Our Lady of the Snows Catholic Church in Reno. According to the announcement that appeared that morning in the *Nevada State Journal*, one of Reno's daily newspapers, it was an "informal ceremony"—meaning not a full-fledged Mass—attended by the immediate members of the family, followed by a wedding luncheon at the home of the bridegroom's parents. The best man was Bill's older brother, Jack, and the matron of honor was Anita Matthews, Helmi's friend from San Francisco. Bill's family included both his brothers' families. Helmi's mother, still living in Kobe, was not able to attend, and Helmi had no other family to invite. All of her other close relatives were still in the Far East.

The newspaper announcement described the bride's wedding outfit ("a smart summer suit of dust rose wool") as well as that of the matron of honor ("a soft green suit with white accessories"), along with the table at the luncheon ("covered with a lace and embroidered cloth, decorated with pastel colored sweet peas and candles"), and dutifully reported that the cake was "cut in the traditional manner," meaning bride and groom held the knife together. Not mentioned was the fact that the bride had been required to stand well apart from the groom during the wedding ceremony at the church. Being a non-Catholic, Helmi, with the loyal Anita by her side, was ordered to remain outside the communion rail, while her husband-to-be, his parents, and his best man were all grouped together in front of the priest at the foot of the altar, on the other side of the rail. This was one of the obligations she had been informed about when she took the formal "instruction" from the same priest a week

Helmi and Bill on their honeymoon, in
Monterey, California, July 1947

before the wedding. She had readily agreed, having been offered no
choice.

Also not mentioned in the announcement was the fact that the offi-
ciating priest was a last-minute replacement. Monsignor Connors, the
local parish priest, fellow Irishman, and good friend and poker buddy of
Bill's father, had hastily agreed to officiate when word was received that
the planned clergyman was suddenly unavailable. This absent clergyman in fact was a relative: Bill's uncle, an older brother of his father.

Monsignor Thomas Horgan, pastor of a parish in northern California, was revered in the Horgan family as a stern and exacting scholar of Catholic doctrine and liturgy. No clear reason was given for his unavailability, but the problem had been quickly and quietly solved. Something seemed to be amiss, and Helmi made another mental note to eventually find out what had transpired—all in good time, of course.

The weekend was not without further irony. On Saturday morning, the day before the wedding, Helmi accompanied Anita downtown for another quick private ceremony. Anita's divorce—from Mr. Matthews, whom Helmi had never even met—had only just been made final. Anita wanted to perform the traditional celebration of freedom by tossing her wedding ring into the Truckee River from the downtown Virginia Street Bridge. Both women stayed in Bill's parents' house the night before, and early in the morning, declaring a need to shop for Anita's outfit, they walked the eight or ten blocks into the heart of town and then out onto the bridge, where Anita—very unceremoniously, as it turned out—yanked the ring out of her purse and without a pause hurled it into the waves thirty feet below. "Good riddance," was all she had to say. As they walked off, she added, "Better luck to you, my dear. I think you're a smarter girl than I am." Then they did indeed go shopping downtown, where Anita picked out her soft green suit and white accessories.

The bride and groom, Helmi and Bill, left after the luncheon and drove to Santa Barbara, California, for a short honeymoon, after which they returned to Reno and took up residence at 1427 Humboldt Street, a two-bedroom white-painted brick house behind a small sloping front lawn, with a separate wood-framed garage and a fenced backyard facing a paved alley. Bill had signed the mortgage two weeks before the wedding. To Helmi this modest frame dwelling was a haven better than any palace, a real American house with big pantry shelves waiting to be filled, nestled on a quiet street, with a grocery store just around the corner, in a middle-sized town protected by the sturdy Sierra mountains on one side and the Great Basin desert on the other. She intended to apply for American citizenship as soon as possible. She would learn to cook American food and she would learn to drive an American car. For the first time she would truly belong where she lived. Her life so far had been spent surviving as a stateless alien in the hidden corners of the world. Now a new life had been offered to her, one she had scarcely dared to imagine for herself. And, for a while at least, she would have it.

The Loud-Mouthed Bishop

Reno, 1948

SOME MONTHS AFTER THEIR HONEYMOON, Helmi and Bill attended a family gathering at her in-laws' home. By now she had become better acquainted with the extended Horgan family, including Bill's two brothers and their wives. Each of these couples already had two young sons. Along with Bill's parents, Jack and Von, plus an assortment of other relations that included the two brothers of the Italian sisters and their own spouses and children, it amounted to a large and all-around very Catholic clan. She had never before been around any sizable cluster of Catholics, and it took her by surprise a bit how much they stuck together. Well, she thought to herself, Jews certainly did the same, although they had mostly been forced to. These Catholics seemed to be more of a tribe unto themselves than she had ever imagined.

She found that she could attend such tribal meetings with her new husband without feeling unduly panicked. She was interested in other people in general, and was not self-conscious about the fact that they seemed to find her interesting or even exotic. She actually enjoyed this perceived status, up to a point. She also found that she had a taste for alcohol, something she had entirely missed out on in her formative years. Drinking, she discovered, could be an excellent social aid—under controlled circumstances. Everybody here seemed to like a good *snort*, as she remembered it described back in Shanghai, and she joined in. The protocol apparently was to stand around talking in groups and subgroups that formed and broke apart and then reformed in new permutations, according to some seemingly well-rehearsed choreography. Often one person served as a sort of magnet for conversation, especially if that person happened to be new to the tribe.

She had a secret that only her husband knew so far. She was pregnant with their first child, the result of well-executed planning. She now found herself with a small group of women, and the subject of conversation was children, since several of the other ladies were already mothers. They talked about their own offspring, but the conversation then focused on Helmi and her own family plans. How soon would she want them? How many did she want? She took care in answering these questions. There was an additional implication, a subtext just below the surface that she could read in the overall tone. This hidden topic, of course, was birth control. She was well aware of the Catholic rules and regulations on this subject, and her impression was that there were two kinds of Catholic families: the ones with ten children spaced barely ten months apart, and the ones with only a couple of kids produced at a comfortable interval marked in years, not months. Sipping her highball—the primary drink of choice among the Horgan clan was bourbon and ginger ale—she made it known to the other women that she would belong firmly in the latter camp. There were smiles of assent all around. This much was good. They were not religious fanatics.

She was also grilled, in a friendly and more general way, on the subject of faith. What were her beliefs? Did she ever expect to join the Church? Very forthrightly, she answered that she had no particular religious beliefs and had no intention of joining any church, adding that her husband had no such expectation of her either. Someone countered that of course her children would be raised as Catholics, wouldn't they? She replied that she understood she had made a vow at her wedding that any children would grow up in that tradition, and this was not a problem at all, because her impression was that this was a fine way to provide a strong moral foundation for them. This was received well, as it was intended to be. What she chose not to add was that any children of hers would be free to believe or not believe once they attained an age where they could make up their own minds about such things. She did add out loud that although she considered herself Jewish, this was entirely a cultural identification rather than a religious one. It couldn't hurt to come right out and address another obvious subtext.

She smiled and sipped her drink. She was reminded of the many Hollywood movies she had seen in Shanghai with scenes such as this, with everyone standing about reciting polite dialogue that advanced the plot. The difference, of course, was that here there was no script to follow, at least not an explicit one. Nevertheless, everybody had a clear role to fill and needed to stay in character and give certain impressions. One could be frank and honest, as long as careful levels of diplomacy were maintained. She thought she could become skillful at this American-style social banter, with practice. It was like wearing makeup, the requisite lipstick and rouge. It was easy enough to put on a good face. The bigger question was whether she could could be happy in the long run as a black-sheep outsider in this Irish-Italian Roman Catholic empire. She gazed across the rim of her glass at her husband, who stood twenty feet away, slightly apart from a group of men, every one of them wearing a suit and necktie, like a uniform. Some of them were laughing, but not him. He didn't like to wear suits, though he had to often. She remembered what he had told her on their way to this gathering, that these things were not much fun for him, and he would not want to stay long. He would prefer to be home, seated in his armchair and reading a book. And, she had to admit, so would she. It was a pleasing habit they had already found they shared—reading for an hour or more in the evening after dinner. Bill was in the middle of a book about Albert Einstein. Her own love was fiction, and a stack of new novels from the Washoe County Library awaited her on the nightstand. She thought suddenly of the opening scene of *War and Peace*, the soiree in Anna Pavlovna's elegant drawing room, where Princess Bolkonskaya, the toast of St Petersburg, though young and relatively inexperienced, manages to make every person she meets feel special just by her natural glow. Did she possess this sort of talent? Certainly not. Yet she believed she was making a decent impression. She tried to catch Bill's eye, and when she did, and he smiled conspiratorially back at her across the room, she felt he was echoing her thoughts. Soon the whole clan would know that they had a child on the way. That would no doubt help too.

Helmi now realized that one of those organic realignments had taken place, and the little group had now admitted a male presence, in the form of a tall and portly white-haired gentleman wearing a somber black suit topped by a black-and-white clerical collar.

"Good evening, ladies," he said in a booming, stentorian voice. "Aren't we all looking lovely?" His eyes passed over each of them, but then landed and stayed on Helmi. His eyelids were heavy and parked at half-mast, but his gaze was nevertheless intense. Her instinct told her to gaze right back.

"And whom have we here? Someone I don't know." He put out a large pink hand, which was surprisingly clammy when she took it. "Charmed, I'm sure, my dear."

Evidently she was supposed to know who this man was. A priest, this much was obvious. One of the other ladies then stepped in and made proper introductions. He turned out to be the bishop, evidently a person of considerable authority. If she understood the hierarchy correctly, he was the potentate of the entire northern Nevada Catholic district. She had actually heard of him. There was a school somewhere named after him.

"Ah, Helmi, is it?" the bishop was saying now, seemingly to himself. "Helmi. Oh yes, of course! I know who you are." A good foot taller, he leaned down much closer to her, and clamped more tightly onto her hand. "You're one who caused so much trouble last spring. The little Jewish girl and all that business with Monsignor Horgan. Aren't you?"

An audible gasp went up from one of the other ladies. Helmi hadn't given much more thought to the hasty rearranging that had taken place back in the spring at the time of her wedding, when Monsignor Thomas Horgan, Bill's uncle who was a parish priest in Sacramento, had suddenly backed out of coming to perform the ceremony with no full explanation being given. It all came clear now. *The little Jewish girl.*

Helmi took her hand back, but made a point of meeting the intensity of his scrutiny with as piercing a look as she could muster. This cleric of the West, this supposedly powerful personage of the Church, had a big mouth. He had just given away what was supposed to have been kept secret, an embarrassing detail that the family would like to have spared her knowing.

"Yes, I suppose I am," Helmi replied, taking care to speak up. She wanted to be heard clearly. She hoped the ice in her voice was clear as well. "Nice to meet you, too."

She made two mental notes. One was to carefully relate all of this to her husband when they got home, asking him to fill in the details. The other was to congratulate herself. She now had something she had been looking for in order to understand what this family was all about. She had evidence in hand that they were perfectly ordinary people. These Catholics were just as capable as anyone else of failing to live up to their own professed high standards. There were two ways she could go with this. One would be to hold it against them. The other would be to use it to gain both hope and confidence that she would get along just fine with them. Here was proof that they were just regular human beings with regular faults. This could be taken as good news.

She enjoyed the rest of the evening and met many more people, but within a reasonable time she found her husband and they excused themselves to leave. Once back in their own new home, she did bring up what the bishop had said and asked Bill for a full explanation. She didn't make it difficult for him. She knew none of it was his fault. Yes, Bill admitted, at the end of the day his uncle had refused to perform the ceremony. He was an old-fashioned, bigoted Irishman. Could she find it in herself to forgive?

"If you mean forgive you," she answered, "for keeping the truth from me, yes, of course I forgive you. If I'd known at the time, it would have cast a cloud over our wedding day. I can see why you didn't tell me." She paused to let that sink in and to enjoy the relief on his face. "If you mean forgive him, the venerable monsignor Uncle Tom, for allowing his prejudice to possibly hurt your very nice family, well—I'm going to have to think about that. I'll let you know."

"Fair enough," he said.

They kissed after they made up. Then they both picked up the books they were reading and spent a quiet hour before retiring for the night.

Mother-in-Law

Reno, 1948

MY BROTHER, Terence Edward Horgan, was born in October 1948. He was given an Irish first name by way of an informal agreement—his father, after all, was one hundred percent Irish and his mother was technically only half-Jewish. She, however, was quick to remind her husband that anyone with a half-Jewish mother would still be considered Jewish everywhere else in the world. She extracted a teasing promise that the next child, if there were to be one, would receive a nice Jewish name from the Old Testament. Meanwhile, Terence's middle name was that of Helmi's father, the Finnish pearl trader whom she had never known.

The surprise for Helmi was that motherhood suited her so well. She had never thought of herself as the motherly type. Back in Kobe during the war, as part of the effort to keep spirits up within their small refugee community, she had taken charge of a few birthday parties held for the younger offspring of her mother's friends, and she had been appalled by the racket, chaos, and general misbehavior of little children. Even earlier, as a teenager in Shanghai, she had concluded that bringing a child into a world filled with so much horror was irresponsible. Yet now, in her first year of marriage in a peaceful and happy American home, she thought: okay, why not? So now here he was, her firstborn son, and she discovered to her delight that she loved him with a fierce intensity she had read about in many books and yet had always vaguely mistrusted. But it was real after all.

Practically the first order of business after bringing little Terence Edward home—they would call him Terry—was to have him baptized. This was a very serious matter among these Catholics. Without this proper ceremony, carried out by a proper priestly official, the child evidently would be blocked from entering heaven even if innocent in every other way. Well, then, by all means, better hop right to it. She said this to Bill as she sat nursing little Terry in the bedroom. He moved closer to her, and then cleared his throat awkwardly. Even in the midst of the motherly bliss of the moment, she could sense something else was coming.

"So," he began. "I'd like to ask a favor. About the baptism."

"I already told you it was fine," she replied. "Just tell me when and where. I suppose it should happen at the church."

"Yes, that's the traditional place. It'll be soon, probably in a week. But the favor is something extra. I want to know if you can allow my Uncle Tom to do the baptism. He has said he would like to come."

"Oh, really?" She didn't take her eyes off the baby at her breast, but for the moment her focus was altered. "You mean the Most Reverend Monsignor Tom, the anti-Semitic Irish bigot?"

"That's who I mean."

She cut straight to the obvious question. "Why?"

"Because it would make my parents very happy. It would help to set things right, from their point of view."

She had already made up her mind, but she decided to tease him a bit more. "What about having Monsignor Connors do it, that nice priest who stepped in to marry us? He's your father's friend, too."

"He'll be there also," Bill answered. "But there's always a main celebrant, and could it be Uncle Tom? Don't do it as a favor to me. Do it for my parents."

"Answer one more thing for me first." She still hadn't looked up. "Let's get all the cards on the table. Did your saintly Uncle Tom also put your parents up to trying to stop our marriage? Did he send them to San Francisco with instructions to break us up?"

There was no hesitation. "Probably. I never asked them. But that's what I think, too. You know, they are very fond of you. They would not have done that on their own."

Helmi did know that. She had sensed from the very beginning, since her first visit to Reno, that they were decent people and that they had indeed grown fond of her, as she was of them. Maybe they were old-fashioned, but they were not bigoted. It had been plain during that difficult encounter in San Francisco that they were not really speaking for themselves. She saw that she could extract some small revenge on the infamous Uncle Tom by refusing Bill's request, but would it be worth it?

She refocused her attention on the baby, who had sensed her distance and was beginning to fuss. She stole another glance at her husband. "Okay," she said, "let him come. A priest is a priest, to me."

The baptism itself was shorter than she had expected, nothing like the rigamarole that had taken place in the same church for their marriage ceremony. This time there were no restrictions on her participation. She was allowed to hold the baby, which was a good thing, because she probably would have walked out with him in her arms if there had been any rule against it. Uncle Tom performed his duties, involving sprinkling water on Terry's bald head and reciting some Latin phrases, somberly and swiftly. He had very little to say to Helmi, and she returned the favor. But judging by the glowing faces of her in-laws, and consequently of her husband also, all was well in the family. Her son was now an official Catholic along with the rest of them. So be it.

Other than discovering the joy of motherhood, Helmi had not, overnight, acquired much in the way of domestic skills. She was still working on learning her way around a kitchen, which had never been given much of her attention. Her life had gone from school to work to marriage, and somehow, along the way, she had barely learned how to boil an egg. Some of her attempts at cooking American-style meals for Bill had already been disasters—frying bacon and eggs, roasting rounds of beef. Why hadn't her mother taught her these things? She knew the answer. Rachel had been concerned with Helmi's basic survival skills, especially her education, and then had needed her to go right to work at age sixteen. There had hardly been time to teach her how to cook. Besides, for most of those years, there had been no bacon, no eggs, no roasts.

Her mother. His mother-in-law. This was a subject Helmi had discussed with Bill since the moment they became serious about each other. She knew well that she was permanently tethered to her mother, despite the new life she had made for herself on the opposite side of the world, and Bill had come to understand this. The link and obligation, in fact, were for her now all the stronger. Helmi had been sending money to Rachel in Kobe since she had first landed in San Francisco and begun her job there. In Kobe after the war, while working for the U.S. Army, she had given Rachel all of her salary every month, just as she had before the war when she was employed by the Thomas Cook travel agency.

Now she and Bill together continued to send Rachel money regularly. In Japan, Rachel was now alone, still operating her small boardinghouse and trying to maintain her connection with members of the remaining Jewish community, but many of them had begun to scatter. Some had come to the U.S., like Anatole Ponevejsky and Moise Moiseeff, both of whom had relocated their families to California and restarted their import businesses. These two brothers-in-law remained in contact with Rachel in Kobe and assured Helmi that they would help provide assistance, if necessary. The U.S. Army continued to use Rachel's boardinghouse as temporary housing, and food and other basic necessities were easier to come by under the American occupation, but in the long term Rachel's prospects were uncertain. The German gentleman Mr. Dudchke, whatever his real name may have been, was long gone.

In the months preceding my brother's birth in Reno, as husband and wife discussed their excitement and expectations for the future, a new plan presented itself. Helmi's life was now with Bill but she was also still bound to her mother and her old life. Why not put the two together? It seemed simple: they would bring Rachel to the United States. She could live with them, at least for a time, and help care for the baby.

Accomplishing this was surprisingly smooth. Helmi was not yet a U.S. citizen, but she was married to one. The paperwork only required both that Bill vouch for Rachel's welfare and accept the obligation for her support if needed. Both Mr. Ponevejsky and Mr. Moiseeff, who had so efficiently organized the Jewish community in Kobe during the war and had subsequently established diplomatic contacts in the U.S., stepped in to facilitate with immigration officials in San Francisco. The documents were filed in the summer of 1948, six months into Helmi's pregnancy, and by September official word was received, one month before her due date, that Rachel would be admitted.

The U.S. Immigration and Naturalization Service counted Rachel as part of the 1948 immigration quota from the Soviet Union, since she had been born in the former Russian Empire. She had no documents to prove this, but with the support of her Russian friends in Japan her sworn word was accepted. She was eligible to sail immediately. Meanwhile, Terry was born right on time. A telegram was sent to Rachel in Kobe with this wonderful news, and the response followed quickly, with an outline of her travel arrangements. On December 10, 1948, Rachel boarded an American freighter named the *Andrea Luchenbach* at the

Japanese port of Yokohama, bound for the port of Seattle. She was seen off by the Sidline family, Boris and Fania and their two sons, Alex and George. The Sidlines had been relocated to Kuruizawa near the end of the war and had moved to Yokohama to open a new dry goods store, replacing the one destroyed in 1945. They took a few photos; hugged Rachel, who had sheltered the family during the horrendous bombings; and promised to someday, somehow, reunite with her and Helmi in better times. The promise would be fulfilled.

After a brief stop in Honolulu, the ship arrived in Seattle on Wednesday, January 19. According to the Department of Justice's official manifest of inbound alien passengers, Rachel was forty-nine years old and had paid the requisite $8.00 Head Tax levied by the U.S. Customs Service. In fact, she had lied about her age. She was actually fifty-three. Rachel had no birth certificate, passport, or official identification of any kind, and she realized she could state any age she wanted. Helmi would later say that Rachel knocked four years off her age thinking that she might have an easier time finding an American husband. A nice trick indeed, had it succeeded. As things turned out, it did not.

Bill Horgan left Helmi at home with two-month-old Terry and drove ten hours to Seattle. He stayed overnight in a hotel, and in the morning met the ship at the pier. He told Helmi later that they both had trouble recognizing each other. Rachel had expected to see the same skinny, greenish-faced soldier she had met in Kobe in 1945. For his part, Bill had retained an image of a timid and frail old lady, the tiny babushka he had interrogated along with her daughter in Kobe. It's tough to say who was the more surprised.

Rachel's Pacific crossing in midwinter had been a rough and chilly voyage. Yet, like her daughter a little more than two years before, she had enjoyed the trip and felt no seasickness. It was a wonderful respite from the stresses of ordinary life. For weeks, she had nothing to do but eat and sit and visit with her shipmates. There were nine other passengers—six U.S. citizens and three others on alien visas, one British citizen and two Japanese. Rachel was the only one traveling without papers of nationality. After passing through Seattle Customs, she stepped into the Seattle terminal together with an unmarried Japanese woman ten years her junior named Yoshiko Kunugi, the director of early childhood education for the Japanese Education Ministry in Tokyo, who was on her way to the University of California at Los Angeles on a one-year visa to do graduate work. The two women had become fast friends on the voyage, comparing notes about their wartime experiences. Miss Kunugi had worked as an interpreter for the Japanese transitional government immediately after the war. As they continued to chat away in different renditions of accented English, the two tiny women, neither taller than four-foot-ten, walked right by Bill Horgan, who was peering over their heads scanning for the feeble old lady he had been expecting. When no more passengers appeared, he finally turned and realized that the lively little woman across the room hugging and saying goodbye to her kimono-clad counterpart was indeed his mother-in-law. He called her name, and as she looked over to see a neatly dressed gentleman in horn-rimmed spectacles, she made her own startling discovery that this was the father of her new grandson, the same emaciated American she had met at the end of the war. Bill himself was slightly taken aback that, impoverished as Rachel was, she had arrived with ten bags that needed to be loaded into the trunk of the car.

During the long drive back to Reno in Bill's gray 1948 Chrysler sedan, the two of them got better acquainted. Rachel made it plain that she was thrilled beyond belief to be in the U.S.A. She asked question after question as the miles went by, about his family background and his hometown of Reno. She made no effort to disguise her opinion that Bill was a fine catch for her daughter—an American and a lawyer. What could be better? Her Russian accent was thick, but her fluid command of English was far different than he remembered. From the postwar months in Japan he had retained an impression of her as a timid, elderly, and war-weary Russian refugee. Yet here was an effusive and vigorous woman, curious and articulate. In turn, Bill took the opportunity to inquire about her past life, and she responded with candor about her childhood memories of Odessa, her youth in Manchuria, and the years raising Helmi in Shanghai. She had very little to say, however, on the subject of Edward Koskin, Helmi's father, and Bill did not press her, sensing that the subject was a tender one. Overall, his initial impression was that she would have no difficulty adjusting to a new life and that, far from being the needy and fragile figure he had come to imagine, she would surely be a great help in raising and caring for his new son.

What Bill didn't tell Rachel was that he was considering putting his law career on hold. In recent months his father had let his three sons know that the hardware store was having difficulties. The three brothers had pledged to do whatever might be necessary, including joining the business and guiding it to expand and thrive in the competitive postwar economy. This prospect was looking increasingly likely. It was not the career he had foreseen for himself, and perhaps the move would only be temporary, but if it helped his father, whom he revered, then there was no question of whether he would do it. It would mean a great deal of hard work, many long hours, and probably not many free days. Having a live-in grandmother for his new child would be just the thing.

As the hours passed and January darkness descended, Rachel quieted and finally leaned over against the window and dozed off. Surely she was exhausted from her journey, although until now she had showed little sign of it. Bill felt lucky that the winter highways were clear of snow or ice. The winding two-lane roads that snaked across the mountain passes in northern California could be treacherous at this time of year. The only frightening moment had nothing to do with the road or the weather. Rachel had been asleep for some miles—snoring fairly loudly, in fact—when out of nowhere she let out a piercing shriek, causing Bill to snap forward and jerk the wheel.

"Oy, Bozhomoi!" she cried out in her sleep, as her body lurched to the side. Bill slowed the car, and when he put out his hand to touch her shoulder she shrieked again. The car had come to a stop at the side of the road. A few tense moments went by before she calmed and showed signs of awakening. He waited for her to sit up.

"You have had a bad dream, Rachel," he said to her. "Are you all right?"

Her answer was something that stayed in his mind for the rest of the evening's drive to Reno, and for some time beyond.

"No dream," she said, shaking her head. Bill took this to mean she was still confused between sleep and wakefulness, but then she turned to him and spoke in a clear and steady voice. "Now, here with you, I feel as if I am dreaming. Before, God forbid, this was my real life coming back."

The Little Theater

Reno, 1949

A N EXPANDED NUCLEAR FAMILY settled into postwar American life in
the little white house on Humboldt Street in Reno—Bill, Helmi,
baby Terry, and Rachel, the live-in grandmother. Rachel took on this
role with enthusiasm, intending to be nothing short of indispensable
to her daughter. Perhaps Rachel had initially lied about her age to the
immigration authorities thinking it might help snare a husband, but in
fact husband-hunting was not high on her agenda. What she sought was
a safe and comfortable home, a haven from the cruelties of a fickle world,
something that had long been lost to her. She was not about to waste
this opportunity, having made it to the U.S. by the skin of her teeth. Her
daughter, by some miracle, had married this generous man and he had
invited her to be a part of their home. Who cared if he was one of those
Catholics? She had known Catholics, both good and bad. This made no
difference to her. She was thrilled beyond belief at her good luck. She
knew how to care for a child, and she knew how to cook. She would
seize this chance and make it work.

Rachel moved into the second bedroom of the house, while little
Terry slept next to Helmi and Bill in the front bedroom. Bill proceeded
with his plan, with Helmi's agreement, to take a leave from his law practice and join his two brothers in helping with their father's store. As for
Helmi, when she became engaged to Bill, she had thought she would
continue working after her marriage—after all, she had good references
from the U.S. Army, as well as from the American Asiatic Corporation,
her employer in San Francisco—but Bill assured her it wasn't necessary. He hoped she would feel completely free to do anything she liked.
He was earning a good living, and after some coaxing he persuaded her

Rachel, Helmi, and Terry, in Reno, 1949.

that she did not need to worry about money at all. She had read about the American housewife's life of leisure and had seen it depicted in the movies, without ever quite believing it. She wasn't even sure that she could adjust to such an existence. Her Aunt Sonya back in Shanghai was the only woman she had ever known who had lived that sort of life, and Sonya had never seemed happy, tied to a husband whose livelihood seemed to depend on the demands of warlords and politicians. Bill, however, was another sort of person altogether. Well, then, all right, she said. She would try it out.

Sure enough, Helmi's first year as a housewife had passed very happily, in the blink of an eye, as it turned out, and here she was now, with a baby of all things. Bill was becoming confident that the plan for the new larger hardware store would succeed and provide for their expanding family. Maybe he would go back to the law once the business was on strong footing. Helmi was willing to continue this experiment in pampered living for the time being. Yet even as she grew more comfortable, she never completely shed the feeling that something unforeseen might drop from the sky at any moment and bring a return to the poverty she had left behind.

Helmi now brought her mother into this new life, feeling both relief and trepidation: relief, in that Rachel's welfare had remained at the forefront of her thoughts, even during the months of her whirlwind courtship and subsequent marriage, and it was better for them both if an ocean no longer separated them; and trepidation, in that she felt, with chilling clarity, the power of the bond tying them together, formed in the crucible of poverty and fused in the fire of war. Here was another facet of this grand experiment, the challenge of incorporating Rachel into the fabric of her new married life. But there was really no choice. This was the way forward.

Helmi had made some friends in Reno, having been "introduced to society" in the fashion of the day. On July 22, 1947, less than a month after her wedding, a notice appeared on the Society and Clubs page of the *Nevada State Journal*, one of Reno's two daily papers at that time, under the headline "Two New Members Are Welcomed by Overseas Club." Helmi had been one of the new members inducted at a meeting held on the previous Saturday. The woman who invited Helmi to join, Madge Tillim, was British by birth and Jewish by heritage. Madge had been one of the first to call on Helmi at home after her wedding, inviting her to attend services at Temple Emmanuel, an Orthodox synagogue to which she and her husband belonged. Helmi had politely declined, explaining that she was the other kind of Jew, proud to identify as such but otherwise with no interest in religious matters. Sensing that another question was in the air, she added that she would not be attending any of her husband's Catholic services either. Impressed by this young woman's frankness, Madge replied that this was all the more reason for Helmi to come to the Overseas Club. She was bound to make some interesting friends.

At the afternoon tea event, several of the women present were indeed interesting, and Madge herself was one of them. She explained that growing up in London she had been trained as a singer and actress, and now she was regularly involved in productions put on by the Reno Little Theater, an active amateur organization. She was impressed by Helmi's bright personality and saw in her a potential participant. Had she ever been involved in theater productions? Helmi laughed and explained that she had performed in a few school plays back in Shanghai, but that was all. She hastened to add that she was tone deaf, with no musical ability whatsoever. Madge assured her that was no matter. She urged her to come to one of the organizational meetings. They would be presenting a wide range of productions in the next few seasons—dramas and comedies as well as musicals. Helmi really ought to come, to see how she liked the people.

The Reno Little Theater occupied a building downtown on Sierra Street, not far from the University of Nevada campus: a former Danish Society meeting hall that had been remodeled into a small auditorium. Founded in 1935 by a visionary theater director and administrator named Edwin Semenza, by the late 1940s the Little Theater was well established as one of the most successful community theaters in the western part of the country. When Helmi came to the meeting, she received an effusive greeting from everyone there. It seemed that her arrival in Reno had generated interest beyond the circle of her husband's family. They all wanted to know more about this British-sounding Russian girl who had come from Japan to marry a local Irish lawyer. They were amazed at her familiarity with American books and movies. For her part, Helmi felt a sense of kinship that surprised her. Here was the kind of church she could belong to, a congregation she could embrace.

For the first year, Helmi volunteered in nonperforming capacities, as an usher, ticket-taker, prop master, or stage manager. She loved being close to a place where make-believe mattered, at least for a few hours at a time. The world of imagination had always been her refuge. Now she found it thrilling to stand in the wings of a real theater. Her new friends began urging her to audition for stage roles. For the 1949 season—after the birth of her son and her mother's arrival and availability as a nanny—Helmi did finally step forward and audition, for a play called *The Women*, a well-known comedy by Claire Booth, notable for its forty-four roles for women and none for men. To pluck up her courage, she took out the report card she had saved from high school in Shanghai and reread the comment from her English teacher: "In dramatics her characterization is distinctly good." She also recalled the interview with her headmistress, when she had admitted that she was better equipped to be a secretary than an actress. Buoyed by a desire to prove that she had been wrong, Helmi sailed through the audition and was cast in a speaking role.

The Women is a satire of life among American housewives of the leisure class. Written in 1936, it had a successful run on Broadway and had been made into a popular 1939 film, starring Joan Crawford and Rosalind Russell. Helmi was given the role of Edith Potter, a catty and gossipy wife bored with her existence and burdened by her children, whose main recreation other than playing bridge and eating lunch is meddling in the personal affairs of her friends. The irony of acting out this part was not lost on Helmi. She had seen the film version in the fall of 1939, not long after her arrival in Japan at age sixteen, when it played at one of the theaters specializing in Hollywood films. Then she had gazed in wonder at the absurd antics of the fatuous female characters, busy carrying on affairs with one another's husbands and verbally stabbing each other in the back. The second act even took place in Reno, where some of the women went to obtain divorces while they continued double-crossing each other. Could that be anything like the way American housewives actually lived? Now here she was playing one of those very characters onstage. Moreover, here she was offstage, in the real-life role of an actual American housewife, in the real Reno. She greatly enjoyed rehearsing and performing the fictional role, hamming it up along with the other forty women in the cast, putting on the requisite air of duplicity and deviousness. At the same time she was already launched in the far more important real-life role, one calling for a person of integrity and loyalty, who loved her family and valued her friends. This was easy to master, because it came to her naturally.

The Women was performed nightly to sold-out houses at the Reno Little Theater for a week in October 1949, just after her son's first birthday. Helmi had been able to attend nightly rehearsals for several weeks prior to this, thanks to her mother's babysitting assistance. A review of the play appeared in the *Nevada State Journal* on Saturday, October 22. The reviewer's tone was snide regarding the overall production ("Generally the cast gave the impression of being archly aware of the audience, with little or no identification with their own roles…"), but he went out of his way to single out the better work of several of the performers: "There were some few of the cast who were outstanding. As the hard-boiled Crystal Allen, Phyllis Saviers was convincing. Helmi Horgan was another who did a good job with thorough ease and ability." As it happened, Phyllis Saviers, whom Helmi met for the first time working on this production, was to become one of her closest lifelong friends. This was the first Little Theater play for them both, and when the cast gathered to celebrate its success the two women resolved to be in more productions together.

Phyllis, tall, lanky, and blonde, had portrayed Crystal Allen, a sharp-tongued perfume counter-girl and conniving husband-stealer, with sass and finesse. Helmi, dark-haired and petite, had made good use of her Shanghailander/British accent to imbue her character with a controlled air of self-centered snobbery. In the opening scene of the play, Helmi—as Edith the catty housewife—had played a game of bridge with three other characters, trading gossip and wisecracks between hands. Over drinks at the cast party, Phyllis suggested getting together with their husbands to play bridge for real. Helmi laughed, and asked Phyllis if it was truly an obligation for a proper American housewife to play bridge. Bill knew how to play and had also suggested that she might like it. The very next day Phyllis came over, and the lessons began. Helmi learned quickly, and found to her surprise that she loved the challenge and strategy of the game. Within a short time the two couples began meeting for regular weekly rounds of bridge. After a few years, Phyllis divorced her husband in order to marry a neighbor from across the street with whom she had been having an affair—a shocking move that put Helmi in mind of that first play they did together—but the regular couples' bridge night, now with Phyllis's second husband, continued on for many years. Helmi would embrace the game as a serious pursuit, becoming an expert player, partnering in duplicate bridge tournaments and bringing home trophies, despite the game's iconic status as a casual pastime for indolent mid-twentieth-century American housewives. It's as if she chose to try on this cliché for size and then turned it inside out. This way of life—keeping house, playing cards—was what America offered its luckiest citizens, and she considered herself the luckiest of all.

Citizen, indeed. The other notable event for Helmi in 1949 was becoming officially naturalized as a United States citizen. Shortly after her honeymoon in the summer of 1947, she had obtained a booklet filled with study questions for the test administered by the U.S. Immigration Service. There was a list of 100 questions to which she needed to know the answers. She studied carefully, since she had learned very few of these facts in school. What is the supreme law of the land? *The Constitution.* When was it written? *1787.* Who wrote the Declaration of Independence? *Thomas Jefferson.* When was it adopted? *July 4, 1776.* Who was president during World War I? *Woodrow Wilson.* What is the longest river in the United States? *The Mississippi.* Her schooling in Shanghai had not provided her with these facts. Who did the United States fight in World War II? This she knew without studying. *Japan, Germany, and Italy.* She had meant to take the test as soon as possible, but the birth

Helmi's certificate of naturalization, 1949.

of her son had intervened. Finally, on August 10, 1949, she stood before the examiner, with her proud husband and her ecstatic mother standing beside her, and answered every question correctly. A document was issued in the 2nd Judicial District Court of Nevada, with her photograph and signature affixed, and that was that. She had official papers. She was an American. She walked out of the Washoe County Courthouse, the same place where she and Bill had obtained their marriage license a year and a half before, this time holding her nine-month-old son in her arms, a documented citizen for the first time in her life. A month later, she was onstage playing someone who took such a thing completely for granted, a spoiled matron who had no reason to give her position as a privileged American even a second thought. Helmi resolved never to allow herself to slip into such complacency. This precious gift was to be treasured and never forgotten.

The Second Son

Reno, 1951

A ND SO THIS PARTICULAR FAMILY, residing in the little white house on
Humboldt Street in Reno, fell into step with the rest of America, striding into the 1950s, although with differing levels of optimism.
Bill Horgan, the head of the household and devout Catholic, hoped
and prayed that hard work would mean prosperity for his family and
his growing business. Helmi, the newly minted citizen, proud mother,
devoted wife, and budding actress, held continued high expectations for
the great adventure she had embarked upon, determined to fulfill her
project of self-reinvention. Rachel, the recent immigrant and new grandmother, viewed the future with a wary eye, focusing just on the day's
meals and diapers and laundry, fearing that to gaze beyond those was to
risk the sight of some unnamed darkness ahead.

Bill worked long hours, six days a week, along with his father and
two brothers to make sure their new expanded hardware store would
succeed. On the seventh day he never failed to attend Mass and exercise his faith. He maintained contacts in the legal world, thinking he
would one day make more of a contribution to that profession. Helmi
performed in more plays, read through tall stacks of books from the
library, learned how to cook and to use the stick shift in their Plymouth
sedan, and expanded her circle of friends. She could do all these things
and still care for her young son because her mother was there to help.
Rachel made good on her vow to be essential to the household. She
scrubbed, she baked, she changed diapers, she washed clothes, and she
babysat. Together, mother and daughter explored daily the gleaming
aisles of the grocery stores, hardly believing their eyes at the sight of

the ever-expanding bounty. Seven kinds of bread. Six brands of canned fruit cocktail. Huge lockers of frozen food, packed with everything from meat and poultry to vegetables and fruit and ice cream and orange juice. Milk, cream, half-and-half, all in three different sizes. Fresh meat of every possible kind, already butchered and trimmed and wrapped. All of this under one roof. Such opulence made the head spin. It was the stuff of dreams. There were three stores within a short distance of the house, and the women found a reason to go shopping every single day. Helmi always had money in her purse to buy a few things that looked new and interesting. Instant coffee, instant cake mix, pureed baby food in twenty different flavors. Heads turned at the sight of these two petite women with a shopping cart and a baby stroller, marveling to each other in rapid-fire Russian as they moved up one aisle and down the next. They were never more conscious of living in a glorious new world than when they made their daily expedition to the grocery store.

By now Rachel had also begun to make some friends of her own, mostly among the Jewish women connected to Temple Emmanuel, the same congregation her daughter had declined to join. Like Helmi, Rachel had been sought out by some of the Temple's members soon after arriving in Reno and invited to social events. She was grateful to make contact with a Jewish community. Just as in Shanghai and Kobe, here was a close-knit group with people from widely differing backgrounds yet sharing a common identity. Rachel began irregularly attending Friday evening services, not with any renewed sense of religious fervor—youthful faith having been iced down long since by cold reality—but out of a simple need to share. This was her tribe. Plus, there were even some women, several of them widows like her, who could speak Yiddish. Just imagine. Such a thing in, here of all places, the wild west of America.

Soon another member was added to the family, once again carefully timed. In April 1951 a second son was born to Helmi and Bill: it was my turn to enter the world. Helmi once told me, with a characteristic smirk, that she had hoped for a daughter this time, to help counter all the males in my father's family. Bill's two brothers each had three sons and no daughters. She had awakened in the hospital—having been totally anesthetized for the birth, in "modern" 1950s style—to my dad leaning over her and gently apologizing, because I was another boy. The Horgan clan would remain a male-dominated society for another generation.

My earliest memories are of that little white house—the sunny kitchen with its windowed breakfast nook, where a big radio sat on a high shelf; the laundry room off to the side that doubled as a pantry, the walls lined with shelves piled with canned goods as high as I could see; the dining room with a long table always covered with a white lace cloth; the living room with a big brown couch, another big console radio, and a huge green overstuffed chair. This is where my dad sat every evening after work with his highball—bourbon and ginger ale—parked on the rounded arm of the chair while he briefly allowed me to crawl into the round space he made by crossing one trousered leg over the other. Once I was upside down, he would squeeze me by pinching his knees together and I would shriek with glee, instantly causing his grip to release, too soon for me. Unlike my calmer older brother, I was by nature a shrieker and a squealer and a wailer, and my dad, though loving and devoted, only had so much tolerance for high-pitched noise. I would be sent off so he could listen in peace to the news on the radio while waiting for dinner.

In the kitchen my mother and grandmother would be teamed up as usual, pots boiling on the stove, a big cut of meat roasting aromatically in the oven, plates and glassware rattling, dishcloths flying, aprons rustling, high-heeled shoes clattering on the tiled floor, and their two voices advising, cajoling, joking, and bickering in sonorous Russian. From the very beginning I loved the sound of that language. To this day, hearing it spoken conveys the household sounds of my childhood, even though neither my brother nor I can understand it anymore. I am amazed to consider that there was a time, during our earliest years before we went to school, when we were bilingual.

Six months after I was born, Helmi donned a hat loaded with plastic fruit and portrayed Carmen Miranda in a single-evening benefit performance for the Reno Century Club titled "Mexican Holiday," in a cast with twenty other women. For many years she kept a framed photo of herself along with some of the other cast members, wearing fake mustaches, sombreros, and serapes. Two months later, she put on a Catholic nun's habit to play a novitiate nun in a Little Theater murder mystery, set in a mountaintop convent, called *High Ground*. This was not that difficult a role to step into, since she figured she knew what Catholics were all about, being married to one. In subsequent productions, among other varied roles, she would portray a world-weary sophisticate in *The*

Importance of Being Earnest, a ditzy American secretary in *The Solid Gold Cadillac*, and a Japanese geisha in a postwar military comedy called *Teahouse of the August Moon*. Helmi was singled out in reviews for her ability to deliver a natural and unforced performance. She found great satisfaction in temporarily adopting a new persona for seven evenings and a couple of matinees, as long as she could then return to a quiet and protected home life. Being on stage and receiving adulation was wonderful in its way, but her theatrical ambitions were well suited to the Reno Little Theater, which lived up to its name—a small space with a small audience, in a small community. She had no great desire to seek fame in the larger world. She didn't trust the larger world. She had survived so far by being stateless, out of view, officially anonymous. Despite the pleasures of performing and receiving praise for her acting talent, her desire was to remain exactly where she was.

And so we became a somewhat normal 1950s middle-class family, with a dad who worked hard, a mom with leisure time to play bridge and perform in plays, two little boys, and a high-strung Russian grandmother. Commercial Hardware, the business my father ran with his two brothers and his father, began to thrive as he had hoped. The big new store they constructed was proving to be a success. Helmi and Bill built a small addition onto the back of the house with a new master bedroom for themselves, moving my grandmother, whom we called Baba, into the front bedroom. They bought a new car, a white 1954 Ford sedan. They got my brother and me a black Labrador puppy and told us we could name her whatever we wanted. We put our heads together and named her Whitey, my first experience with irony. Our parents socialized by playing bridge and attending cocktail parties, and Baba was our live-in babysitter who baked us fabulous Russian pastries and waited on us hand and foot. She spoke to the dog in Russian as often as she did to us. Despite this cushy and comfortable arrangement, we were trained to be alert to Baba's nervousness, her quick propensity to panic. She was forever looking over her shoulder, waiting for disaster to strike. Any loud noise could elicit from her a choked gasp and a hand clutched to her chest, signs that an outsider, unaware of how tough she actually was, might well have perceived as symptoms of a heart attack. Little boys though we were, Terry and I learned early on to tread carefully around our beloved Baba lest we take the blame for causing her to die of fright.

Helmi in Carmen Miranda costume, with unknown fellow actresses, in Reno, about 1950.

Rachel was herself finally naturalized as an American citizen in August 1954. She kept her certificate proudly framed and displayed on her bedroom wall for the rest of her life, and she saved in a dresser drawer her official citizenship booklet from the Department of Justice along with carefully folded congratulatory letters she received from the Washoe County sheriff and U.S. senator George W. Malone.

In 1955, when I was four, we got our first television set, a massive piece of mahogany furniture with a flickering black-and-white screen around which we all sat mesmerized. The TV was no doubt the main reason that our early Russian vocabulary deteriorated so fast. Terry and I grew up watching Pinky Lee, Howdy Doody, Phil Silvers, Jackie Gleason, and Ed Sullivan. It seemed Ed Sullivan, every Sunday night, featured a different Jewish comic, and we grew to love Myron Cohen, Shelly Berman, Mort Saul, Phyllis Diller, Henny Youngman, and the team of Mike Nichols and Elaine May, who may not have actually been Jewish but successfully pretended to be. Our mother couldn't seem to get enough of these assorted wise guys and gals who cracked jokes in a tone of weary resignation that we boys recognized, without needing to be told, was intimately connected to us. These were our people. We understood this self-deprecating brand of eye-rolling humor, delivered with a deep sigh. Our devout Irish Catholic dad loved them too, which only reinforced my early conviction that being Jewish had nothing to do with where you were born or what you believed. It depended entirely on who you lived with.

Our parents would occasionally enjoy weekend outings to San Francisco to visit friends, and these would often include an evening at a nightclub called the hungry i, where some of these same TV wisenheimers could be experienced in the flesh. On some of these trips Helmi also had brief opportunities to reconnect with people from her former life, visiting with the Moiseeffs, Moise and Esther, and their son and daughter, Gregory and Simonne, along with Anatole Ponevejsky and his wife, Gita, and their two daughters. Together they celebrated their status as members of an exclusive club, Jewish survivors of wartime Japan. Another old friend who had made her way to San Francisco was Anne Bernstram, Helmi's former schoolmate from Shanghai. She was now Anne Bashkiroff, having eventually married the same imperious Russian gentleman who had accosted the two girls trespassing on the grounds of the Grosvenor House apartments in the French Concession so long ago. With Anne, Helmi shared memories of a time that few others understood, the chaotic years in prewar Shanghai when glimpses of life elsewhere in the world came mostly from the movies. Anne had arrived in the U.S. by way of South America, after her own series of adventures. Yet Helmi's patience with reminiscing was limited. Even with a childhood friend, she had little appetite for nostalgia. Her instinct was to focus on the present. After a short visit, she wanted nothing more than to cross back over the mountains to her family and her new life.

On another of these early-1950s San Francisco trips, Helmi and Bill attended a cocktail party hosted by a connection of Bill's from Harvard

Law School in a large Nob Hill home. They were engaged in conversation with the host when Helmi caught a familiar-sounding voice from across the room, that of a man speaking in low and measured tones. Edging her way closer, she listened more carefully. Yes, she knew this voice—not the person it belonged to, but where it came from.

She sidled up to the man, who was tall, neatly groomed, and elegantly dressed, casually holding a cigarette and conversing amiably in a small group. She waited for a break in the conversation before tapping him on the shoulder. He looked down at her in surprise.

"Yes?" he said. "What can I do for you?"

"Pardon me for intruding," she replied. "You're from Shanghai."

His eyes widened further. "Why, yes, I am." He paused. "Do we know each other?"

"No," she said. "My name is Helmi." She held out her hand. "You have the Shanghailander accent. I heard it across the room."

"Well, you are absolutely right. Delighted to meet you," said the gentleman, taking her hand. "My name is Robert Raven. Indeed, I was born and raised in Shanghai. Everyone thinks I'm from England, though I've never been there. You too are from Shanghai?" He laughed. "I think I hear it now in your voice also."

"Yes indeed, I am." But now she was distracted by the name he had given. "Might you be any relation to Frank Raven?"

His eyes narrowed, and his smile flattened. "Frank Raven was my father."

"We rented from him, my mother and I. From the Asia Realty Company, which he owned. Your father was my landlord. This is a small world, isn't it?"

There was a pause while he gazed at her, and Helmi sensed she was being sized up. This was an instant reminder of the Shanghai days, when people were not always what they appeared to be. Frank Raven had been well known around Shanghai in the mid-1930s, when Helmi was a schoolgirl, as one of the wealthiest American businessmen and civic leaders in the city, having established a real estate and banking empire early in the century. He had cashed in on the booming economy and easy opportunities and had owned and built property all over the city, from luxurious mansions and sumptuous apartments to thin-walled tenements with no heat or proper plumbing. It was to his company offices just off the Bund that Helmi, as a schoolgirl, would travel

on the bus to hand-deliver the monthly rent for the Hongkou tenement
sublet by Auntie Anna and her mother.

A famous philanthropist as well as a teetotaler, Frank Raven had
been celebrated in the Shanghai press of the 1930s as one of the upstand-
ing and uncorrupted barons of power in the Far East. Yet his greatest
fame, finally, was as a criminal. In 1935 his financial empire collapsed in
the wake of a major corruption scandal, and Raven himself was indicted
for fraud and embezzlement. Millions of dollars from both American
and foreign investors were lost, a financial collapse that helped lead to
the loss of Western financial control over Shanghai. Frank Raven served
two years in an American prison.

Finally the man spoke again, sounding more relaxed. "I'll make a con-
jecture. I'm supposing you rented one of the townhouses my father built.
There were many in the French Concession."

It was her turn to smile. She saw he had made a judgment about her,
based probably on her smooth British-Shanghailander accent, plus the
fact that they were meeting at a San Francisco cocktail party attended
by other members of his tribe, the upper crust. He took her for one of
his own. He must have thought she was British, or else an American like
himself with a Shanghai-British education. Her social ease, along with a
lack of any discernible foreign accent, meant she surely wasn't one of the
many impoverished Russians who lived in his disgraced father's hastily constructed cold-water flats in the northern International District of
Shanghai. It might be fun to fill him in on just how mistaken he was. Or
should she go easy on the fellow? His own life had probably been made
difficult by the humiliation his father had suffered.

"Well, no," she said, "not exactly a townhouse. Our home was in Wayside, north of the river." His look changed now to one of real puzzlement.
He had no idea who or what she was. She decided to leave it that way.

"So nice to meet you, Mr. Raven," she said. "I'm afraid I must go
find my husband." She turned away to look for Bill elsewhere in the
room. She was ready to leave now. This is how it was for her whenever a
reminder of the Shanghai years came along. She had no desire to linger
on those memories. It was much more interesting to look forward rather
than backward.

Later on, Helmi would learn more about this man, Robert Raven. He
became a distinguished diplomat, holding a number of posts in Asia for
the U.S. State Department, and after retirement he taught English to

foreign students and did volunteer work in California prisons. It seems he did his best to atone for the disgrace of his father. She always felt glad afterward that she had not added further to his discomfort that evening in San Francisco. Perhaps it was rude to walk away. But by explaining more of herself, she might have forced him to apologize for circumstances that were not his fault. She had left him with a mystery to ponder, which was far better.

Reno I

First Communion boys class, Our Lady of the Snows School, Reno, 1958.
Top row, center: Monsignor Connors; *top row, far right*: altar boy Terry Horgan; *second row, second from left*: the author; *first row, fourth from left*: Danny Horgan.

The Eternal Fires of Hell

CHRISTMAS MORNING, 1956. I am five years old. We have opened our presents under the tree, including those from Santa Claus, for whom, the night before, my brother and I had left a peanut butter and jelly sandwich, a bowl of strawberry Jell-O, and a glass of milk on a TV tray in front of the fireplace. When we got up, the milk and Jell-O were gone, and nothing was left of the sandwich but a single piece of crust. Our red and green Christmas stockings, hand-knit by our Irish grandma and empty when hung last night, were now filled with candy. Terry noticed, and did not hesitate to point out, that a couple of the packages from Santa were wrapped in the same paper as those from our Jewish grandmother. He also whispered that our dad often leaves uneaten the crusts of his sandwiches. None of this matters to me. Terry is eight years old and a skeptic. I am still a true believer.

It also doesn't matter that my mother and grandmother are Jewish. They always seem just as happy as the rest of us to celebrate Christmas, at least as it pertains to presents and food and family. Later today, after breakfast, Terry and I will attend Mass at noon at Our Lady of the Snows along with our dad. Helmi and Rachel naturally will stay home. Then in the afternoon we are all scheduled to gather, along with our aunts and uncles and cousins, at our grandparents' house for the big annual Horgan family Christmas dinner. I am eagerly looking forward to comparing my inventory of gifts with that of my cousin Danny, who is closest to my age and the only one who will fully appreciate my shiny new cap gun with fringed leather holster, a surprise gift from— who else?—Santa Claus.

We are having breakfast, including festive Russian pastries—sweet coffee cake and tiny melt-in-your-mouth meat pies—baked by Baba sometime in the dark early morning hours (I have already formulated a quick theory, to present later to my brother, that she may have been awake in time to loan Santa some wrapping paper). Helmi and our dad drink coffee, Baba has her usual strong tea, and Terry and I are treated to hot chocolate. Whitey, the black lab, now a year old, lies in the corner of the kitchen with a festive red ribbon around her neck, chewing on a new rubber toy. Our parents have exchanged gifts—Terry and I paid no attention to what they gave each other—and thanked us lovingly for the bath salts and polka-dot bow tie bestowed by us, with Baba's shopping assistance. As for Baba, we have given her the identical beribboned, boxed set of mysterious powders and perfumes that we are presenting to our other grandmother later today, on our mother's suggestion. To judge by the wet kisses and Russian endearments we received, this was a gift fit for a queen. All in all, we are the picture of a contented, mostly American family on Christmas morning.

My brother chooses this moment to throw a wrench into the proceedings. "Mom," Terry says to Helmi across the table, his mouth full of half-chewed *piroshke*, "you should come to church with us. Sister Imelda says so."

This is met by a moment of thick silence. Both my parents gaze in astonishment at Terry, coffee cups suspended in the air. Sister Imelda is Terry's second-grade teacher at Our Lady of the Snows school, attached to our parish church, staffed by Dominican nuns. He has to wear a uniform consisting of a white shirt, brown sweater, brown corduroys, and polished brown shoes every day. I go to kindergarten at Mount Rose public school and get to wear sneakers and jeans with my favorite cowboy belt. Next year I'll go to first grade at Our Lady of the Snows, and the mention of Sister Imelda calls to mind those ugly uniforms and the nuns tightly wrapped like mummies in their black-and-white habits with only the fronts of their faces showing. What a thing to bring up on Christmas Day.

Helmi is in her bathrobe and slippers, her dark hair brushed back from her face. She is not "made up," as she likes to put it, but her eyes glare brightly at my eight-year-old brother.

"Is that so," she says at last, not in the tone of a question. "Well, Sister Imelda knows full well that I am not a Catholic. That's why I don't go to church."

I expect this to close the door on the subject. But my brother isn't finished. "She says that doesn't matter. She says the whole family ought to come to church together. She says you'd like it, and it would be fun."

This—the word *fun*—triggers something in me. I have watched other families come to church in dense numbers—moms, dads, kids, babies, grandparents, all packed together in a single pew—and have felt a pang of envy. They never seem like they are having fun, exactly, but there is a kind of pride on display. Maybe we could have that too. I also feel an unexpected urge to join forces with my brother. So, with no more forethought, I jump into the discussion.

"Yeah!" I say. "We should all go. It'll be fun!"

Terry takes my cue, and together we wheedle and whine on this theme for a minute or so. Baba, who was seated next to Terry, has hastily risen and gone to fuss over things in the sink.

Dad at last puts down his fork and clears his throat. "Boys," he says quietly, "just because Sister Imelda is a teacher, it doesn't mean she tells us what to do at home." He looks at his watch. "I want you both to run and get dressed, because I'm taking you to Mass very soon."

Suddenly Helmi stands up, wiping her mouth with a napkin and tossing it onto the table. Has she "reached her limit"? This is the phrase she uses when, for instance, Baba drops a load of wet bread dough on the floor, Terry and I burst into hysterics, and the dog responds with a barking frenzy. But now something remarkable happens.

"Okay," she says. "Have it your way. Let's all go." She stares each of us down, Terry and me, and then fixes her gaze on Dad. "I mean it," she says. "Let's all get dressed." She speaks in a tone we all know well, meaning it's time to shut up and do what we're told.

So we do. Terry and I run to our room and change into our Sunday clothes, then dive together into the bathroom to brush our teeth. When we arrive back in the kitchen, the three adults are there already, dressed to the nines, Helmi and Baba in high heels and out-to-dinner type dresses and our dad in a coat and tie, something we almost never see. If more discussion has taken place behind the bedroom walls we haven't heard it, but it's clear that serious purpose is at hand. Helmi and Baba even have hats on. Dad must have reminded them that women always cover their heads in a Catholic church. We all climb in the car— our white four-door Ford—and ride in silence. Terry wears a stunned expression the whole way. Clearly he was not expecting this outcome.

When we file into the church the five of us take up most of a pew. We are near the back, unlike some of the other familiar clans who parade up the center aisle to the very front. I am keenly aware of both my mother and grandmother as the Mass proceeds. They sit together in identical straight-backed postures, purses gripped in their laps. Neither moves while the rest of us stand, then kneel, then sit for a while, then stand and kneel again, during the various parts of the proceedings. The church is packed to the gills, unlike on a regular Sunday, and I know that there are plenty of others here who only come on Christmas Day, or maybe that and Easter Sunday. Still, Helmi and Baba, at least to me, stand out like sore thumbs. My mother wears a grim expression. I wonder what she's thinking. Has she done this simply to quiet our foolishness? Or might she be wondering if some sort of enlightenment will be experienced? To me, at age five, what goes on here is thrilling and also quite scary—the priest in his flowing golden robes, the Latin mumbo-jumbo, the magical transformation of a little circle of bread dough into the actual flesh of God and the wine into Jesus's real blood, which Monsignor Connors slurps audibly from the gleaming golden chalice. But when I look at Helmi during these portentous moments, nothing changes in her stony face.

Baba is another story. She gazes all around the room, beaming. She always loves it when people gather for happy reasons. I know that in some ways she is a believer. I have witnessed her, through the doorway of the bedroom in the middle of an afternoon, pressing her hands together and wringing them at the ceiling while mumbling in Russian what can only be an aching entreaty to the heavens. She also goes to Temple on many Friday nights, where they have a different but equally weird set of rituals.

The next big event is when most of the congregation files solemnly forward to take Communion. I won't be initiated into this bizarre activity until next year, in first grade, so I sit quietly next to my mother while the parishioners, including my dad and brother, parade up the aisle with downcast eyes to receive the white wafer squashed against their tongues by Monsignor Connors's big pink thumb. Out of nowhere Helmi reaches down and takes my hand and gives it a squeeze. I look up, and this time she faintly smiles at me and lifts an eyebrow. I take this as an acknowledgment that this part of the Mass is creepy.

Later on we congregate at Grandma and Grandpa Horgan's house with the rest of our relatives. Passing through the living room with cousin Danny in our matching cowboy gear (how did Santa know to give us the same surprise?), I catch a snippet of adult conversation. Somebody asks Helmi why she suddenly decided to go to Mass, and her reply is crisp, in her clear English diction: "I decided to try it. Just once. Once will be quite enough."

Before dinner, we are herded into the living room for a group photograph, and as we fall into place—women all in armchairs, men standing behind, kids cross-legged on the floor—a surprise is presented. Baba, it turns out, has brought a gift for the other ladies, something she proudly announces she has made in her hobby class at the Golden Age Club. A beribboned box is unpacked and out come some large clusters of dried cranberries that, apparently, have been strung together and fashioned into enormous earrings. The five women—Helmi, Baba, Grandma Horgan, and my two aunts, the pair of sisters married to my two uncles—all struggle to attach these things to their ears, amid exclamations of what even a five-year-old can tell is fake delight. The earrings are supremely silly-looking. They look like adornments worn by some primitive tribe in the *National Geographic*. Those of us on the floor can't help breaking into a round of giggling. Nevertheless, Baba is extremely pleased with her gift. Helmi, with a look of steely resolve and possibly worry, leads the way in thanking Baba and complimenting her on her handiwork, and my other grandma and two aunts follow her example. There is a great deal about the adult world that is a mystery to me, but I understand that Baba is often perceived as ridiculous and even pathetic. My mother, on the other hand, is considered a force to be reckoned with and her wishes are respected.

The camera has been mounted on a tripod in the middle of the room. Somebody shouts out, "Heads up, everybody! Merry Christmas! Shut up and smile!"

Most of us do, and the shutter clicks.

~

IT IS A YEAR LATER, and I am now enrolled at Our Lady of the Snows, wearing the school uniform every day. My first grade teacher, Sister Mariana, is young and friendly and knows how to laugh, and I like her just fine. Most of the other nuns are not to be trifled with. Sister Imelda, the one who encouraged Terry to nag my mother about attending

Christmas Mass, is small and wiry and bespectacled, and flits up and down the halls at amazing speed, accompanied by the steady clicking of the strands of black rosary beads tied around her tiny waist. She never looks anyone in the eye and doesn't seem capable of smiling. Sister Winifred, who teaches in the upper grades, is short and rounder, with a large, pudgy, pink face, and she seems to have a perpetual cold: a glaze of yellowish snot often blocks her nostrils, and she uses a filthy handkerchief that is tucked into her billowing white sleeve.

One afternoon, we are marching into the building from our lunch recess after filing into military-style lines outside. As our first-grade troop peels off and turns down the hall toward our classroom, out of nowhere Sister Winifred grabs me by the arm and yanks me out of formation. She bends over to put her face close to mine and for a second I think I will pee in my pants, but the terror of what further tribulations this would cause enables me to hold the urge in check.

"Listen to me, young man," Sister Winifred says in a husky whisper. "I have a message to send home with you." I try not to stare at her crusty nostrils, only inches away. She takes hold of both my earlobes, locking her hold on my head.

"You tell your mother," she goes on, "that without faith she risks the wrath of God. The Lord is merciful, but those who refuse to believe cannot enter into Heaven. There is the glory of Heaven, and there are the fires of Hell." I know she speaks these words with capital "H's," because they are always written that way on the classroom blackboard. "Now you go home and tell her what I said." She releases me and shoves me back into line with my marching classmates.

One thing we know already in the first grade is to obey every order of the nuns, no matter how weird, so I plan to do what I am told. Walking home from school, I find I am curious to see my mother's reaction to this threat. She represents a formidable opposing force that I have no name for, but in my limited experience it carries considerable weight. We have had very few theological discussions at home, but I know this much: my mother considers herself Jewish, which is what Jesus was when he was a boy and before he founded a new church, but she doesn't believe in any of it, because she doesn't need to.

The moment I choose is at the dinner table. I do my best to quote Sister Winifred word for word. As expected, all conversation stops. My brother looks at me with wide-eyed interest. My dad rolls his eyes. Baba covers her mouth in horror and releases a stifled squeak, like a little bird. Helmi puts down her fork.

"Oh, really?" she says. "So Sister Winifred thinks I don't deserve heaven." Her tone is surprisingly cheerful, as if she had been paid a compliment instead of threatened with eternal damnation. She takes my hand across the table, with a bit more pressure than just a gentle motherly squeeze. "Sweetheart," she says, "Sister Winifred doesn't know me very well, does she?" Her voice is even more British-sounding than usual, just like on the previous Christmas when she had declared that one visit to Mass would be quite enough. "I do know what hell is, perhaps even better than Sister Winifred. I have seen it, right here on earth. And, believe me, I'm not going there. But you don't need to tell her." Without letting go of my hand, she looks at my dad, who meets her gaze. "Your father will be glad to explain this to Sister Winifred."

"Yes, I will," he says.

"Now," she says, with a big smile, "we will drop the subject."

I wonder if soon I will no longer have to attend Our Lady of the Snows School.

The Chesterfield Girl

NO SUCH LUCK, as it turns out. I will remain in Catholic school until I finish the eighth grade. And I will learn, long after the fact, that my dad did make that trip to the school, probably the next day, to remind the nuns of certain facts, and no further mention is ever made of my mother going to Hell. No one ever accosts me in the hallways again.

Helmi is overall quite happy with Our Lady of the Snows School. She loves the strict discipline and the uniforms and that we have to wear polished shoes instead of sneakers. She even likes some of the nuns, especially the ones who know how to have fun and can demonstrate a sense of humor. Sister Walter, for instance, joins the kids in the school-yard in the winter and happily participates in snowball fights. Terry and I seem to be learning our basic reading, writing, and arithmetic, and if these need to be accompanied by relentless Catholic indoctrination, so be it. After all, she promised to allow her children to be raised this way, and a promise is a promise. Terry and I, along with our cousins and classmate pals, both become altar boys, which requires memorizing the Latin Mass and being driven to the church on many early mornings, a chore Helmi eventually takes upon herself because our dad is so slow-moving in the morning that he can't seem to get us there on time. She pitches in at Catholic bake sales and rummage sales and spaghetti feeds, bringing Baba along as an extra hand, who of course loves it all. Helmi doesn't mind any of this, as long as she doesn't have to go to church.

Time passes. My parents build a beautiful new house, designed by an architect friend. It has plenty of room for all of us—our parents, Terry and me, Baba, and the dog. It has a big patio, hidden from the street,

Helmi and her Reno pals, about 1965. Phyllis Crudgington, the Chesterfield
Girl, is in the front, at left. Phyllis Goldwater is in a striped top, wearing
sunglasses, and Helmi is standing directly behind her.

where all summer Helmi and Baba practice barbecuing. We have a pond
in the backyard with families of ducks and geese.

Our dad continues to works six days a week at the hardware store,
and with the long hours put in by him and my grandfather and my two
uncles, the business thrives. They build a big new store, and every year
all of us kids help with the annual inventory by pushing each other
around the aisles in shopping carts, counting hand tools and hinges
and batteries and fasteners. Our dad is still a lawyer on the side, too,
and assists friends with preparing cases. He sometimes spends all day
on Sunday, after church, working on a legal brief. He becomes involved
with the founding of the Nevada Civil Rights Commission and helps
draft the state's first anti-discrimination legislation. He loves his books
on astronomy and physics and decides to build a telescope from scratch;
in the garage he makes a stand out of a post mounted in a tub of concrete on which he begins grinding a pair of six-inch lenses. He drinks a
single highball, bourbon and ginger ale, every day after work.

Helmi has a cadre of friends with whom she laughs and gossips and
smokes and sips sherry on many afternoons. When I come home from
school, one or another of them of them is often perched on the couch
in the living room. After emerging from our walk-through pantry with
its walls of canned goods, I am trained to stop and say a brief hello on

my way to my room to change my clothes, aware that whatever topic was under way is on hold until I am again out of earshot. Baba is rarely included in these parlays. Most often she is in the kitchen bustling around with her apron on or else off in the darkness of her room. Sometimes the conversation I'm interrupting is serious and conducted in low tones, and then I can tell that Baba herself, the problem of Baba, is the subject of discussion.

Helmi acts in more productions at the Reno Little Theater. She has a leading role in *Teahouse of the August Moon*, playing a Japanese geisha named Lotus Blossom. The play takes place during the U.S. Army occupation of Japan, precisely the time Helmi was there. We all go to see the show and watch in amazement as she tiptoes across the stage in a kimono and wooden sandals and a tall black wig with chopsticks sticking out of it, delivering her lines in a delicate voice with an expertly rendered Japanese accent. She is praised in newspaper reviews, and at the end of the drama season she wins the theater's best actress award, called the Golden Egg. The statuette takes a place of honor on our bookshelves.

She continues her habit of making a biweekly trip to the county library, each time returning an armload of seven or eight books and checking out an equal number. I like to accompany her, either on a Saturday or after school, but I can't make it through very many books—even slim Hardy Boys novels—before the next due date. Where does she find time to read so many? At night, she tells us. While the rest of us sleep, including our dad, she sits up in bed and reads. She has always done this, she says, and she probably always will.

When we move into our new house, our next-door neighbors are the Crudgingtons—Phyllis and Cleve. As a family they are as different from us as they can be. Their son, Winky (who is really Cleve Junior, but no one calls him that) is a couple of years older than Terry, and their daughter, Sandy, is a couple of years older than me. My mother met Phyllis when she first came to Reno, which resulted in a famous family story. They were introduced at a cocktail party, and Helmi immediately remarked that Phyllis's face was familiar from the past. Phyllis had never been to the Far East, so they couldn't have met. After a moment Helmi said, triumphantly, "I have it. You're the Chesterfield Girl!" And indeed she was. Phyllis was tall and glamorous, and in her youth she'd had a brief career as a model. In the late 1930s she had been photographed in a green Robin Hood costume for a Chesterfield cigarette advertisement

Helmi on the beach at Lake Tahoe with cigarette, about 1954.

that had been used widely in magazines and on billboards around the world. This was the image Helmi had admired as a schoolgirl while riding the bus in Shanghai. She had not forgotten that beautiful face, which had beckoned her to a world achingly out of reach. Now, because of sheer luck, Helmi lived in that world. Chesterfields would always be her brand of choice. And amazingly—fittingly, she sometimes allowed herself to think—the Chesterfield girl now lived right next door.

The Crudgingtons become our friends, despite the differences between our families. Cleve and Phyllis drive a white Cadillac with huge fins and taillights shaped like rocket engines. They dress like movie stars. Cleve wears plaid sport coats and Hawaiian shirts, and his business is publishing books and pamphlets promoting the Nevada gambling and tourist business. Phyllis, twenty years past her modeling days but still slender and platinum blonde, favors tight gold Capri pants and lots of jewelry, and in the summer she walks around in a bikini. My mother says she is very brainy. She is locally renowned as an expert bridge player and makes money teaching other people to play. The Crudgingtons do surprising things. Cleve sunbathes on his patio wearing only a wash-cloth on his crotch. Phyllis likes to play chess. She and Cleve some-times have loud shouting matches late at night that keep us awake next door. Winky and Sandy each have their own record players for their collections of 45s by Elvis Presley, Bill Haley, Fats Domino, and Chuck Berry—fantastic songs that we love and also know the nuns would con-sider deeply evil.

Sometimes we all get together on weekends. The adults chain-smoke and drink cocktails. Cleve likes to cook and with loud enthusiasm par-ticipates in the kitchen chores with my mother and Baba, his rapid-fire laugh resonating through the house, while Phyllis and my dad end up in the living room huddled intensely over a game of chess. He says she is a better player than he is. We kids gather outside, playing kickball in our adjoining yards or roller-skating on one of our patios, or we end up at the Crudgingtons' house listening to loud, sinful music.

My Irish grandparents own a narrow lot on the shore of Lake Tahoe, and the year I turn seven they build a cabin to share with their three sons' families. Our family gets two weeks there every summer, plus Terry and I often join some of our cousins or our grandparents for their slots, which can add up to half the summer at the lake. The families go in together on a motorboat and we learn to water ski. For Christmas the grandparents buy all the grandsons season passes to a nearby ski hill. During snow season we take skiing lessons on Saturdays and hit the hill again on Sundays after Mass, graduating from the rope tow to the T-bar and finally to the grownup chairlift.

We are provided a comfortable and carefree life that Helmi never knew existed. She has no interest in skiing, whether on water or snow, but she relishes the fact that we can enjoy these activities. She doesn't mind that we are growing up taking this kind of life for granted. To her it is an astonishing stroke of good fortune that she can raise children who see the world, at least for a time, as a genuinely happy place.

We know nothing of the lives she and Baba led before we were born. Our ignorance is monumental. We have never experienced hunger or privation or war. These are things we have read about in books and seen in movies. We have hot water every day and toilets that flush. We have never seen the sky darken with planes loaded with bombs. We have never watched city blocks go up in flames. We mock our mother for her obsession with cleanliness: taking our Catholic school uniforms to the dry cleaner so they will remain as crisp as the day they were bought, washing and polishing the linoleum floors and pounding out every speck of dust from the rugs, scrubbing the bathrooms with bleach and removing the kitchen garbage every evening so there is no hint of an odor other than the sweet and savory aromas of carefully prepared meals and fabulous baked treats. We ridicule our little Russian grandmother for her nervous fears and mysterious demons, her twitching and jumpiness, her leaping in horror at the slightest ripple in the fabric of daily life. We are told that her "condition" is a sickness to be treated, like the flu. She takes special medicine to stay calm. She cannot bring herself to come out of her room to watch Premier Khrushchev pound the table with his shoe and say that he will bury us, even though Helmi corrects the translator on the TV: he is not speaking literally, he is using a colorful Russian metaphor. It doesn't occur to us that Baba's terrified outlook, nutty as it appears to us, might have a rational basis—that her intuitive view of the world may in fact be based on experience and not be so crazy after all.

We continue on, my brother and I, believing that nothing truly fearful can penetrate our comfortable world. Our mother encourages this belief, seeing it as a gift to be savored for as long as it can hold up. Our dad puts his stock in his religious faith along with the power of brains and hard work. Baba, however, doesn't disguise the fact that she is perpetually on the lookout for something terrible, some evil coming to get us all. We laugh at her, and we feel sorry for her. Helmi, in particular, grows more and more irritated by her mother's hand-wringing and constant worrying, her nameless and unfounded fears.

Howling in the Night

OUR HOUSE IS STOCKED like a grocery store and built like a fortress. One room is a long passageway that we call the pantry, leading straight off the entrance by the driveway, the door everybody uses, so this is your first impression when you enter the house: shelf upon shelf, up the walls on both sides from floor to ceiling, loaded with enough nonperishable food to last for months, probably years. We are just one family, my brother and me, my parents, and my grandmother, but our supplies would feed an army. Rows and rows of canned fruits and vegetables, endless cans of soup, every possible variety of beans, white tunafish, brown tunafish, Spam, clams, sardines. Boxes and more boxes of crackers and cookies and cereal and cake mixes, hanging baskets of potatoes and onions. On its own shelf, a deep supply of canned condensed milk, sweetened and unsweetened. Also vast amounts of paper products—Kleenex, napkins, toilet paper, piled high and wide. Then, once you finally turn the corner into the kitchen, you'll find the table always loaded with fresh fruit: apples, bananas, oranges, pears. It is as if the house itself is making a declaration of its bounty, its ability to provide: *Here is a home, safe and fortified, laden with life's essentials. Here lives a family prepared to withstand any hardship.* As my mother likes to say, no matter what else happens, we'll be the last ones to starve.

My parents had the house designed and built to their specifications, which we understood meant mostly to my mother's specifications. It's very different from other houses in the neighborhood, with its low profile, flat roof, and no windows facing the street. People sometimes say it looks like a bunker. All the doors are concealed behind sections of gray brick walls. Deep in the interior is a room designated exclusively for books, with built-in shelves stacked with our mother's novels and our dad's law books. We call it, naturally, the library. The backyard slopes downhill to a small pond rimmed with weeping willows, and the bedrooms all face that way, each room with its own door to the outside, designed as if for easy escape.

Like the books on our parents' bookshelves, the stock of provisions seems permanent, built into the very structure of the house. Nothing ever runs out. My mother and my grandmother make sure of this by going to the store every day. Not every other day, or once or twice a week. Every single day.

We are not the only well-provisioned family I know. Some of my friends' houses also have amply stocked pantry shelves. A few even have an actual bomb shelter, a semi-secret room connected to their basement, loaded with emergency supplies as a hedge against a nuclear attack by Nikita Khrushchev. But these provisions are kept hidden, stashed out of view and not meant to be shared. At our house they are all on proud and fully public display. My mother laughs at the bomb-shelter people. When the bombs finally come, she says, there won't be anywhere to hide.

Cooking goes on perpetually. Baba spends most of her waking hours in the kitchen. Though my mother is barely five feet tall, Baba is even shorter. At nine years old I can almost see eye to eye with my grandmother, and probably I outweigh her. Thin, wiry, perched on a high stool at the kitchen counter, singing to herself softly, sometimes in Russian and sometimes in Yiddish, in a flour-dusted apron that comes down to her ankles, she can sit for hours flattening dough with a wooden rolling pin, flinging handfuls of flour onto the breadboard, her arms white up to the elbows, clouds of flour exploding to the side and spattering onto the floor. Her specialty is baking: *bulka*, a dense rolled coffee cake made with jam and nuts and thick sugar icing, or *piroshke*, bite-sized meat-and-onion pastries with a flaky crust rolled so thin you can see through it. My mother, if she isn't off rehearsing one of her plays or taking a book break on the couch in the library, will be helping out, perhaps tending the stove or chopping vegetables at the table but more likely sweeping up the mess that my grandmother is making as fast as it occurs. All the while, they both chain-smoke unfiltered Chesterfield cigarettes and mutter back and forth to each other in one of their foreign languages.

My mother is a cheery person most of the time, yet around Baba her face can go dark in a split second. Outwardly, it is about neatness. Helmi makes it clear to all that she detests untidiness, in the kitchen or anywhere else. Standing with her broom behind Baba in the kitchen, she will turn toward whoever happens to be nearby—fourth-grade me, for instance—and roll her eyes dramatically. But there is another kind of tension between them. We dimly understand that they are tethered by past tribulations bigger than battles over a messy kitchen.

We grow up knowing only a few simple facts. They are Russian and they are Jewish. They were very poor and survived terrible things. They came to the United States from Japan at the end of World War II. Why they lived in Japan was only one of the abiding mysteries. We knew that our dad was a soldier with the American army occupation. Our parents were married soon after the war, and Baba joined them in Reno when my brother was a baby, before I was born. This, for most of the years we have lived together, is all that I know.

When my brother and I try to pin our mother down to ask about her life before Reno and before us, she is almost always too busy to answer, or pretends to be. She is thoroughly occupied with inhabiting the life she has made for herself, the happy life of an American wife and mother. She enjoys a fine reputation in the community, among neighbors, relatives, and friends, for being sophisticated, glamorous, and witty. She drinks cocktails at five, wine with dinner, and beer on a hot summer day. She volunteers at the hospital and the Goodwill. She continues to honor her commitment to send my brother and me to Catholic school and to Mass every Sunday because she promised to do so, but she readily reminds us that we are Jewish because she and Baba are Jewish. "If the Nazis ever come back," she'll say with a smirk, "that's all they'll need to know." She holds the past at a distance and maintains that she has neither the time nor the inclination to talk about it.

Prying information from Baba is almost as difficult. Her adjustment to a new life has been less complete than Helmi's. We will eventually come to understand that the effort required to keep her private terrors under control has exacted a price on both her sanity and her relationship with my mother. Mounted on her kitchen stool, bearing down with her bony elbows on a sticky mound of dough, puffing away on her cigarette, she works hard to keep at bay a mortal fear of the

world. We have became accustomed to her fearful shrieks at anything
unexpected—a pot boiling over, the dog underfoot, a thunderclap over
the Sierras—and are adept at mimicking her accent and replicating her
cry of distress: *Oy Bozhomoi!*

~

It's 1958. My parents have taken a two-week trip to the East Coast, visiting both Washington, D.C., and New York City. Being a member of
Nevada's first Civil Rights Commission, our dad has been invited to a
meeting with important people, including President Eisenhower. This is
a momentous family event. My big brother, now eleven, has been taken
on this adventure and I have been left home. I was told that I was too
young to appreciate the trip. There seemed to be some undercurrent at
work, some other reason to leave me behind in the care of my grandmother, although I had no idea what the reason could be.

While they are gone, I have several conversations with my brother,
conducted over a scratchy long-distance phone connection, where I grill
him about every aspect of the trip: the height of the skyscrapers in New
York, the size of the White House, the floor of Congress. I want desperately to be on that trip. I know full well that I am not too young to
appreciate it.

Later, I will learn from Helmi that although my grandmother was
technically watching over me, I actually had been left behind to insure
that Baba herself was not alone in the house for those two weeks.

I knew that Baba had been starting to act extra strangely, even for
her. What I didn't know was that for some time she had been regularly
seeing a psychiatrist and was considered a risk for what in those days
was called a "nervous breakdown." We had noticed books sitting out on
our parents' nightstand with titles like *How To Live with a Neurotic*. I
didn't have a clear sense of what a neurotic was, but I knew full well it
referred to Baba.

One evening, soon after my parents and brother had left on their
trip, I turn the corner from the hall into the doorway to the kitchen
and what I see freezes me in my tracks: there is Baba kneeling on the
floor in front of the stove, weeping, wringing clasped hands skyward in
a perfect picture of abject misery. Holding my breath, I watch her for a
few seconds. Her arms are fully extended and her clenched fists trem-
ble while tears stream down her face. She is mumbling softly, her words

seemingly aimed at the ceiling, or beyond it. I hear her say through her sobs, "Please, please, I beg of you."

This frightening image of suffering sends an icy jolt through my insides. I connect it in my mind with familiar tales of Christ's agony in the Garden of Gethsemane, except that this display of pain, happening right in front of my eyes to my own grandmother, seems much more real. Baba is not a militant non-believer like our mother, but we have never known her to be truly religious. In any case, whoever she is talking to now, God or somebody else, it is not a happy conversation.

I back out of the door quickly and try to catch my breath. This is my very first glimpse of the world of adult-sized unhappiness, and I feel terrified by its apparent power. The fact that I have no inkling of what troubles her somehow makes it all the more frightening. I know I have to do something, if only to combat my own fear. So I turn around and go back down the hall, wait a few moments, and then about-face and head again toward the kitchen, this time producing a range of artificial noises—I hum, stomp my feet, whistle, call out to the dog. The idea is to give her plenty of warning and time to recover herself. And it works, at least for the moment. This time, when I turn into the kitchen, she is back on her feet and has opened the oven door to check on whatever she was making for our dinner. I greet her as heartily as I can, considering I'm still shaking, and all through our dinner I keep up an awkward effort to act especially cheerful. I can see that she is straining to do the same. I have never participated in this kind of social artifice before—a forced change of mood borne out of mutual necessity.

Within a couple of days another event occurs, even more frightening in its way. I awake in the middle of the night to the sound of ghostly howling, coming from somewhere in the house. At first I assume it's the dog. Or rather, I hope it's the dog—except that the dog, being mild-tempered, has never been known to howl. She rarely even barks. Once I am fully awake, I realize it has to be Baba.

I get up and go down the hall to the door of her room and listen. She is producing a noise unlike anything I have ever heard in my life, except maybe at the movies or in the House of Mystery at the county fair: the sort of sound I have always imagined might emanate from the Banshee of Ireland, the legendary Celtic ghost my brother gleefully told me about late one night in front of the fireplace at the family cabin at Lake Tahoe. What am I supposed to do? I want the rest of my family to be here in this moment, but they are thousands of miles away, sleeping soundly high up in some fancy skyscraper hotel. I can't go back to sleep with that sound in my ears. So, in the semi-darkness, I push open the door.

"Baba?" I call out. "Please stop."

She doesn't stop. She keeps it up. A bit of light comes through her window from the street, and I can see her quite clearly. She has rolled herself in the sheet, wrapped up tightly like a mummy, with her head completely covered. This is unquestionably the creepiest moment of my young life. I could easily go running from the house and awaken the neighbors, the Crudgingtons next door or the Springers across the street. Why don't I? Maybe the reason has to do with the recent incident in the kitchen. I feel connected to her now, almost responsible for her, in some way that I don't fully understand. I don't want to leave her by herself. I feel a strange mixture of terror and fascination. So, I go in and stand next to her bed.

The sound she makes is like that of a wounded animal. Low to high, then low again. Instinctively I reach out to touch her, but then think better of it. So I simply stand there and listen, and wait. Finally she subsides, and at last she ceases moaning. I wait for my heart to stop pounding, and then I back out of the room carefully, feeling as though I have just passed some mysterious test. As I lie again in bed, unable to go to sleep, I begin planning how I will tell my brother about this. I know he will come home from the trip with plenty of stories to tell. Now I have one also.

When I relay the saga to my mother after they are home, she is quiet at first, then takes hold of my shoulders and looks me straight in the eyes. "I will never, ever do this to you again," she says. Tightening her grip, she adds, "Believe me." And I do. Not long after, Baba has to be hospitalized for several weeks. We are told she has finally suffered a "nervous breakdown." Now I didn't need to ask what this means. I have seen it for myself.

Black Sunday

Autumn 1961. I am ten years old and Terry is thirteen. Exciting things have happened. A Catholic, John F. Kennedy, young and handsome and energetic, has been elected president of the United States. The nuns had us on our knees all through the fall, saying extra rosaries for his campaign, and we can tell ourselves that we helped get him elected.

The previous year America had hosted the Winter Olympics in Squaw Valley, California, just over the hill from Reno, and our family got to attend for free. Both our dad and our mother were the reasons why: Dad, despite his bashful nature and rumpled clothes, had become a prominent citizen. Elected president of the Reno Chamber of Commerce, he took charge of a booth at the Reno airport to welcome Olympic athletes coming from all over the world. And, because of her fluency in multiple languages, my mother worked in the booth as a greeter and translator. She did so well handling Russian, Japanese, German, and French that she was asked to use her skills again in Squaw Valley during the Games. We attended the opening ceremonies in the ice arena, a show put on by Walt Disney. They gave us tickets to see the figure skaters and ski jumpers, and we were in the stands in the ice arena when the U.S. hockey team shocked the world by winning the gold medal. These Winter Olympics were said to have helped defuse the rising tensions of the Cold War. Our mother, we believe, had a hand in this when she presented bouquets of flowers to actual Russians and spoke to them in their own language.

Then, in the summer, we experienced another rare adventure, accompanying the Crudgingtons on a two-week ocean voyage. Cleve concocted the idea and talked us into it. We would man a luxurious sixty-foot yacht and sail among the islands of southwestern Canada. As a former Navy

officer, Cleve was qualified to rent and captain a boat out of Seattle and
staff it with a crew. He formulated a daring plan to fudge the nautical
regulations and list all of us as official crew members—our mother, dad,
Terry, and me, along with Cleve, Phyllis, Winky, and Sandy. Baba didn't
make the crew list. Having weathered her nervous breakdown, she had
been given clearance to stay home alone and take care of the house and
the dog. Terry and I were thrilled and amazed that our parents went
along with this scheme. We had never known them to circumvent the
laws of the land or sea.

The trip replaced our family's regular two-week stay at the Lake
Tahoe cabin. Terry and I got the impression that Cleve and Phyllis
seduced our parents into going along with it by selling the trip as a rare
educational opportunity for us kids. We would catch salmon and go
crabbing and pluck oysters, while navigating and sightseeing at our leisure among the snowcapped peaks of the San Juan Islands. We all drove
to Seattle, then early one drizzly morning gathered at the dock to board
our yacht, called the *Sailfish*, which turned out to be a partially converted
fishing boat. It was a far cry from luxurious. The berths were cramped
and dank, the diesel motors noisy and smoky, and the galley and bathroom facilities smelly and dilapidated. Nevertheless, we loaded our luggage on board and cast off. After passing through the Ballard locks, we
were required to have a customs inspection, and this was when our dad
took Terry and me belowdecks for an awkward, whispered lecture. It
turned out that Cleve had stowed several cases of booze—Scotch, bourbon, gin, vodka—beyond the allowed limits and in violation of international regulations, and we needed to know about it to help protect the
secret. It was a tough sell for our dad. His tactic was to explain to us
that, as the official crew members, we were obligated under maritime
law to obey all orders from our captain whether we agreed with them
or not.

"We're smugglers," said my brother, enjoying the chance to voice a
moral dilemma. He was entering the seventh grade and had lately
expressed an interest in becoming a priest. Our dad, after an uncomfortable pause, said, "I suppose, yes. More like accomplices to smuggling,
you could say."

"Are we pirates?" I added. My belief, which thrilled me to the core,
was that listing us all as fake crewmen defined us as blackguards of the
high seas. And pirates, of course, need to stock plenty of rum. Rolling

his eyes, he said yes again. No doubt the issue had been discussed at length in the topside captain's quarters, and Cleve's need to carry an ample and varied bar stock had been deemed sacrosanct. Anyway, we got away with it. The customs agents, whose inspection we felt was surprisingly cursory after all our sneaking around, did not discover the booze, stashed in the engine room under a greasy tarp, and we sailed safely and fully stocked into Canada.

It was clear from the very beginning that Helmi took a skeptical view of this entire enterprise—and not just the smuggling. You could tell from the look on her face that the boat and everything that went with it—the smoke, the slime, the sludge—held no appeal for her whatsoever. We knew she was going along for the rest of our sakes, chiefly for the sake of our dad, who had maybe fallen the hardest for Cleve's adventure pitch. What we didn't understand very well was that she had already had her share of ocean voyages. She had steamed from Shanghai to Kobe alone, under dangerous wartime conditions and with no papers to guarantee her safety, and she had traveled again from Japan to San Francisco on an American freighter after the war. There was no glamour for her in sailing the high seas. She would have far preferred to stay at home on dry land. But she put on her game face and tried to make the best of it.

The trip, in my nine-year-old estimation, was spectacular. There were a few setbacks. Illness, for one: my brother spent several days in his bunk—seasick, we thought at first, but actually with the flu, only getting up to run to the tiny, stinking toilet to puke up everything he tried to eat. There were several heavy rainstorms which forced us to drop anchor in protected bays. We suffered a major breakdown: one of the two diesel engines failed after the first week, and parts had to be flown in to a tiny logging town on the Canadian coast that had a bar but no restaurant. We also ran aground once in the middle of the night while anchored, waking before dawn when the whole boat suddenly heaved sideways, throwing us out of our bunks, and we discovered the tide had gone out from under us in a tiny bay paved solid with golden-colored oysters. Through it all, the adults drank and played bridge. Helmi and Cleve cooked up fish stew and clam chowder in the tiny galley, while Phyllis and our dad mixed cocktails and played rounds of chess. My dad brought along a sextant and practiced navigating by the stars at night and by naval charts during the day. Every one of us—even I, the youngest sailor on board—got to take a turn manning the wheel.

When we returned home after two weeks, weather-beaten and exhausted, Baba treated us like long-lost refugees, greeting us with tears of joy. She had suffered through the two long weeks, no doubt fearing every day to receive the grim news that we had been shipwrecked. I felt great pride—a nine-year-old's dream—in having manned the ship, braved the elements, and mastered the high seas. Even my brother, after barfing his way through the first week, had recovered and managed to have a good time. Our dad had loved learning to navigate. We all saw that the trip in many ways had been an ordeal for Helmi, who loved her comforts, but even she was willing to declare it a success once she was home, safe and sound.

I began fifth grade in the fall assuming that more great adventures lay ahead. The family seemed charmed. Our parents, in their different ways, were locally famous. Terry and I had become seasoned sailors. The future was bright.

~

OCTOBER. Out of nowhere, suddenly there are strange doings in the house. Late-night phone calls. Intense whispered voices. Terry and I are sent out of the room abruptly at odd hours, doors are shut, conversations between our parents are conducted out of earshot. This ought to be a festive season, with Thanksgiving coming up, then the Christmas holidays. I have a private worry that maybe it's the return of the Nazis our mother warned us about. Whatever big thing is happening, my brother and I are kept out of the loop. But not perfectly. Terry has crept around a few corners and reported what he can. One night, lying in bed in the dark, he says out loud, "Dad said he has blood in his poop." Baba, if she knows what's going on, reveals nothing, although her face betrays something fearsome even beyond her regular demons. This goes on for a week.

One evening at the dinner table, there's another phone call. My mother answers, then looks ominously over at our dad, who brusquely orders us boys to our bedroom. Baba joins us on the way out, without being asked, and shuffles rapidly into her room. On our way down the hall, Terry turns abruptly and tiptoes back, circling around the brick partition in the living room to a spot off the kitchen where he can eavesdrop. I don't have the nerve to follow him. Whatever is up, my gut sense is that a blatant violation of parental orders won't help. I also have a brand-new feeling: I don't even want to know. So I keep going and sit down on my bed.

After a few minutes, down the hall and into the room come my parents, followed by my brother. Terry catches my eye, and he looks pale, and I see that he now knows everything. Somewhere in the shadows behind them stands my tiny grandmother, exhaling her steady whimpers of anxiety. Dad sits down on the bed next to me and says, "Boys, come here." He pays no attention to the fact that Terry has followed him from behind. Helmi stands next to him, rigid, wearing a stony face, a blank stare that I can only look at for a few seconds, but that we will grow used to seeing more in the next few years.

Looking not at us but at the wall, our dad says, "Okay, here's what it is. I am very sick. I have cancer, in my stomach. We've been waiting to hear the results of tests." His voice is barely above a whisper. "It's going to grow, we knew that for sure. It was either slow or fast growing." He looks up at my mother. "Now we know. It's a slow-growing cancer. They say I have probably five years more." And then he bursts into tears. Something I have never even imagined. The sight of my dad crying shocks me more than the news he has delivered. "I'm not going to die yet," he blurts out, through heavy sobs.

Not much has stuck with me as to what anyone said then or exactly what happened next. We must have all sat up for a while and then gone to bed, and probably no one slept much. The next few days were no doubt difficult. I'm sure there was a measure of relief on the part of my parents, since they had been waiting to hear news of the tests and may have had reason to expect worse. I'm sure we all pretended to go on as usual for some days, maybe even weeks, trying not to believe that as a family we were now under a kind of spell, or a curse. But the change was unmistakable and profound. The future was now something to dread rather than welcome.

~

AND SO TIME PASSES. It just does, no matter what anyone wants. Terry, across the seventh and eighth grades, continues to think about becoming a priest. I follow him along through the grades at Our Lady of the Snows, moving from one nun to the next, some of them smart and fun, some stereotypically sour and humorless. We are both conscientious students, models of good behavior, extremely cognizant that our

Rachel (*far right*) reaching for the bridal bouquet at George and Simonne
Sidline's wedding, San Francisco, 1962. Photo provided by George Sidline,
forty-six years after the fact.

primary duty under these trying circumstances is to cause no trouble, be
no problem. We still have our pals and relatives. We still water ski in the
summer and snow ski in the winter. Efforts are made to help us grow up
in as normal an atmosphere as possible.

   December 1962. I am eleven years old. We—my parents, my brother
and me, and Baba—take a family trip to San Francisco to attend someone's wedding. We stay overnight in a fancy downtown hotel, and the
streets are shiny with rain. The wedding itself is lost to memory. We
are all dressed up as we take a cab to another, even bigger, hotel for the
reception. There is a huge room decked out all in white, and a band with
the members wearing tuxedos. Many people hug each other, and quite a
few of them are speaking Russian. I have no idea who is getting married,
but clearly this is an important event for both my mother and grandmother. I will find out decades later that the bride and groom, strangers
in a billowing white dress and a black tux, are Simonne Moiseeff and
George Sidline, the younger children of two families who lived in Kobe
through the terrible war years with Helmi and Rachel, were reunited
after sixteen years, fell in love, and were now joining themselves as well
as their families. Two more vivid images of this event will remain with

me. One is of my parents dancing together: or rather, my mother dancing, while my dad just sort of stands there, turning back and forth and holding onto Helmi's hand while she twirls around and around with a smile on her face. They are enjoying themselves, despite this dark thing that hangs over our family. It is probably the last time they ever danced together. The other image is equally vivid. When it comes time for the bride to throw her bouquet over her shoulder, the unmarried women hastily gather in a group. They are all young women, except for one: my grandmother. Baba is sixty-six years old, but she has maneuvered herself into the assemblage, and when the bouquet is thrown she actually leaves her feet for a second, attempting to catch it. She misses the bouquet, and people snicker at her. I understand why, but I also feel bad for her. I really wanted her to catch it.

~

OVER TIME, friends and family try to regard us in all the ordinary ways, but we know we are marked. We live under a thick cloud of dread. Our dad endures surgeries and radiation treatments, and he loses a great deal of weight. He begins to stoop far forward when he walks. His hair stays on his scalp but goes gray very rapidly. He continues working, but his days grow shorter. He leaves the dinner table quickly, without ever eating much, and it becomes routine to hear him in the bathroom at the far end of the house, vomiting violently. He regularly visits his friend, the bishop of our Catholic diocese—the successor to the loud-mouth bishop, a fellow intellectual Catholic—to discuss the Big Questions: how to face death, how to prepare for eternity in the presence of a difficult-to-please God. He has to abandon his telescope project in the garage, but he still spends time with his books on physics and astronomy. He talks about how much he looks forward to a full understanding of the structure of the universe when he is finally released from the corporeal realm. When he says things like this, Helmi averts her gaze. In times past she might have rolled her eyes, but she doesn't do that anymore.

Helmi no longer takes part in theater productions nor does much else in the way of fun. She still goes to the library every two weeks to exchange one armload of books for another. She sleeps even less than she used to. She stays awake reading half the night, although she rarely acts tired. She maintains a few close friends. Phyllis and Cleve still come over from next door, and, just like in the past, Phyllis will challenge our dad to a game of chess while Cleve helps Helmi in the kitchen. He is one of the few people who can still provoke a laugh out of her. The other Phyllis, her first theater pal—formerly Phyllis Saviers, but now remarried to a prominent lawyer named Bert Goldwater—is her closest pal and confidante. She and Bert come over at least once a week to play bridge, and we can see that they are monitoring our family dynamics carefully, keeping tabs on how everyone is holding up. They are particularly watchful of Helmi as she juggles the tasks at hand: taking care of our dad, monitoring Terry and me, and paying close attention to her own mother's needs. Baba walks around the house sighing and fretting, hand-wringing, and casting her weary eyes upward to a blank ceiling and beyond that to an opaque and silent sky.

Weekends are the worst. Saturday mornings Terry and I want to sleep in, but the sounds begin early: feet clomping and echoing up and down the linoleum in the hallway, the washing machine chugging through one load after another right outside our shared bedroom, then the baritone hum of the dryer. Eventually one of the doors opens with force and determined footsteps come marching in. There's the sound of a laundry basket hitting the floor, and then one of us—it varies indiscriminately from week to week—is subjected to what we have come to see as a bizarre ritual. Our mother, under the pretext of needing a convenient place to fold laundry, begins piling it up on top of one of us as we lie there. She is sending us a message, without having to say a word: You lazy slobs cannot lie there sleeping, or pretending to sleep, while the tough work of this household goes on. No son of mine will get away with snoozing the day away. So we get up and find things to do. We make our beds and dutifully put our folded clothes into our dresser drawers. We have breakfast and then wash our dishes. We do whatever other chores have been assigned to us. Feed the dog, wash the car, mow the lawn, clean the garage. There is a strange emptiness filling the house. Our dad has gone to work early, the way he always has on Saturday, but in place of laughter and chatter between our mother and grandmother there is mostly grim silence. They go about their same cooking and cleaning routines with minimal conversation. I get the feeling that they are testing out what it will be like when my father is gone for good. This is what we'll have: a home, but a joyless home.

Terry and I get out of there as soon as we are allowed. He goes off to his Saturday afternoon magic club, or to the public library to do homework, or—horrors!—to the parish rectory to discuss his possible future career as a priest. I tend to leave the house without any clear agenda, being more of an improviser with my time. Typically I grab my bike and pedal across town to see my cousin Danny, if I know he is home. Danny, besides being a relative, is my first best friend. Together we have a knack for cooking up fun. He lives on the edge of town and has a big yard attached to a horse pasture, and his family owns three horses. Danny teaches me how to handle the smallest and gentlest one, named Mocky, and to my amazement we are allowed to ride off by ourselves toward the foothills and arroyos south of Reno for entire afternoons, a couple of eleven-year-old cowboys roaming the wide-open spaces. It's a taste of pure freedom, of complete physical escape. A huge gift, in fact. I am given the chance, for half a day, to be a carefree kid.

Sundays are different. Our dad is home, sleeping in or trying to sleep in. A heavy atmosphere hangs over the household. Terry and I are expected to get ourselves to Mass, usually at 11:00 a.m. Dad is sick enough to have been given a special dispensation from attending Sunday services, but we are still obligated to go. One or the other of us might be assigned to altar boy duty on any given Sunday, which our mother takes extremely seriously, but even on a day when neither of us is on duty we must both be washed, dressed, groomed, and out the door in plenty of time to be at the church at least ten minutes before the service. It has long been impressed upon us that our mother's intent is to fully honor the promise she made to raise us as Catholics. Now, with our mortally ill dad to care for, she approaches this commitment with more grim vigor than ever. She seems to feel the need to parade us right to the steps of the church and march us all the way to the altar rail, as her way of contending with a God she does not believe in yet still feels needs to be appeased, because our dad remains a devout believer. A God who showers nothing but pain on the world, yet who demands complete devotion, a God who regularly dishes up mass murder and mayhem and at the same time capriciously selects individuals for special suffering. Our dad gets down on his knees and prays to this mysterious God, and therefore her children must also. If the weather is bad she will drive us, but usually we walk.

One Sunday in late spring, a beautiful sunny morning, Terry and I trudge down the street toward our weekly religious commitment, wearing our shined shoes and pressed trousers and clean shirts, each of us occupying our private silence. He is now thirteen, I am eleven. The distance between us seems much vaster than a mere two and a half years. This morning, in my estimation, has been particularly bad: heavy silence pervading the house, except for an occasional wearisome sigh emitted by our grandmother hiding in her bedroom. Helmi barked out the order for us to get moving while parked in the kitchen with a cigarette, drawing long puffs and blowing out the smoke toward the closed cupboard that held the TV, eyes downcast, forehead creased in anger or worry, or both. We dressed ourselves hastily and hit the door faster than usual, knowing better than to say anything to her.

A few blocks along, something wells up inside me. I decide to give vent to my sour mood. "Geez," I say. "What a crappy place to wake up to."

I wasn't expecting any reply, but my brother immediately says, "Yeah, Sundays are shitty." For someone considering the priesthood, these are strong words. Then he adds, "I call it Black Sunday."

I take this as an invitation go on whining. "What if we just don't come home? What if we stay out all day, until the house is dark and everybody's asleep? I don't want to go back to that. It would serve them right."

I don't expect him to pay much attention to me. Probably he'll slip right back into his adolescent reverie, pondering whatever it was he was thinking about before I spoke up, whether his future career in the priesthood or the glories of Sandy Crudgington's boobs. But now my big brother, age thirteen, does something surprising.

He stops, puts an arm over my shoulder, and makes me stop walking. Then he turns me toward him, captures me with his eyes, and gives me a shake: not hard, just enough to engage my attention. "Look, I know Mom is being a wicked witch," he says. "She can't help it. Dad is getting sicker every day. It's making her insane. We don't want to make it worse. We have to be there. It's our job."

Lately I have thought that Terry and I have practically nothing in common. He is a teenager, which most of the time seems like an entirely different species. Now it hits me that I have a choice. I could be the little kid I was a minute ago, and go right on whining about the things I hate at home. I miss our mother, who used to grab any chance to laugh out loud, but now skulks around the house ready to bite everybody's head off. I miss our dad, who used to take us to Sunday Mass and spend the rest of the day grinding his telescope lenses in the garage, then drink a highball in his easy chair and, after dinner, join the rest of us to watch the Ed Sullivan show, but now can't get out of bed except to crawl to the bathroom and puke. I even miss our nutty Baba, flitting around the kitchen in a whirl of pots and pans instead of cowering in her bedroom hiding from her version of God, the vengeful tormentor of the Jews. I could easily be that pissy little kid and throw a serious fit, right here in the middle of the street. In a heartbeat I could burst into noisy tears, really cut loose. Or not. I could admit that Terry is right. This, to eleven-year-old me, is the biggest surprise.

"OK," I say then. It's all I can think of, but it's enough. He loosens his grip, and with his arm still around my shoulder we walk on. We go to church, we say the usual prayers for our beleaguered family and for our put-upon selves, and then afterward, like good boys, we go straight home.

The Empty Chapel

Aᴜᴛᴜᴍɴ 1963. I am in the seventh grade at Our Lady of the Snows school. My teacher is Sister Hyacinth, a tall, lanky nun with fierce eyes and a pointed nose but a decent sense of humor. The first week, on Art Day, she had us make collages out of torn-up magazine ads. She picked the best ones to display on the bulletin board and awarded prizes. Out of little bits of glossy paper I made a buffalo standing in a field, with a tiny human mouth, shiny with lipstick, that I snipped from a grinning model in a hair-color ad. Sister Hyacinth gave it a gold star.

It's a late afternoon in November, and we are at our desks taking turns reading aloud—I doubt anyone who was there will ever remember from what book—when the door to the hallway opens suddenly and in pops the head of one of the assistant parish priests. He motions Sister Hyacinth over to the door and they confer in hasty whispers, and her hand jumps to her mouth to cover a gasp. She tells us crisply to rise from our seats and march quickly to church along with the rest of the school. The president of the United States has been shot. We will all kneel together and recite rosaries.

We have been made keenly aware that John F. Kennedy is our first Catholic president. He is also young and handsome and charismatic, with a bushy head of hair—in all of these ways a stark contrast to the only other commander in chief I have lived under, the elderly and bald President Eisenhower. As we pray for the wounded president, it flashes through my mind that my parents met Mr. Kennedy once when, still merely a U.S. senator, he passed through Reno on a campaign trip. Our dad was a president himself at that time, though only of the Reno Chamber of Commerce—still an important enough post to warrant his greeting a nationally known figure at the local airport. Helmi came home that day with a dazzled look in her eye, and couldn't stop talking about how charming a man Kennedy was in person.

In the church, lined up in the pews, down on our knees, we recite out loud the endless strings of Our Fathers and Hail Marys, with probably no one—not even the priests and nuns—concentrating much on what we are saying. The news given to us was sketchy: he was in Texas, outside, riding in a car. Our voices rise upward through the air, those of a handful of adults along with a couple of hundred first through eighth graders, in the faint hope that we are being heard somewhere beyond the church's brick walls. Suddenly there is a commotion up in front on the altar: another priest has come in from the side door. After some more hasty whispering, our recitation is abruptly halted. We were instructed to pray for the living, but today we aren't going to pray for the dead. We are told, simply, to go home.

I ride my bike home and go in the back door, past the shelves on both sides piled, as always, with canned goods, and there in the kitchen on the couch in the corner is my mother, staring at the TV on the opposite wall. Up on the screen, Walter Cronkite sits at his desk in his rumpled shirtsleeves, looking totally worn out, dark circles under his eyes, his voice hoarse. Helmi has her legs tucked under her, a handkerchief held to her nose, and she is softly weeping. The only other time I have ever seen my mother cry is a blurred memory—when she walked out on the stage in that play long ago—but then she was only pretending. She motions with her hand for me to sit down next to her, and she suddenly seems small and fragile. I'm only twelve, but already I am several inches taller than she is. It has taken an outside event this terrible to open a crack in the wall she has built around herself. We continue watching the news unfold together for another hour or so before my dad and my brother come home. Through all this, there is no sign at all of Baba. As usual, she doesn't want to come out of her room.

~

WINTER COMES ALONG with the new year, 1964. Gloom settles over our house, as it has over the whole country, yet ours is a special variety. It's as if an unpleasant relative has moved in with us, a nasty new family member whose bleak spirit is made up of various dark forces borrowed from each of us—Dad's grim disease, Helmi's anger, Baba's terror, and

Terry's and my teenage frustration. This spirit hovers in every room, like a bad smell.

The bright spots are fewer and farther between. Terry, thank God, no longer wants to be a priest or a magician. He has joined the football team at the Catholic high school, and his new obsession is lifting weights so he can bulk up. For Christmas he got himself a set of barbells, and he spends every evening out in the garage pumping iron. As for me, I have taken up playing the guitar. In the fall I took five or six lessons at the local music store, partly as a way to get out of the house but mostly because of the Beatles. Their album (*Meet the Beatles*) was the first record I ever bought with my own money, and I am fixated on learning their songs. I have quit the lessons, because the teacher wanted me to read notes on the page. I would rather sit on the floor in my bedroom and teach myself the chords to "She Loves You" and "I Want to Hold Your Hand," two of the numbers they played on *The Ed Sullivan Show*. When I think I have the songs figured out, I take the guitar into the garage and strum them for my brother, while he grunts and sweats with his barbells. We are in different worlds, but we share one big thing: we have found our ways to escape when we need to. And as time passes—spring, another summer—we find lots of ways to stay out of the house. We mow lawns for pocket money. Terry goes to summer school and joins a gym. I hide out at Lake Tahoe with my cousins.

Fall again. New trouble is brewing with Baba. She has become a problem that we are all tiptoeing around. She mostly only comes out of her room for meals, although at night we can sometimes hear her padding up and down the hallway, muttering to herself in deep-throated Russian. Once in a while she emerges to try to help Helmi in the kitchen, but she's not actually any help, judging by the arguments that ensue. She doesn't go to Friday night Temple anymore. Her Golden Age Club friends come around once in a while to coax her out for some activity, but from everybody's face it's plain that this is a chore being performed as a favor to get her out of Helmi's hair. It seems like something we just have to live with. I start to wonder if she'll end up back in the loony bin, where she was a few years ago.

I'm in eighth grade now. One day when I come home from school at 3:00, I can tell that I'm interrupting a serious conversation between Helmi and her friend Phyllis Goldwater. They are sitting in their usual spots in the living room with their usual glasses of afternoon sherry, and when I walk in they both look up at me with stiff smiles and don't say anything. It's a cue that means, "Please go to your room and leave us alone." So I do. I follow up with what I have done at times in the past, though, which is to tiptoe just far enough back down the hall to pick up what they are talking about. It can be helpful to check in with what is ostensibly off-limits. And sure enough, it's a big deal. Phyllis is explaining to Helmi that she and her husband, Bert, have come up with a potential solution to the Baba problem. They have found a nice little apartment close by, but not *too* close by, and they are prepared to help pay for it if necessary. Baba needs to move out and live on her own, for the sake of Helmi's sanity and our dad's health and our family's well-being. Baba is not nearly as helpless as she appears, in Phyllis's opinion, and Bert concurs. Her supposed helplessness is a habit she has formed, a convenient identity. So this move is something necessary to try. Anybody can see that the current situation is untenable. To be honest, says Phyllis, it should have happened long ago.

Helmi is silent for a minute, and then tells Phyllis that she has almost never lived apart from her mother. She feels tied to her. Shackled, is more like it. Phyllis replies that this is precisely the problem. For just a second, I feel a wrench in my gut. They actually might kick Baba out of the house? But in the next instant I'm over it, and I see that Phyllis is very possibly right. We need some way to ease the crazy tension in our house—as Phyllis says, you can cut it with a knife. Phyllis goes on to say that she will talk to Baba about it herself, to take the burden off Helmi. She has thought this over thoroughly. She insists.

I make it a point to buttonhole my brother later to give him a report, and he agrees with me. Why not try it? A few evenings later, Helmi sits us down after our dad has gone to bed and Baba is safely out of earshot, and informs us of Phyllis and Bert's plan. She isn't exactly asking for our opinions, but neither is she simply presenting a done deal. She says she is thinking it over. We are careful to act suitably surprised, but we are just as careful to let her know that neither of us will raise any objection. If this will let some of the steam out of the house, we are all for it.

So, a couple of weeks later, on a Saturday morning, we pack up Baba's stuff—Helmi, Phyllis, Terry, and me—which doesn't amount to more than one load in the station wagon, and help her move into a furnished one-bedroom apartment on the ground floor of a four-unit building about ten blocks away. Baba's attitude, as Phyllis had suggested, is better than expected. She seems to have signed on to the notion that this is a helpful step. She even tries to pretend that she likes her new digs, saying nice things about the curtains and kitchen linoleum and the tile in the bathroom, although everyone present knows she can't possibly mean them. I feel a weird admiration for this little spark of bravery. Who knows how long it will last? She says she wants to have Terry and me over for lunch very soon, and we all act as if this will be a nice housewarming celebration. We help her make the bed and put away her dishes, and then we drive away while she stands on her concrete stoop and waves goodbye. Helmi, at the wheel of the station wagon, keeps her eyes on the road and stays silent. Phyllis, on the front seat next to her, pats her on the shoulder and says, "Take my word for it, this is really for the best."

~

1965, ANOTHER NEW YEAR. Nothing much is different. With Baba out of the house we all breathe a little easier day to day, though nobody says this out loud. Terry is in his second year at the Catholic high school. In the fall he makes the junior varsity football team, playing guard on the power side of the offensive line. But something weird is going on with him. He was always a top student, but this year his standardized test scores have dropped like a rock. He says he isn't learning anything. Then there is a scandal. One of the JV basketball coaches is caught trying to fondle one of the players. They keep it out of the newspaper, but it spreads through the network of families. Suddenly there is serious talk of letting Terry go to public school next fall, to give him the best shot at colleges. This might mean the same for me. I'll graduate from Our Lady of the Snows this spring, and I have a slim hope that I can go to a public junior high school for ninth grade. A glimmer of light in the darkness.

Our dad is getting thinner by the day. Also slower and weaker. He has to give up things that he loves. He hasn't touched the telescope lenses in the garage for at least a year. He is no longer the president of the Reno Chamber of Commerce. One night at dinner he tells us that, a while back, he was approached by a group of businessmen who wanted him to run for U.S. Congress, but of course—he actually laughs at this— he had to say no. He still goes to the hardware store six days a week, but his workday has shrunk to a few hours. This year he puts a lot of time into a big legal project having to do with a civil rights case in southern

Nevada. A hotel down there was explicitly discriminating against Black people, enforcing a policy of denying them all services. This policy was challenged, and a lower court upheld the hotel's right to deny serving clientele based on their race. All through the summer, along with engaging in the Catholic school debate taking place at our kitchen table (with Terry and me arguing the negative side), he meets regularly with a group of other lawyers, drafting a brief that will be presented to the Nevada Supreme Court to challenge and overturn the lower court's ruling. Our dad says that, on the question of civil rights, Nevada is as bad as Mississippi. His job is to draft a brief called an amicus curiae, which sounds to me like a Gregorian hymn to sing at a High Mass but, according to Dad, means "friend of the court"—a supporting argument that will be considered in the decision that he doesn't have to present in person. We are amazed at how much energy he puts into this effort, considering he is down to skin and bones and can barely eat anything, and that he has to walk bent over nearly double from constant pain. How does he do it? One answer is that he only sleeps about three hours a night. He is pouring over law books and filling up yellow legal pads long before dawn. Late in the fall, the other lawyers get to finally argue the case at the state Supreme Court. On the day the ruling is to be issued my parents dress up and drive to Carson City, the state capital thirty miles away, to sit in the courtroom. Dad wears one of his suits that used to fit but is now about three sizes too big. Helmi puts on a stylish dress and paints up her face, the first time she has done this in a long while. The court overturns the lower ruling: Dad's side wins. That night we actually have a celebratory dinner. Our dad is totally exhausted, can barely sit up at the table. But he is proud. He says this contribution to an important cause is something he was hoping to leave behind. Everybody knows what he's talking about.

We also win the other case: Terry and I get to go to public school. The transition to junior high is even more thrilling than I had hoped. I can wear jeans and sneakers every day. I can pick out any color shirt I want, and I don't have to keep it tucked in. The other kids at first view me with suspicion, since I have come over from what they call the "nunnery," but it only takes a few weeks to start making friends. I can't believe how advanced they are. Lots of them are already paired up as boyfriend and girlfriend, and certain corners out behind the gym and the janitors' storage shed are officially designated for making out. I am very far behind in this department, but I have begun playing in a rock and roll band—we have already had a few gigs at YMCA dances—and this gives me a modicum of cred with my classmates.

Terry has transitioned well at the high school level, although he has found that if he wants to graduate he'll need to make up for lost time. He is forced to take two math classes at the same time and is totally buried in nightly homework. He also goes out for the debate team and discovers that he is a wiz at it. This brands him as something of a nerd, although I have to admit that debate talent does have practical value. It dawns on me that while I was hunched over my guitar for the past year he was actually paying close attention to Dad's work on the legal brief and picking up tips on how to argue persuasively. His knack for what he calls "rational discourse," as opposed to my rhetorical style of whining and pestering and losing my temper, was a definite factor in securing both of us the right to go to public school.

We get through the holidays. This year we pick Baba up from her apartment and bring her over for Christmas dinner like a visitor. Deep anxiety is etched in her face with dark lines and creases, but she tries hard to cover it up. She enjoys volunteering at the hospital as one of their "Gray Ladies," wearing a special hat and apron and delivering mail and meals to patients' rooms. She still goes to Golden Age Club and sometimes even to Friday night Temple. Just as Phyllis said, Baba is tougher than we thought.

In the winter of the new year, 1966, Dad has had to cut back his work schedule to just a few hours in the afternoons. Some days he can't go in at all, and we don't even see him emerge from the bedroom. Helmi keeps on her feet, moving around the house from room to room, taking care of business, while we try to stay out of her way. Her jaw is set, her eyes are fierce, her smile and laughter all but gone. Nobody knows how long this will go on. If you were to tell me it has been five years since Dad got sick, my answer would be that I can hardly remember when he wasn't.

One blustery day in March, we come home from school and Helmi tells us that Dad is in the hospital. Just for tests, she says. He has been having bad headaches, and the doctors want to rule some things out. Tomorrow he'll have a barium scan, where they inject a kind of dye into his bloodstream and take x-rays of his brain. After dinner, we go to visit him in the hospital. When we walk into the room, he is lying on his back under just a sheet with his knees raised up. His face is gray and sunken, and in this setting he looks even more like what he is—a very sick person. Suddenly, before any of us can say anything, one of his feet pops out of the sheet and his leg starts twitching violently up and down in the air. I realize we're getting a look at what he goes through when he's closed up in the bedroom. The conversation that ensues is short. Helmi asks him if he has slept during the afternoon, and he tells her, "Of course not." She lets out a heavy sigh that seems to carry a lot of meaning. She tells him, not in a way that shows much conviction, that maybe he'll sleep tonight if he takes his codeine pills. He answers that they don't help anymore. Then she tells us to give him some news. Terry and I talk about some of our stuff—he is the school debate champ now, and is getting ready to compete at the national level. He has also received an early acceptance letter for next year from Stanford University over the hill in the Bay Area, a genuinely big deal that actually gets Dad to smile. My news is less thrilling. I have learned a bunch of new Beatles tunes. Also, I have been told by some of my teachers that I would be a good candidate to attend some fancy prep school next year in California, maybe even with a scholarship, but I have made it crystal clear it's the last thing I want to do. Helmi backs me up on this. Dad looks over at me and says, very softly, just what I want to hear: "Well, then that's it, isn't it? Don't do it."

The next day, a Friday, I am sitting in my English class. We are reading *David Copperfield*, and every day we take turns reading sections out loud. I am right in the middle of delivering a nasty speech by Uriah Heep, using my best Snidely Whiplash voice, when there's a knock at the door and in walks the school principal. He stops the reading and signals for me to come with him. My thought is that if we have to discuss the prep school thing again I'm now armed with the supporting words of both parents, including my gravely ill father. But when we get to the office there stands my Uncle Jack in his green Commercial Hardware Company shirt, with a grim look on his face. He can be here for only one reason. He informs me that he's taking me to the hospital. Something has happened with the x-ray tests.

We ride in total silence, which means the news must be bad, but I don't ask any questions. I have the feeling Uncle Jack himself doesn't know exactly what's going on. Finally we get there and park and head up the steps of Saint Mary's Hospital, run by the same Dominican nuns that run my school. We ride up the elevator and then go down the hall of the ward that houses Intensive Care. There stands Helmi, my brother, a couple of doctors in white coats, and a tiny nun in full black-and-white regalia, who turns out to be Sister Seraphim, the head honcho of the hospital. She is fiddling with the enormous loops of black rosary beads hanging at her belt. When we walk up, she says, in a scratchy voice, "Well, this is just not good, not good at all. Hopefully it'll be over quick." This is a trait I have noticed in many nuns: they don't mince words.

Here's what we find out. The fluid they injected into Dad caused convulsions in his brain. He is not expected to recover. Somebody decided we all needed to be there to see him. One of the doctors guides us into the Intensive Care Unit, which is dark and full of electronic machinery on wheels and blinking lights. They pull back a curtain and there on a gurney lies Dad. He is curled up on his side with only a thin sheet covering him. His eyes aren't quite fully closed and you can see that his eyeballs are rolled upward. Nobody says anything, so I break the silence by saying the first thing that occurs to me: "He looks cold. Maybe he needs a blanket." I feel a hand on my shoulder. It's my brother. "It's OK," he says.

Eventually we go home with Helmi and have dinner. Dad isn't there, and he isn't there Saturday morning either, and I wonder if we are all having the same thought: this is what we have been waiting for, this is how it's going to be. I think about what I have pondered lately, that he has been sick since before I was nine years old, and I almost can't remember a time when he wasn't.

One night later, deep in the middle of the night, the phone rings, and hardly a minute later the sliding door to our shared bedroom scrapes open and the overhead lights blaze on like a silent explosion. "Your dad's on his last lap," our mother announces, very loudly. She's trying to be stern and businesslike. "Get up. Let's go."

All the way to the hospital her words are ringing in my ears: *last lap*. Not her style at all. Maybe using a dumb phrase like that helps her keep a grip on herself.

This time we are led to a different hallway, and there is only the one doctor, the brain scan dude. He shakes his head and says that it's just about over. Then he corrects himself and says it is over. We can go in. Helmi and I start to move forward, but Terry stays back, shaking his head. He doesn't want to go, and nobody can argue with that. I don't want to either, but I feel like I'm in a movie or a play, and the stage direction says to go with my mother, and so I do.

He is lying in a bed this time, with his head propped up, a sheet and blanket folded neatly under his arms. His eyes are really closed now, and his jaw hangs open just a little bit. Now I know why they always say that a dead person looks calm and peaceful, because that's how he looks. He hasn't looked that way in a long time. I make a mental note to tell my brother this, and maybe he'll feel a little better. Helmi, next to me, also seems very calm. She must have thought about this moment a lot, and now it's here and time is still moving. She reaches out and touches him very gently on the forehead. Then she takes off her wedding ring and puts it on his pinky finger. Maybe she thought about this ahead of time, knowing that's the only finger it would fit. She doesn't cry at all. I think maybe she is, right now, the bravest person I have ever seen, and I'm glad I came with her. Then she takes my hand and without a word we turn around and leave.

Out in the hall, she finally says something to us, and it's surprising. She says, "I think you two should go upstairs to the hospital chapel. It's what your dad would want." Terry and I look at each other, but we both know not to question her at all. So we obey. We march to the end of the hall and get in the elevator and go upstairs and get out and head down the next hall, like a couple of zombies.

The chapel is small, only about five rows of pews, with a tiny little altar up front with the standard crucifix and a big blue and white statue of Mary, the mother of Jesus. This makes sense, since the hospital is named after her. There is another giant statue of her, painted all white, mounted over the hospital's front entrance.

Nobody else is in the chapel. We do what we are expected to do, kneel down in one of the pews. Terry closes his eyes and starts in on some prayer. I take a minute to look around the room. The walls are pale blue, which is probably supposed to invoke the Blessed Virgin with her loving and protective nature. But to me the color is cold, and I feel a shiver. I decide then to just wait. At a moment like this, there should be some other feeling coming, some help from somewhere. But there's nothing. Just the same bloody Jesus hanging on his cross, and Mary up there, frozen in place, her painted eyes a blank stare, her arms locked outward in a futile gesture, as if to say, "What can I do? I'm just a statue." I keep waiting, while my brother next to me prays. I can't think of a

prayer that means anything. I'm down on my knees, the chapel is supposedly a holy place, but right now, in the deepest part of the night,
except for the two of us, it's totally empty.

After that we find Helmi again, who has been talking with the
doctor. She thanks him, I don't know what for, and we head off. Outside it's getting light already. She has my brother take the wheel. Instead
of going straight home like I expect, after checking her watch she has
him take a detour to stop at our church, next door to my school. We all
three go inside the church, and I'm very aware that she hasn't stepped
in here since that one weird time when we dragged her to Christmas
Mass. Somehow she finds Monsignor Connors, the same parish priest,
our grandfather's poker buddy, who stepped in to officiate at her marriage eighteen years ago. It's Sunday morning and she has calculated that
he will just be getting ready to say his regular 7 a.m. Mass. How in the
world could she have the presence of mind for this? Standing in the
church aisle, she gives Monsignor Connors the bad news in a matter-
of-fact way. He takes hold of her hand awkwardly and says he will say
Mass for our dad. She doesn't cry. She barely even blinks. Her face is like
stone. She thanks him curtly, and we leave. We don't stay for Mass. No
doubt she'll send us later to perform our normal religious duty. Back in
the car, sitting in the front seat next to Terry, looking straight ahead, she
says, "I think that's what your father would have wanted." After another
minute she says, "Okay, let's go home and have some breakfast."

The Old Man at the Window

A WEEK LATER WE HAVE THE FUNERAL. The whole big extended family, grandparents, aunts, uncles, cousins. Plus lots of other people, everybody in shades of black. Dad was an admired pillar of the community. A high funeral Mass, with organist, incense, the works. The coffin at center stage, right in front of the altar. It's closed, on Helmi's order. The altar boys are guys I know well, who are counting on a tip of at least five bucks apiece.

The bishop himself officiates the Mass, with his pink satin beanie on his bald head. When it's time for the sermon, he steps to the lectern and delivers a stern message, in his clear, booming voice, all about receiving final judgment before the all-seeing eye of God at the throne of eternity. I think about how Dad dragged himself over to this person's house every week for the past couple of years to discuss the finer points of theology. No doubt much of the talk centered on getting ready to die. Now it has happened, and we have to sit here and listen to the bishop lecture us about baring our naked souls at the moment of death in the blinding light of eternal truth, which in its perfection is neither merciful nor merciless, but simply *is*. The longer he goes on, the more I hate his message. There's nothing comforting about it. I am sitting next to Helmi in the pew. She has put on a hat with a little veil down over her eyes, in deference to the church laws, and she sits motionless. I feel like I am reading her mind. Like me, she wants the bishop to shut up.

Finally it's all done: holy water has been sprinkled on the casket, incense burned and smoke spread all through the room, hymns sung by the little choir upstairs, out of view behind us. Out we go, back into the bright glare of day, into the limousine, and off to the cemetery, leading a

caravan of vehicles that winds through the streets. Two cops on motor-
cycles accompany us, and at intersections they hold back traffic so the
procession can stay together. At one corner, as we turn, we notice a
shiny red Corvette convertible with the top down, and at the wheel is
the college-age son of one of Helmi's friends. He is first in the line held
up by the cops, and as we make the turn we pass close to him. He has
slicked-back hair and dark glasses, and his face betrays extreme irrita-
bility at having to wait. When Helmi spots him she emits a familiar
sound, a drawn-out harrumph of bemused sarcasm, which she reserves
for those who merit her disdain. Not quite a laugh, yet it comes with a
half-smile. Whatever else she knows about this dude's failings, today's
transgression is clear: although his parents were at the funeral, he has
chosen not to accompany them.

After we make the turn, she says, to no one in particular, "He always
was a little shit." She states this matter-of-factly, a merciless judgment.

The cemetery occupies a treeless slope, with scrubby grass that might
look better later in the year but in March is mostly dry and dormant.
We gather at the grave site. This time Monsignor Connors is in charge,
and things move along swiftly. Some prayers are said, more holy water
is sprinkled. The casket is covered with an American flag because Dad
was a veteran of World War II, although he always told us that he spent
most of the war in a hospital bed with dengue fever. At the end of the
service, two guys in military uniforms carefully fold up the flag and present it formally to my mother. She receives it stoically. Baba, seated next
to her, whimpers softly and dabs her cheeks with a handkerchief, but
Helmi's eyes remain dry. We accept hugs and handshakes and sympa-
thy and condolences, and then leave with the coffin sitting on the ground
next to the open grave.

We pile back into the limousine and are ready to take off when a
face suddenly appears at the window. Helmi rolls it down, and an old
man with yellowish teeth and wispy white hair leans in and grabs hold
of her wrist. His hand is wrinkled and skeletal-looking, and his arm is
trembling. His head comes further in the window, and we see that he is
weeping. He is wearing a black coat and a black-and-white clerical collar.
Yet another priest. Then he says in a shaking voice, through his tears, "So
sorry. Just so sorry." Helmi says nothing, but just lets him grip her arm
and pump it up and down. Finally he lets go and pulls away. Terry and I
look at each other. He whispers to me that it was Old Uncle Tom, as he

is known in the family, our grandfather's brother who is a parish priest somewhere in northern California. We know the family lore: he was the one who refused to officiate at the marriage of our parents because Helmi was Jewish.

"That poor man," she says, as we drive away. Her voice trembles a little. "I think he's never forgiven himself, after all these years. What a terrible shame." And then her eyes mist up. She sniffles a couple of times and wipes her nose with the back of her hand, then takes a long breath and composes herself again. She is back to her steely self within a few blocks. But we all noticed it: those were the first tears she had shed all day.

The Kitchen Table

SIX MONTHS LATER, late one evening in the fall, I head into the kitchen for my midnight snack, something from the pantry—maybe I'll open a can of peaches along with a fresh box of Cheerios—but when I turn on the light I'm startled to see Helmi sitting at the table. No book or magazine is in front of her. The TV in the cabinet on the wall isn't on. She has just been sitting here by herself in the dark. I had assumed she was already holed up in her bedroom behind the closed door.

I have just started high school, making new friends, seeking out any and all distractions, practicing the guitar with my door closed. Terry is off at college (Stanford, five hours away), where I know from our phone conversations he is fully appreciating the distance. Helmi has remained in what we assume is a state of mourning, a continuation of the same old black mood. All summer we moved warily around her, trying our best to avoid any transgressions, doing the dishes, obeying the curfew, causing no trouble, but anyone can see that everything pent up inside her could blow at any moment. Failing to fold clean socks and underwear or, even worse, failing to pick up dirty ones from the floor would invariably invoke her wrath, followed by a deep, guilt-inducing silence. Now, however, it's just the two of us in the house, she and I, a strange condition that we are both trying to get used to. In that way, there's a new balance. Neither of us has anyone else to commiserate with, and neither of us is outnumbered. Plus, in this big house, we can give each other plenty of space. We seem to have made a silent agreement to steer clear of each other.

Still, this time the right thing seems to be to sit down across from her with my late-night bowl of cereal. I would feel too awkward turning around and walking out on her. I take a couple of spoonfuls, and then our eyes meet. I'm immediately struck that her usual dark look isn't there. I don't feel accused of anything. She stares straight at me, and whatever she sees isn't the usual fifteen-year-old adversary. There's a softness in her face that I remember from long ago.

And then, just like that, she bursts into tears.

On the one hand I'm shocked, and on the other hand I'm thinking, well, it's about time. Nobody has seen her cry since the Kennedy assassination. But I don't say it. All I can come up with now is to put down my spoon and reach across the table and take her hand. She grips my hand back, hard and steady, and, for probably a full five minutes, she weeps.

Finally she eases up and goes over to grab a paper towel to dry her eyes. I should have thought of that, I guess, but then I'd have had to let go of her hand, and holding on to it seemed to be important, judging by the strength of her grip. She sits back down and blows her nose.

"I'm glad you're here with me," she says then, in a voice I'm not used to at all. It's not an order, or a warning, or a recrimination. She doesn't sound weary, or frustrated, or put-upon. She sounds calm. She reaches for my hand again. "Thank you for being here," she says. She smiles at me, maybe for the first time in a couple of years.

I'm thinking, do I have a choice? But I don't say it. In fact, I don't say a single word. I just sit there and let her hold my hand for as long as she wants, still staring into my face with that weird new look, until she finally gives me a quick extra squeeze and lets go and heads off to bed so I can finish my bowl of Cheerios with canned peaches. The cereal is totally soggy, but I finish it anyway and then head to bed myself, knowing that things are different now.

The Silver Fox

IT TURNS OUT I WAS RIGHT. Helmi and I get along much better. I'm less nervous that I'll commit an infraction worthy of a lecture, and she moves around with more of the old spirit. She has her friends over, Phyllis from next door and the other Phyllis also, of course, and they drink sherry in the afternoon and laugh sometimes, like they used to. She brings Baba over fairly often for dinner. Sometimes they even cook together, though this is getting harder to do because Baba is clearly getting loopier in the head and can't be trusted with anything complicated. We have discovered that, at home by herself, Baba mostly eats TV dinners and Campbell's chicken soup. Helmi is worried about her, and the next unspoken subject is what will become of her down the road.

Late at night, by myself, I sometimes wonder where we go from here. Helmi is a widow now, just as her own mother was. It occurs to me, in a way I resist considering too deeply, that my brother has escaped and it will fall on me to be the one to stay closer. Helmi has had Baba, her own widowed mother, as a responsibility, a weight on her shoulders, since long before I was born. These things happen. Will I have a similar job? This is as far as I want to ponder the subject, but there it is, and it isn't going away.

Meanwhile, time goes forward. I traverse the deserts and mountains of high school. I get a driver's license. I learn that I can't drink as much beer as most of my friends without throwing up. On TV, astronauts orbit the earth and sail toward the moon. War is waged in Southeast Asia. I still play guitar. Music replaces religion. On Saturday nights I go to hear every band that comes to town, and on Sunday mornings I sleep in late and skip going to church. The emptiness of the hospital chapel has stuck with me. Helmi stops making me go, with a quick, dismissive wave of her hand and the words, "That's up to you from now on."

Terry is home from college one weekend, and over breakfast Helmi announces, to our amazement, that she is thinking about buying a new car. Our brown Ford station wagon doesn't seem useful anymore and is hard to park and maneuver around. We heartily agree. She suggests we go down to the Ford dealership and talk about trading it in, an idea that thrills both of us into scurrying to get dressed. On the way to the dealer, we kid her about what to get. A Thunderbird, maybe a Mustang. Of course, not in our wildest fantasies can we really picture anything like that residing in our driveway, but there's a sudden spirit of fun among the three of us, pretending to consider such possibilities. In my mind, I'm already envisioning the likeliest outcome: yet another frumpy vehicle, albeit smaller, in yet another drab color.

The salesman is perfect. A central-casting character, right down to the mustache, plaid sport coat, and wingtip shoes. His first announcement is that he can give her an excellent trade-in value for the wagon, better than he would normally be allowed to, since his supervisor, who is more of a stickler, happens to be out of town—but only for this week. Without even looking at him, Helmi replies, "That's nice," in a tone that even the salesman can tell means, "Who do you think you're kidding?" We head out to the lot and stroll toward the rows of cars, Fords all— Galaxies, Falcons, wagons, T-Birds, pickup trucks. In the middle of the very first row we come upon a Mustang, candy-apple red, shiny, sleek, beautiful, brand new, and what occurs then is an astonishment on the order of a major earthquake. Helmi stops, faces the car, and puts a hand to her chin. "That one is sure cute," she says. "What do you boys think?" What do we think? Terry and I look at each other and make an instant, telepathic pact—don't blow it. He jumps in first, not fully trusting me. "Well," he says, in his best imitation of someone making a thoughtful and careful evaluation, "it is nice and compact." My turn. I decide to show a modicum of honesty, without going overboard: "It's a great color." She still has her gaze aimed at the car, so I take a chance and go one step further: "I think you'd look good in it." The salesman smells his opening, explaining that the car has a smooth automatic transmission (correctly identifying her as someone with no interest in a stick shift) and a 289 V-8, Ford's most dependable engine, and is fantastically comfortable to drive. He opens the door, to reveal more red—red carpet, red seats, red trim on the inside of the doors. Helmi climbs in and sits down, to see how well her feet reach the pedals. She puts her hands on the wheel, looks up at us, and smiles.

"Okay," she says. "I'll take it."

For a minute, even the salesman doesn't know what to say. But then he gathers himself and leads us back into the dealership, sits at a desk, draws up some paperwork showing Helmi the trade-in value of the wagon against the sticker price of the Mustang, takes her check, shakes her hand, and hands her the keys. The next thing we know, Terry and I are crammed together in the tiny rear seat, rendered speechless, and Helmi is driving us home in her snazzy new red Mustang.

For a brief time, we consider the possibility that she did this somehow for us. But after while, we have to give that notion up. She did it totally for herself. The Mustang was the first step in a campaign to forge a new identity.

It would remain her prized possession for the next twenty years.

~

FALL 1967. Dad has been gone for a year and a half. One day, I come home from school and Helmi is on the couch with Phyllis Goldwater. The minute I walk into the room their giggling conversation ceases and they both give me the old look that means "scram," so I do. Good for them, I think. Let them enjoy their private jokes. I'm not interested in eavesdropping anymore; that's how far we've come. Something is up, though, enough to put a blush on both of their faces.

The very next weekend, early on Friday evening, Helmi is prepping to go out. She explains that she is planning to have dinner with the Goldwaters, and she checks with me to see if I have plans ("I do"), and if I'll be out late ("I won't, I promise"), and then she says she may be later than usual, but not to worry about her, because they'll be up at Lake Tahoe. All of this is delivered in a nervous tone that I can't help noticing. She goes back to the bedroom several times to check her hair and change her earrings. Finally she heads off in her Mustang, reminding me that there is a dinner that I can heat up in the fridge and to keep my promise not to be late.

I beat her home, but not by much. While I'm having my snack, she sits down at the table, plucks off her earrings and sets them down, is quiet for a minute, and then says, in a way that sounds rehearsed, "Guess what? I've met someone interesting."

"Oh?" I say. "In what way?" My tone elicits from her a derisive snort.

"Very funny," she says. "I don't know why I should even tell you. It was at the Goldwaters', at a dinner party. I knew it was a setup. The whole thing was designed for us to meet and get to know each other. He's a very nice person. Divorced. But very nice. So there. I told you. Now, good night."

From that point, things escalate. The new dude, as Terry and I come to refer to him, turns out to be the dad of one of my brother's former high school classmates named Cliff McCorkle. The suggestion to set the two of them up was actually made by another one of Terry's classmates, his best buddy, Harold Thompson. The new dude is named Jack McCorkle (great, I think: just what the family needs, another guy named Jack), and he used to be the advertising director for one of the big hotel/casino empires, but there was a corporate shakeup and he lost the job; he is currently studying to take the state real estate exam. He has been divorced for two years. He and Helmi are almost the same age; he is actually two months younger. All this information comes straight from his own mouth, one night a few weeks later when Helmi invites him over for dinner. Baba is there with us too. Helmi obviously wants him to see what my grandmother is like up close, so there will be no misunderstanding of what he might be getting into. Baba is fidgety and quiet all through the meal, nervously eyeing him with blatant suspicion. I find the guy likable, especially his directness in talking about touchy subjects like his forced change of career and his divorce. He is different from my dad in virtually every way—tall, broad-shouldered, handsome, and youthful, despite his bushy hair being prematurely gray. He has a loud and boisterous laugh, and we can see that he finds Helmi endlessly fascinating. Baba, however, isn't charmed one bit. She shoots him venomous sidelong glances and gives him low muttered responses to his innocent questions. Lately she is going beyond eccentric, as Helmi puts it. Nobody really understands what her relationship to the world is these days. We get reports from her Golden Age Club friends that she is showing increasing signs of slipping off the rails. Helmi sees her nearly every day, helping her with grocery shopping and everything else. Baba's eyes seem to sink deeper into their dark sockets every time I see her. She has reverted to speaking to Helmi mostly in Russian.

~

ANOTHER SATURDAY NIGHT, a month or two after this dinner meeting. I'm out with pals as usual, and I'm home almost on time, give or take thirty minutes. I come into the house quietly; grab a quick hit of the potent, concentrated breath freshener I keep stashed at the back of a shelf in the pantry, right by the door, to kill any obvious beer or marijuana breath; and step gingerly into the kitchen. Helmi had said she was going out also, to dinner and a movie with Jack, but she isn't back yet. The clock says 12:30 a.m. I go down the hall to make certain, and, sure enough, she's not at home. A half hour later I'm sitting quietly with my Cheerios in the kitchen, perusing the cartoons in the latest *New Yorker* magazine, when the back door opens and then shuts with almost no sound. A pause, a couple of light footsteps, and there she stands, looking startled.

"Oh," she says, "you're here."

"Yep," I reply. Hey, fun, I think to myself. We're turning the tables. She was hoping to sneak in late.

She clears her throat, which only adds to the awkwardness.

"How was your evening?" she asks, unconvincingly.

"Oh, fine," I say. "Just a bunch of us hanging out. Did some jamming." One of these days, maybe I'll find a way to explain to her that playing guitar really loud for several hours after smoking a joint and downing a couple of beers can be a truly cathartic experience when you are sixteen. Not tonight, though.

She takes a step further into the room, and it's only then that I take full notice of her. Her hair looks peculiar, squashed down very flat in the back. She reaches up a hand reflexively and touches the back of her head. No question about it. She has been lying down. I feel my eyes go wide and my face heat up, and suddenly it's all I can do not to spit out my Cheerios. I turn away fast. Holy shit. I know now she was hoping to tiptoe to bed unobserved.

I could be a terrible wiseass and deliver something snide: *And just where have you been all this time? Gee, it must have been a long movie.*

Instead, looking down at the magazine, doing my best impression of a disinterested teenager, I say, "How was your night?"

Another short silence, while she either breathes easy or evaluates my possible layers of meaning. Out of desperation, I even fake a yawn.

"It was fine," she says at last. "Well, then, good night," she adds, and off she goes, her hair still mashed down but her dignity intact.

I take a deep breath. Why do I feel like the one who has dodged a bullet? Staring at the magazine page, I consider what just took place. Maybe I'm still stoned, but this seems like a moment of tremendous import. She hasn't just gone on a dinner-and-movie date with her new boyfriend. I now have strong evidence, if not irrefutable proof, that they have been getting it on.

This could be serious. This could have real consequences for the future.

Mazel Tov

SURE ENOUGH, a couple of months later, we are in the living room, having a wedding. The date is the 4th of July, 1968. Independence Day. Helmi is in a shiny silver-blue dress, and Jack is in a spiffy tailored suit and shiny silk tie, looking like a model in a men's clothing catalog. Helmi has taken to calling him, affectionately, the Silver Fox. The rest of us are all spruced up as well. Terry and I wear coats and ties for the first time since our father's funeral, two and a half years ago. Baba is there also, dressed up in satin with a white corsage pinned at her shoulder yet glowering suspiciously the whole time.

She has never warmed up to this fellow who came out of nowhere to marry our mother. He is as unlike our dad as anyone could be. Bill Horgan was thoughtful and reserved, and also short and clumsy, and he wore rumpled, ill-fitting clothes even before he got sick. Jack is hearty and jolly and brash, and also tall and athletic, and he is always impeccably turned out. While Bill gave both Helmi and her mother a miraculous opportunity to live safely and comfortably in the U.S.A., in Baba's eyes Jack is pulling Helmi away. He has not been particularly warm toward his new mother-in-law—understandably so, given the blatant skepticism he has received from her. We all can tell he views Baba as loony and difficult, because that is what she certainly is.

It's also clear that he has accomplished something remarkable: he has brought Helmi back to her former self. For most of the past seven years, my mother has not been the person I remember from my childhood, who laughed eagerly and often and met the world with clear-eyed optimism. That person went virtually missing from our lives, and now she has returned. Still, Baba can't get herself to trust this interloper, this slick, fast-talking character in fancy suits—Silver Fox, indeed—who has barged into our lives and moved into our house. That's how she sees things and, bless her weary and pessimistic Russian heart, she is unable to conceal it.

Everybody else is here, too: my father's two brothers and their families, both Phyllises with their current husbands, neighbors, ladies from the bridge club, pals from the Reno Little Theater, even the young woman who cleans our house every two weeks and has become a confidante of Helmi's, and who has brought along her one-year-old baby, whose father has yet to be identified. My other grandmother, now also a widow, is also here. My Irish grandfather died a year after my father, from a much faster cancer, bringing the clan together for another funeral in the same church that hosted my father's. There will be more of these to come.

All we know about Helmi's first wedding, to our dad, other than that it was hyper-Catholic and took place in church, is that there was nobody there who knew her at all except her one recent friend from San Francisco. This time she is surrounded by a crowd of people who love and respect her and, with the exception of her own neurotic mother, who offer full and unconditional support for this new venture. The officiant at the wedding is Judge Gordon Thompson, the uncle of Terry's classmate, Harold Thompson, who first suggested setting Helmi and Jack up on a date. Judge Thompson also happens to be the Chief Justice of the Nevada Supreme Court, who issued the opinion, in 1964, that established the enforcing power of the Nevada Commission on Civil Rights, which our dad helped write. He has since become a good friend of the family, and cheerfully offered his services since it's a national holiday and the Supreme Court is not in session.

The ceremony is short and sweet. Do you, Jack? Yes. Do you, Helmi? Yes. Okay, you're married. Almost that quick. As an altar boy I have assisted at dozens of weddings by now, the kind that involve a long Catholic Mass with hymns and organist and sermon and plenty of Latin mumbo-jumbo—similar to the kind of wedding my mother endured long ago before my brother and I existed, when she stood patiently alone outside the altar rail waiting for it all to be over. This one is much better.

When Judge Thompson declares them a married couple, a rousing cheer goes up in the room. Champagne is poured for everyone. Even Baba, my little grandmother, takes a glass, raises it aloft, and manages to mutter "Mazel tov," before reverting to her untrusting attitude and steely gaze. Fine. Let her be unconvinced.

Terry and I grew up seeing with our own eyes how heavily loneliness and widowhood weighed upon our grandmother and made her dependent on our mother. When Helmi became a widow herself, she might have leaned on us in a similar way. There is a good chance that we have now been liberated from the prospect of such a responsibility. Even from inside my cocoon of teenage selfishness I am able to perceive this as a gift. In my mother's face I see joy and pride, buoyed by her instinctive determination to make the most of unforeseen occurrences. The reason for her joy is hope for the future, and not just her own: there is an additional hope that now she will never have to become any kind of burden on us. It doesn't seem accidental that we are gathered on Independence Day.

So when I lift my glass and join the group toast, I'm doing so out of gratitude. There may be a few other doubts scattered around the room, in other minds besides Baba's, that this will be a successful match. Helmi's new husband, Jack the brash Silver Fox, is nothing like the old one, Bill the thoughtful introvert. But whatever lies ahead for them, the very least we can all do is stand together on this holiday afternoon and join them, facing forward.

Reno II

Virginia Street, Reno, looking north, about 1956. The Mapes Hotel is in the background across the Truckee River, with the Sky Room nightclub on the top floor. University of Nevada Special Collections and University Archives, Gus Bundy Collection #1985-08. Used with permission.

Freedom

A s luck would have it, things worked out. These were Helmi's
exact words, many years later. Outwardly she preferred attribut-
ing life's ups and downs to sheer chance. "You never know," she would say
with a shrug and a sigh. "Who can tell?" And yet anyone could see that
she knew well the power of dogged determination or, by the same token,
careless indifference.

From all appearances, her marriage to Jack was a great success. It
lasted through fat and lean years, small ups and downs, major tragedies
and joys, for thirty-four years. She frequently said that Jack was bound
to outlive her. He was younger than she, after all—by six months. She
was proud of his youthful vigor and good health, even well into his seventies. She had no intention of becoming a widow ever again. Of course,
one never knew. Who could tell?

Her close friends all agreed that the success of their marriage was
largely due to Helmi's devotion to the cause. She doted on Jack, spoiled
him rotten, treated him like a king. In my remaining year of high school,
once he moved in with us, I saw that this was true. She took to cooking him big daily breakfasts, a new phenomenon in our house, because
he had grown up on a farm where breakfast was of paramount importance. She ironed his shirts, also a new phenomenon, because he wanted
to be impeccably dressed when he stepped out into the world each day.
He liked to go to bed early and rise early, and he would leave the house
at the crack of dawn, well before I took off for school, to tend to his
real estate wheelings and dealings. She would accompany him to the
door to see him off and then, straightening his tie or snagging a loose
hair or speck of dust from his sport coat, then holding the door so he

wouldn't have to put down his briefcase or the fat manila file under his arm, she would utter in mock-formal tones: "Farewell, brave warrior. Return either with your shield, or upon it!" And they would exchange a lingering kiss. Meanwhile, I kept my mouth shut over my morning bowl of cereal, believing that she was making fun of this silly daily ritual at the same time that she reveled in it.

For his part, Jack thrived on her energy and humor, her spirit of fun, and her gentle but loving mockery of his careful grooming and spotless wardrobe. For all his seriousness and attention to his self-image, Jack quickly learned to be a good sport and appreciate her ironic view of the world. He came to believe that her exotic history along with her sharp mind provided her with a kind of feminine wisdom that he admired tremendously. Years later, he would say that he was surprised at how much she had changed him.

At first I thought there was no way this guy, this so-called Silver Fox, would fit into our lives. He was politically conservative, for one thing. He opposed rules and regulations, especially if they had anything to do with commerce, believing that each person should pull themselves up "by their bootstraps." Phrases like this bounced off the walls at meal times. My dad, on the other hand, had helped write landmark civil rights legislation. Did my mother simply choose to ignore such a profound difference? Finally it dawned on me that I wasn't the one who needed to adapt. I was about to head out the door. By the skin of my teeth, in the fall I was going off to college, joining my brother at Stanford. The adjustments I needed to make were minor and temporary. I was leaving home.

Helmi buttoned her lip when it came to politics and finances. She had seen, in her own circle of friends, how sour things could turn over these issues. She also must have seen that she could have an effect on him gradually, over the long haul, like wind and water eroding a landscape. That was exactly his description of her effect on him, thirty-five years later, after she was gone. Farm boy that he was, through her he learned to love Italian opera, to appreciate Jewish humor, and even, once in a while, to vote for a Democrat. He stated flat-out that she had made him a better person.

Some of the differences with this new husband she enjoyed unreservedly. Jack liked to shop, for instance. Every year, in early spring, he would gather up last year's business uniforms—suits, sport coats, shirts,

neckties, everything but shoes—bag them up for Goodwill, and take
Helmi to San Francisco for a weekend to replenish his wardrobe at his
favorite haberdasheries. She loved helping him pick out matching ties
and shirts, properly contrasting coats and pants, ideal fabrics for the seasons. This was a novelty she had never known, an experience entirely
missing from her life so far—a man who loved clothes! It helped, of
course, that he had the slim build and silver-foxy good looks to make
the most of such treatment. And it didn't seem to be vanity, exactly, that
motivated him. Decent clothes were necessary for business, was how he
put it. Besides, he had left the farm long ago with no intention of going
back, along with the dungarees and T-shirts and seed-catalog caps he
had grown up wearing every day. Another thing Helmi loved was how,
on the weekends when he would work in the yard, trimming shrubbery or pruning trees or cutting the grass, he still always looked sharp,
in khakis and lightweight knit shirts, always neat, always tucked in. He
stated publicly he would never wear a pair of jeans or a sweatshirt. In
this way, she was proud to say, with a wink and a laugh, he was the man
of her dreams. I thought back to my dad, who avoided yard work like
the plague and who, before he got sick, used to stretch out in a lounge
chair on the patio, beer in hand, perhaps delving into one of his rec-
reational texts about quantum mechanics, wearing his favorite Sunday
afternoon post-church getup—a dingy pair of gray mechanic's cover-
alls, which Helmi repeatedly stated she would dearly love to throw out.

Off I went to college, my own duffel bag stuffed with little more than
jeans and sweatshirts, following my brother to California, the hotbed
of tie-dyed psychedelia, student unrest, and the Grateful Dead, all of
which I would partake of, to varying degrees. Driving away from Reno
in early September, I reminded myself how lucky I was to have been
granted this freedom. Only three years before, none of us were able to
look optimistically toward the future. Now the pieces had fallen into
place, for my mother first, and then in turn for the rest of us.

The only one left out of this happy equation was my grandmother.
Baba, still ensconced in the tiny little apartment to which she had been
exiled in order to make Helmi's life easier, was left wondering where she
was supposed to fit in. She was not enjoying any particular new freedom
connected to any particular new life. The deck was stacked against her,
and time was not on her side.

The Rest Home

I BEGAN BRINGING newly made friends home from college, beginning with the first Thanksgiving break of my freshman year. Many of them had come to school in California from far away—New York, Hawaii, Colorado, Minnesota, Texas—and Reno was a quick half-day drive over the Sierras. Moreover, some of my friends, even if their hometowns were close by in California, were not as ready as I was to go home for weekends or vacations. It turned out, to my surprise, that Helmi's house—Helmi and Jack's house now, although she actually owned it—was considered a haven by many of them.

I had grown up thinking of my mother, except for those five years of my father's illness, as a fun-loving person. Quick-tempered, intolerant of stupidity, hyper-demanding of cleanliness and punctuality, but still fun-loving and almost always ready to laugh. Bringing home college friends gave me a new understanding of two qualities in her that I had either overlooked or taken for granted: a deep interest in other people, especially if they were smart or quick-witted or talented in some way, and an equally deep need to win such people over, to impress them. Taken together, I perceived that these traits made her an extraordinary charmer.

Helmi had the ability to size somebody up quickly, zero in on his conversational predilections, determine the type and depth of his sense of humor, and, by the time dinner was over, charm him right down to his socks. In the car going back over Donner Pass to California, I would hear a stock speech from every one of these guys, about how my mother was more interesting—and *interested*—than his own mother. It even got to the point where some of them would visit Reno and stay at my house on their own, when for one reason or another I wasn't there. These guys brought out the actress in her, the immigrant who could successfully present herself as highly sophisticated, able to match wits and quips with the best of them. At peak moments, even her Shanghailander British accent would temporarily return, giving her the aura of an exotic blue blood, precisely the image she wanted to project.

For his part, Jack was a good sport and put up with this parade of visitors and interlopers—and with Helmi's social intensity—with calm amusement. After all, he was deeply interested in Helmi himself and both loved and admired her talent for winning people over. He had been in advertising and now was in the real estate trade, and he understood full well the power of personal charm.

My mother's welcoming charm was less forthcoming when it came to female friends. My brother learned this lesson first, and I was close behind. Terry met someone in his freshman year who soon became a very important person in his life. During Dianne's first visit to Reno, sleeping in the room that had been my grandmother's, she was awakened on Saturday morning by a peculiar sensation—something hitting the foot of the bed. She peeked out of the covers, and there stood Helmi next to a basket of laundry, folding T-shirts and underwear and pairs of socks and dropping them in a pile right onto the mattress—just what she used to do to us back in our teenage years, as a not-so-subtle message to get our lazy asses out of bed. In this case, however, she was doing it to someone she had only met the evening before. Helmi had fixed a nice dinner and had been a gracious, if not entirely exuberant, hostess. She had maintained a polite though somewhat formal demeanor throughout the evening, but Dianne hadn't minded. She had felt that she was under a keen spotlight, but she understood that as a visiting girlfriend she was required to endure a certain scrutiny from Helmi. This folding of laundry and dropping it right on her feet as she slept, however, was something else entirely. Dianne was a highly perceptive person, and she would go on to earn a PhD in psychology and become a professor and recognized expert in the behavioral sciences. She and Terry would be married within another year or so, and she would work hard over the ensuing decades to develop a good relationship with Helmi, which meant accepting certain rules of deference. She would always remember this moment. Lying in bed in the guest room, she perceived what she was up against and steeled herself for the challenge. She closed her eyes and pretended to stay asleep until all the laundry had been folded and my mother finally left the room. She felt that a clear message had been sent: this is my house, and I control things here and run things my way. Go along with this, allow me to assert myself, respect my authority over my children even if they are so-called adults, even if it means pretending that you don't notice, and all will be well.

I took a lesson from this event, with my brother's experiences once again paving the way for me. I didn't bring a girlfriend home to visit until my senior year of college, and then only because we had begun living together. All was fine for a day or so, until the second morning while I was in the shower and my sweetheart came out of the guest room and thought she would join Helmi for early morning coffee and a friendly chat. At the kitchen table she was subjected to an intense interrogation, the details of which were given to me on our drive back over the pass on Sunday. Helmi had fixed her with a piercing glare and had pressed her for information about our relationship and future intentions, making her wish that she had not come. My mother, in her opinion, had a dominating personality and I was lucky to have escaped from her clutches. At that moment I had no reason to doubt her assessment. I made a timid attempt to defend my mother, citing her well-known sense of humor, which I had to admit had been strangely absent all weekend, plus her background as an immigrant, which I feebly offered as a reason for her apparent objection to premarital cohabitation. Our relationship eventually ended, for reasons far beyond that one difficult weekend. But it would be a long time before I had the gumption to bring home another female friend.

When my brother and I compared notes, we realized that to Helmi no girlfriend or wife could ever be good enough for her sons. Helmi had managed to dodge much of what fate had thrown in her way, but in at least one sense she was unsuccessful: she would always be a Jewish Mother.

On some of my trips home, I began to notice that Helmi avoided bringing up the subject of my grandmother. I would have to ask how Baba was, and my mother would avert her eyes for a second, then look straight back at me and say, in her steeliest low register—the voice of doom, Terry and I used to call it—"You'll see for yourself." I would book a lunch date with Baba, which involved sitting down in her cramped kitchen or on her squeaky couch with a fold-up TV tray in front of me, munching a burned grilled cheese sandwich or a bowl of Kraft macaroni and cheese, and getting "caught up." Her cooking skills had begun to fall by the wayside, along with her interest in tracking a conversation.

I would tell her about my friends and my classes and the band I was playing in, and she would listen patiently with a vague smile on her face. When I finally shut up, we would get to the part she really cared about.

"How is Helmi?" she would ask, conspiratorially, leaning in close and clutching my arm. If Helmi's voice of doom could drop to a near baritone, Baba's tone of secret dread was almost a true basso, laden with pungent breath and gravelly foreboding. "You must tell me, Davidochka." Now she was actually whispering. "Is this man good to her?"

"This man? Jack, you mean. Oh, yes. He's very good to her. They love each other very much." I gave her a grin, but I was cringing inside.

Something was definitely going wrong in her head. By the summer after I graduated, when I had come home to work at the family hardware store while deciding what to do next—they had bought out my mother's inherited share of the business by way of a prescient family legal agreement set up by my father—things with Baba had become far more troublesome. That spring she had started a fire in her kitchen by leaving a pan of grease burning on the stove. She had to give up her role as a hospital Gray Lady because she could no longer be trusted with the simplest tasks. She had taken to wandering off and ringing strangers' doorbells in her neighborhood, announcing that she was lost and couldn't remember where she lived.

One weekend, Helmi and Jack treated Baba to a Broadway touring company's performance of *Fiddler on the Roof*. Jack, who naively thought that she would react positively to the wonderful music and relate to the tender story of Tevye the milkman and his impoverished family, had come up with the idea. Helmi later said that she had felt a premonition of trouble, but decided to hold her tongue.

All was well at first. But the third wall did not hold. When Tevye began to sing "If I Were a Rich Man" and launched into his dance with his family and the other residents of their impoverished *shtetl*, before anyone realized what was happening Baba had leaped from her seat—they had put her on the aisle, thinking she would feel less constrained—and hurtled toward the stage, arms outstretched, crying out loud in Yiddish for her mother and father, and probably for her murdered siblings as well. She had been intercepted, with the help of a couple of ushers, and carried bodily out of the theater. Poor Jack, many hours later, still astonished, would say, "She thought it was her family up there. She really, truly did."

Helmi and Jack McCorkle, in Reno, 1968.

"Oh, I doubt that, Jack dear," answered Helmi, wearily. "I think she just wanted to get on that stage."

Not long after this incident, we sat down at the kitchen table, Helmi, Jack, Phyllis and Bert Goldwater, and me—Terry was now married and attending graduate school in Michigan—to discuss options. Jack was his usual frank self. She should not live alone anymore. And by no means could she move in with family. She was suffering from serious dementia. She needed to be moved, he said, to a place with around-the-clock care. Helmi contributed very little to this discussion. Her face and clenched hands betrayed a powerful emotional cocktail of fear and guilt. I did my part and chimed in, backing Jack's opinion. Baba should be cared for safely so life could go on smoothly for the rest of us. I saw that Phyllis and Bert had been brought in by Jack to bolster the case, and it seemed that some careful planning had already taken place. Because she was a naturalized U.S. citizen and totally indigent, Bert explained, her care could be paid for by Medicaid.

This was a delicate moment. Helmi looked around at each one of us, and then gave a half-hearted chuckle. "You've all ganged up on me," she said. She took hold of Jack's hand, but her eyes were on Bert across the table. "I could say to you that this is impossible. I could say that I have taken care of my mother all my life, and before that she took care of me, through terrible times, and there is no way I am doing this."

For a moment Jack's face went pale. I knew that he had always kept a distance from my grandmother, and that he thought of her as a peculiar and mysterious creature. Having grown up on a small farm just north of Portland, Oregon, he had trouble connecting to this crazy little person from the other side of the world. I realized now, from his stricken look, that he was truly afraid of the potential power she wielded over Helmi— over all of us, for that matter. I saw that if anything could ever drive a wedge into their marriage, this might be it.

Bert kept a steady gaze on my mother. "Of course you could say that," he said to her, very calmly. "But for her sake and for your sake and for Jack's sake, you shouldn't." It was true what everyone always said about Bert, that he was a great lawyer.

Helmi looked at him now with her mouth set tight. I thought she might start to cry, but she held herself in firm control. After one more short pause, she said, "OK. I believe you."

After that, Bert took the matter firmly in hand, just as he had in setting Baba up in her apartment, and within a few weeks the deal was done. Baba was moved to what was called a "convalescent center," a twenty-minute drive from Helmi and Jack's house. She went with surprising willingness—surprising to me, anyway. When I went to visit her in her new digs, she seemed more cheerful than she had in years. She gave the food rave reviews and appeared to have made lots of friends. The staff all found her cute and endearing. It appeared that she told them all kinds of fanciful tales of her past life—many probably at least based on the truth—and she was revered as a unique and charming inmate. This made the situation somewhat easier on Helmi, whose routine now included visiting her mother almost daily.

Tiny as she was, feeble as she seemed, thin as a little bird, highstrung with high blood pressure to match, Baba didn't seem as though she would be there for long. But, as she had proven at previous times in her life, she was far tougher, at least physically, than anybody gave her credit for. She would remain a resident of the Reno Convalescent Center for the next fifteen years, finally dying there, at age ninety-four, their longest-tenured resident. By then she would no longer know who she was, or who Helmi was, or who any of us were. This state of affairs caused everyone consternation and sadness, my mother most of all, of course. Baba was the only one who didn't seem to mind.

The Next Life

YEARS GO BY IN A FLASH. One day you wake up and realize that your adult life is under way. You have responsibilities, commitments, an expanded view of the world and your place in it. You move away, begin a professional life, marry, become a parent. And you watch your parents, as long as they survive, age as well.

My own son was nine years old when it hit me that I was exactly the age that my father had been when he first became sick with cancer. Five years later, my son was fourteen, and suddenly I was the age at which my father had died. From that moment on, I would outlive him. I would be older than he ever got to be.

My mother, as she aged, remained healthy and energetic. Jack likewise. They were a famously happy couple in Reno. For several decades, she waited on him hand and foot, cooked up a storm, continued every two weeks to check out and read cover-to-cover an armload of books from the public library, played bridge weekly, drank sherry with her longtime pals in the afternoons, and got by on very little sleep. She volunteered at the hospital, filling my grandmother's shoes. She saw her mother almost daily for fifteen years, reporting very little about their visits to Jack or to anyone else, giving us all reason to assume that there was not much to report.

Jack had success in his real estate career, and their lives were comfortable. He would occasionally kid her that she might have to go back to work as a secretary or translator if the bottom ever fell out of the industrial property market, but this never came about. Jack skied in the winter and worked in the yard in the summer. They took vacations to Mexico and to Europe. They continued their annual spring shopping spree to San Francisco for Jack to update his professional wardrobe. He remained the "silver fox," and she his fondest booster and supporter. As the years went by, even their views on politics grew closer. Through sheer strength of will and relentless sarcasm, Helmi nudged Jack from the right more toward the center, and after many years possibly even a few steps to the left.

As she grew older, Helmi seemed to bask in the reputation she had forged for being both fearless and fearsome. Her opinions were blunt and uncompromising. Her actions were bold, her patience thin. Yet her consistent readiness to laugh was probably her most recognized and admired trait. She relished a flair for the dramatic, and she enjoyed doing surprising things.

For one trip to San Francisco, Helmi and Jack and some friends had made a dinner reservation—a year in advance—at a legendary gourmet restaurant. The group of four arrived early, as instructed, and between courses, with accompanying wines, they were given a short tour of the kitchen. Stepping in careful single file among the ovens and steaming pots, they were greeted by chefs and sous-chefs who gave descriptions of the complex dishes being prepared. After pausing next to a large pot and hearing a mouthwatering account of the fragrant sauce simmering on low heat within, they were ushered forward again. Helmi, taking a quick look around to make sure no one in authority was watching, stuck a finger into the pot and quickly pulled it out, then slurped the sauce off her finger and hastily dropped her arm back to her side. The only witnesses to this deed were her dinnermates, who were at first stunned and then, when it was clear that no one else had seen her and they would not be thrown out of the place, greatly amused. This event was cited by her friends as classic Helmi behavior. She had an audience, a stage, and a golden opportunity to exploit. She determined that the attendant risk was manageable. She may have been simply showing off, fueled by several glasses of wine. Or she may have been acting out a sardonic commentary about a supposedly incomparable dining experience, which required a reservation a year in advance and warranted a different wine with every dish in addition to a guided tour of the kitchen. Was it her intention to cut this snooty restaurant down to size? Or was she acting impetuously for the sake of a good laugh? I think probably both.

~

IN THE FALL OF 1987, Helmi and Jack took their monthlong tour to the Far East, at Jack's behest. My own son had been born in February of that year, and in the spring Helmi had come alone to our home in Montana for a few days to visit and meet the baby. A topic much on her mind at that time was Jack's persistent efforts to get her to agree to take a trip to Asia. He had become greatly interested in her life story and had developed a belief that she would open up and give more details of her past— which she had long resisted—if he could put her back, if only briefly, where she had come from.

Sitting on the couch with my infant son in her lap, she heaved a sigh as she related to Beth and me this battle of wills that was taking place. "Jack is very sweet about it," she said, "but he's not giving up. He comes home all the time with new travel brochures to show off. He seems to think that all kinds of fond memories will come floating up the minute I'm standing on the street in Kobe, or in Shanghai. I have told him over and over that I have no shortage of memories, very few of which are fond, and none of which I have any desire to relive." She seemed adamant in her resistance, and when she departed I had a clear impression that she would eventually wear Jack down and put to rest his idea of returning her to the scenes of her roots. But it turned out it was the other way around. By midsummer the trip was booked. This was a rare instance of Helmi conceding defeat. On the phone in the fall, shortly before they departed, she said to me, "I guess this has to happen, or he'll never stop nagging me. I just hope we come back in one piece. I got out of there once, and I hope I can get out again."

The first week of their tour was spent in Japan, visiting the cities of Tokyo and Kyoto. Kobe was not on the AARP itinerary, but Jack arranged for them to leave the tour for a single afternoon in order to take Helmi there. Nearly everything was startlingly different to Helmi, beginning with the high-speed bullet train from Kyoto to Kobe. She had been in touch with a friend from the past, Sole Bruggeman, who had stayed in Kobe and now operated a small private international preschool for the children of foreigners, primarily wealthy Europeans. Sole picked them up at the rebuilt and unrecognizable train station and took them on a tour of the modernized city. The harbor was still there, with its industrialized waterfront, yet there were astonishing changes. Elevated highways, stadiums, skyscrapers. A thousand-acre artificial island had been built offshore in the center of the harbor, using landfill taken from the surrounding hillsides, and it had been fully developed with a large hotel, a new hospital, sports and convention centers, museums, and shopping malls and connected to the mainland by a multilane causeway. A second island, even larger, was under construction slightly to the east of Kobe in Osaka Bay, which would soon be the site of a new international airport.

Just as in Tokyo and Kyoto, there was no sign anymore of the vast destruction of the war. Helmi and Jack rode a cab up the hill to view Helmi's old neighborhood. A few familiar landmarks remained. Down the street from the alley where she and Rachel had lived was the same Islamic mosque, and the Catholic church five blocks over was still there, too. Perhaps the synagogue, further down the hill, where her mother regularly congregated with the other Jewish families, would be there also. Helmi felt no particular need to see it. She was not gripped by a nostalgic need to remember and reminisce, as Jack may have hoped. The alley where Rachel's rooming house had stood, off Ikuta-Suji Street, was now taken up by a complex of modern condominiums. Helmi dutifully posed for a snapshot standing in the alley, but she felt surprisingly little connection to this place. This was where she had been born, true enough. But she had never felt at home here. Could she ever explain this to Jack, who had grown up so differently, born into a place where he actually belonged? Probably not.

They had a nice meal in a pleasant restaurant with Sole, her childhood friend, even making an effort to laugh a bit about the old days, and then took the bullet train back to rejoin their tour. They spent one more night in Kyoto. Helmi's nervousness now grew into trepidation. China was next. The first stop would be Shanghai.

China was very different. Jack, who had not traveled much in his life, had been shocked and discomfited by the sheer density of population in Japan but also pleased and excited to see the extent of the country's modernization. He loved the bullet trains, the freeways, the high-rise hotels, the man-made commercial islands. China, from the moment they landed in Shanghai, seemed even more densely packed with people and at the same time far more primitive. This was 1987, before China's explosion of economic expansion and development. The airport was dark and dingy. The taxicab was a rattletrap. Their hotel, operated by the government, was cramped and uncomfortable and poorly heated. The bed sheets were smelly and the pillows lumpy. There was no hot water in the shower, but steam intermittently rose from the toilet when it was flushed.

On their first morning, they were led as a group to the Bund to gaze at the harbor-front lineup of former colonial edifices, whose arched doorways and colonnaded facades were now dark and uniformly stained with grime. They were served tea in the musty lobby of the old Palace Hotel, one of the few buildings not boarded up, the same place where Helmi's cousin Sonya Jensen once regularly socialized with her wealthy non-Jewish friends. Afterward, they all crossed the Bund and strolled through Huangpu Park, formerly the Public Garden where the Chinese had once been forbidden to enter, now bare and unkempt and missing its European-style bandstand and wrought-iron benches. Helmi showed Jack the approximate place overlooking the river where she used to escape the noise and smells of the city and sit with a book.

It was then that they received grudging permission from their official guide to briefly leave the tour and travel by cab north across the Garden Bridge and into the old International District along the Huangpu River, Helmi's former neighborhood. After twenty or so blocks, the cab reached Helmi's old corner of Broadway (now Dongdamin Lu) and Congping Lu, and they stepped out onto the sidewalk. The street smell nearly overwhelmed her, calling up the memory of coolies carrying on bamboo poles over their shoulders the infamous honey buckets loaded with household sewage. There were no such coolies in evidence now, but clearly the local sanitary conditions were not much better. She felt in a daze as they crossed the street and found that eight-foot gatepost that had marked the entrance to the alley behind her tenement. She stood dutifully for her photos. There was no other trace of her former home. A sensation of panic rose in her throat.

"Okay, you got your pictures," she said. "Now let's get out of here."

But Jack wanted one more photo of the neighborhood, nearer the waterfront at the end of the block. As he lifted his camera to photograph a building near the piers, they were accosted by a local policeman who demanded, in halting English, to see their passports. He must have been watching them for some time. Helmi's panic rose again. Here they were, away from their tour, far from the city center, the area officially sanctioned for foreign visitors. It was only after they displayed their hotel key, along with their AARP I.D. cards, that the Chinese officer handed

back their passports, with a stern warning that they should return to
their group immediately.

Helmi was unwilling to stop and call attention to themselves any further, even to hail a cab. Wearing their sturdy walking shoes, purchased
in Reno for the possibility of just such urban hiking, they traveled the
full distance back down the long avenue on foot, at a steady pace, with
their heads down. Helmi noted to herself, without saying it out loud
to Jack, in the fear that it might spark another unauthorized excursion,
that this was the same route she had taken many times on her way to
the Thomas Hanbury School for Girls. When they reached the Garden
Bridge, she knew that the school was only five blocks north and was possibly still standing, but she kept her mouth shut. They crossed the river,
rejoined their tour, and Helmi extracted a promise from Jack that they
would not, under any circumstance, venture out on their own again.

The rest of the China tour was mostly uneventful and free from
worry. They toured the Forbidden City in Beijing, saw the Terracota
Army in Xian, and visited numerous other sites. Some of the hotels,
particularly those owned by non-Chinese corporations, were a great deal
more comfortable. After three weeks they returned home, to Helmi's
great relief. For the rest of the trip she had not shaken off the unnerving
sensation of being back in Shanghai, and she would not do so for a long
time. She had caught a nasty respiratory infection that she attributed to
the dank and chilly Shanghai hotel room, and the symptoms stayed with
her for weeks, reinforcing her belief that she was once again lucky to get
out of there alive, just as she had been all those years ago.

~

In early February 1991 Helmi called me at home in Montana early
one morning. When I answered, she spoke my name in a low tone that
I recognized immediately as the cue for bad news, the voice of doom. I
was two months short of my fortieth birthday, with a four-year-old boy
at home. I had last visited Reno the previous summer with Beth and our
son Tai. "What's up?" I replied, steeling myself.

In the same voice, with an entirely flat affect, she said, "I'm calling
to let you know that Baba died. Last night, about four in the morning.
Respiratory failure. Quickly, I was told, without any pain." Then, before
I could reply, she preemptively answered several questions I was sure to
ask. "I'm fine," she said. "There is no need for you to come. I told your

brother the same thing. There won't be any service. She is to be cremated. The ashes will go to the Jewish cemetery. Jack and I had made
plans to go to San Francisco on the weekend, and we'll still go. It will do
us both good to get away for a few days."

Once I could get a word in, I told her that I would be happy to help
in any way I could. She thanked me and said she would let me know,
but for now there was no need. Then she asked me about my wife and
son, and I told her everyone was fine. It then became one of those odd
conversations where, by silent mutual agreement, the actual subject of
the call is henceforth avoided. As I was giving her bits of news about my
son's latest adventures in preschool, images of my grandmother scrolled
through my mind. I saw her standing above me in our old house on
Humboldt Street when I myself was of preschool age, her damp curls
held in place by what appeared to be giant paper clips, muttering to me
in husky Russian to stay still while she brushed my hair with quick,
powerful strokes. I saw her in her Gray Lady hospital volunteer uniform, with a proud smile on her face, holding the Certificate of Appreciation she was given when she was politely asked to retire. I saw her
rushing the stage during *Fiddler on the Roof*, sprinting with arms outstretched, mistaking the actors for her long-gone family. I saw her as she
might have looked as a young woman, bright-eyed, vivacious, making
her perfectly timed entrance to a party and jumping up to sit on the
edge of the grand piano, as she had once told me she did. And I saw her
as I had last seen her, tiny, shriveled, pale, hairs growing out of her chin,
sitting up ramrod-straight in bed and glaring at me with fierce, unrec-
ognizing eyes. For a moment I wondered what Helmi was really thinking at the other end of the line, what images might be running through
her mind as we maintained our artificial chat. She had her own associa-
tion with my grandmother that was longer than anyone else's, longer by
decades than that of any other family member, spanning in fact Helmi's
entire life. If any two people in the world knew each other well, it was
this mother and daughter. Yet we all saw that Baba had remained in
many ways a mystery to Helmi, as well as to the rest of us. Baba's fears
and superstitions were all her own, too deep and well-fortified from
years of practice for even therapists and psychiatrists to truly understand. Helmi's grief, I knew, was likewise private and not to be shared,
for her own reasons. Perhaps she also felt the liberation, or at least the
possibility of it, that she had long hoped for. I'm sure she saw that there

was nothing more to do now besides continue to press forward, just as she had always done. So, without any more discussion of the actual topic in front of us, eventually she said a polite goodbye, and I did also, and that was that.

Baba's ashes were interred in the Jewish cemetery in Reno. Years later we learned that Helmi sponsored a tree to be planted in Israel in her mother's name, just as Baba had sponsored them in the names of her own parents, her brother, and her sister.

~

JACK MAY HAVE BEEN a silver fox, but Helmi resisted going gray, coloring her hair golden brown—several shades lighter than her former dark brunette—until she was nearly seventy. She maintained a sardonic view of the aging process. Having acquired a taste for salty language in the many decades since becoming a fully assimilated American, she was happy to tell anyone within earshot that the notion of the "so-called golden years" was "nothing but a bunch of shit." Grandmotherhood was not a fate that Helmi accepted without a struggle. When Tai was small she told Beth and me, just as she had told my brother and his wife regarding their own two children, that she had no desire to babysit anyone who was still in diapers. As time went by, it became clear that she had no desire to babysit at all. This was not a major issue, since we lived several states apart. But it did affect family relationships. Our mother far preferred that Terry and I visit her in Reno without our respective families in tow. That way she could have us to herself for a weekend, or however long we could give her. When we did bring our families, she was always polite to my wife and to Terry's wife, but our kids sometimes seemed to be unwelcome reminders of the passage of time. They were sternly instructed never to use the terms "Grandma" or "Grandpa." Instead, Helmi announced that henceforth she should be addressed by any and all grandchildren as "Obasan," and Jack as "Zaydeh," terms borrowed from Japanese and Yiddish, representing two cultures that she somewhat mockingly declared fostered greater reverence and respect for elders than did modern-day America.

Her life's focus had been to wage personal war against a host of foes—fear, poverty, widowhood. But the ultimate enemy was time, over which there could be no victory, only surrender in the long run. She held fast to what truly mattered to her—her husband, her friends, her stack of library books by the bedside. That Terry and I had grown to adulthood and now had families of our own was merely evidence that the battle against time, though futile, still needed to be waged.

When Helmi turned seventy-five, Terry and I paid a visit without our families. I had recently acquired a video camera, mostly for recording my son's birthday parties and other family events, and I brought it along on the outside chance that she might be persuaded to let me record some of her life story. When I showed her the camera, she smirked and gave me her familiar cold stare.

"Oh, I get it," she said icily. "You want to catch me now, before it's too late. You're worried that I'll drop dead or go senile."

I told her that I merely thought it would be a good use for my new camera. This was the best answer I could come up with. In truth, in the back of my mind was a possible day in the future when we would all regret not having pinned her down for more information.

Without saying any more, she stepped out of the room. Figuring the subject was closed, I put the camera down and went to her kitchen to fetch myself a beer. When I returned a few minutes later, she was standing there again. "Luckily for you," she said, "I happened to get my hair done this afternoon." I saw that she had quickly spruced up, with fresh lipstick and a pair of her favorite earrings. "Okay, Mr. DeMille," she added mockingly, "I'm ready for my close-up."

Helmi then sat down on the couch and, with no further prompting, proceeded to deliver an unbroken, nearly ninety-minute monologue straight into the video recorder. I propped the camera up on the coffee table in front of her, and Terry and I simply sat back and listened. It was a virtuoso performance, as if she had carefully thought through both what she wanted to say and what she wanted to avoid saying—as if she had been given ample time to prepare the performance, which of course was not the case. With a steady voice, deepened now to a near-baritone, and with the same clear diction she had learned from her British schoolteachers, though with the Shanghai-British accent much abated after more than fifty years, she presented detailed memories of both China and Japan. The crowded Shanghai tenement shared with her mother and aunt and cousin, the "honey bucket" being collected every morning, the pungent smell of the streets, the relentless noise of rickshaws and hand carts and bicycles and streetcars and buses. Her mother's obsessive hovering, keeping her out of school out of fear of dirt and disease, insisting that she speak English at home as well as Russian, taking her on rare outings to the Public Garden to sit and watch the huge ships coming into port from seemingly every country in the world. Then finally being allowed to attend school at age nine, the British school where all classes were, again, in English. Learning that by excelling in school she might overcome the stigma of being a refugee and a Jew, that she could in fact become almost like the other girls from Britain or America, that she could even win the school essay contest by appropriating another girl's life. The terrifying days when the Japanese bombed the city and their home burned and they fled to her cousin's house. Her mother's decision to move back to Japan, allowing her to stay and finish high school in occupied Shanghai. The offer of the American college scholarship, which she was unable to accept, then relocating to Kobe to live with her mother, finding work in a travel agency until the war began, followed by four harrowing years as stateless non-citizens trapped in Japan. The cold wartime winters, the lack of food, the terrifying American bombings. The German officers who had to be housed by her mother. The rumors of a new atomic bomb. The emperor's shocking surrender announcement, broadcast over the radio in his tinny voice. The arrival of the Americans, including a shy, anemic-looking intelligence officer from someplace called Reno, Nevada. Working for the U.S. Army as a secretary and translator, being helped to secure one of the first U.S. visas issued in Japan after the war, coming to San Francisco, living at the Evangeline Hotel for Women, sending a Christmas card to the Reno soldier, marrying him a mere seven months later, moving to Reno, becoming an American, having her two boys, feeling eternally grateful for her good fortune.

Throughout the narrative she sprinkled in details: the signature stench of the Shanghai streets; the Japanese sky blackened by bombers flying in tight formation, filling the sky from horizon to horizon; the morning sun glinting off the Golden Gate Bridge as she sailed beneath it into San Francisco Bay.

And then, just as abruptly as she had begun, she was finished. "Okay, there you have it," she said. "Now turn that thing off." She got up and went to the kitchen to fix herself a drink.

Almost all of it was new to us. We had heard fragments of the story over the years, but not enough to make sense of it all or to put anything into context. When she stopped talking, my brother and I were both stunned into silence for a moment; then we chased her into the kitchen and begged for more. There had to be plenty more to tell, from every step of the saga.

"Get out of my way," she said. "Jack will be home soon, and I need to fix dinner. You got what you wanted, right?"

We thanked her then, and I asked if maybe sometime we could sit down and record more of her story. "Maybe," she said. "Perhaps there'll be another opportunity someday. For now that'll just have to do. And if I drop dead one of these days"—she gave that smirk once more—"you can thank me all over again for this time."

I went home to my family, and Terry to his, and three more years went by in a flash. We each visited a number of times after that, but the chance to sit Helmi down comfortably again and persuade her to tell more somehow never presented itself. This was her last interview.

Helmi's Shadow

ONE EVENING IN EARLY MAY 2002, I sat in a right-hand window
seat on a jet from Salt Lake City descending into Reno. The usual
landing was from the north, passing smoothly over Pyramid Lake, but
when winds were strong from that direction the approach was from the
south, and the plane would drop in low over the Virginia foothills, often
encountering considerable turbulence in the process. This was the way I
came in that night. As we approached, the plane suddenly banked hard
to my side and gave me a clear view of the dry hills directly below. The
sun had descended behind the Sierras to the west, and the landscape
was bathed in rosy twilight. The plane bucked us up and down as we
continued the steep descent between the mountain ranges, and I tried to
focus my eyes on the ground in an effort to steady my nerves.

I was flying in on short notice because my mother was dying. Helmi
had suffered a stroke six weeks earlier and had steadily deteriorated
since. During that time I had already made four trips to Reno and had
seen this clearly for myself. This time the news was dire: she would not
last long. Jack McCorkle had called at midday, and I was on the first
available flight.

Straight beneath me I recognized the lights of Virginia City, the historic mining town and site of the Comstock Lode, the great silver strike
of the 1850s that hastened Nevada's statehood and helped finance the
Civil War. As we completed our steep turn I had a clear view of the road
that snaked from Virginia City down into Washoe Valley over the pass
known as Geiger Grade. Several of the road's tight switchbacks had
turnouts on the downhill side, wide spots on the curves marked by triangular scars of bulldozed earth, where slow vehicles could pull over or
even stop for a view of the valley. Nothing much had changed in fifty

years—the road had been resurfaced, probably many times, but other than that it was still the same narrow, winding road. As we dropped even lower, just before the plane straightened out, I had a perfect bird's-eye view of a scenic viewpoint perched on a tight curve that faced straight west toward the Sierras, and I could see that a car had indeed stopped there, no doubt to take in the view of the sunset. It hit me that I was possibly looking down on the exact spot where my father, in the spring of 1947—on the day they announced their engagement—had taken those photographs of Helmi proudly posing in her spiffy western outfit, and where she had her first hot dog. Maybe down below someone was posing for a similar picture at that very moment.

~

HELMI'S STROKE had occurred in the passenger seat of a friend's car while riding home from an afternoon of duplicate bridge. She had suddenly gone silent mid-conversation and keeled over sideways, banging her head against the window. In a panic, the friend had not thought to go straight to the hospital emergency room, which was relatively close by, but instead had driven Helmi all the way home, about a twenty-minute journey to the west side of Reno, where she knew Helmi's husband was waiting. Once there, Jack had helped carry Helmi, still frozen in silence, to his own car and had driven her all the way back into town and finally to the hospital. Over an hour passed before she received medical attention.

Both Terry and I had flown in the next day. When I arrived at the hospital, Helmi lay calmly on her back in the bed. She turned her head and her eyes flashed in recognition. I took hold of her left hand—I'd been told that her right arm was paralyzed—and felt once again the familiar force of her unblinking gaze fixed upon me. She startled me then by suddenly saying, with a sigh, "What a way to go." Her tone conveyed to me the full weight of her particular take on existence—fatalistic, ironic, unflinching. I feebly answered, "Come on now. Nobody's going anywhere." But she gripped my hand so tightly and held my eyes with hers so firmly that I gave up the idea of arguing any further. As it happens, those were the last coherent words I or anybody else would hear her say.

Over the next weeks, she went downhill rapidly. During those first days in the hospital, various members of the medical team seemed eager to certify her as qualified for release. She was given swallowing tests, and

the consensus was that she passed, although at least two nurses vigor-
ously disputed this assessment. She simply spat out much of the food
she was given. The bed space was needed, we were told, and once stabi-
lized she would need to begin physical therapy, the next stage of recov-
ery. So after a day in intensive care and two more days under hospital
care, she was sent downstairs to do just that. She was no longer speaking at all, and she had failed most of the cognitive tests. When she was
given a pad and paper and told to write her name—she was left-handed,
and her arm on that side continued to function well—she slowly wrote
out, in a surprisingly careful hand, a string of five or six totally unrelated
letters, briefly surveyed her work, and slapped the pencil down with a
self-satisfied smile. This was the last time I saw anything like a happy
look on her face. In the physical therapy ward, she was taken out of bed
regularly and put through exercises designed to rehabilitate her paralyzed side, but she seemed terrified by the difficult activity, the enthusi-
astic young therapists, and the other patients on the ward. Results were
negative. She grew weaker instead of stronger. By the time I flew home
on the fifth day after her stroke, the word was that if she did not respond
better she would be sent to a nursing home.

Sure enough, the next time I was able to visit, this is what had
occurred. Jack had chosen a nursing facility for Helmi that was a thirty-
minute drive from his house. There, she lay day after day on her back,
still eating very little and growing increasingly agitated. Friends came
regularly to visit her, but she no longer seemed to recognize anyone. She
seemed to age decades in a matter of weeks. Sometimes she would suddenly grasp upward with her good arm at something over her head, as
if she saw a bird flying through the room. A couple of her old friends
stated that she would stare at them with her former customary intensity, even with a hint of a conspiratorial look, and they felt sure that
she was aware of far more than she let on. When she refused food, or
spat it out, they concluded that she was deliberately weakening herself
so as not to prolong this terrible situation and the pain it was causing Jack. They tried to reason with her, to cajole her out of this willful
attempt to weaken herself. I understood what these loyal friends meant.
They knew her as stubborn, strong-willed, and always in control. On
my subsequent trips to Reno across the next couple of months from my
home in Montana, it was tempting to sign onto this theory, but finally

I couldn't become a believer. Her gaze was intense all right, but it was not a look of recognition. I held her hand and spoke to her, but I didn't expect her to listen to me.

~

THIS TIME, AS I WALKED OFF THE PLANE, I knew things were different. She had been sent back to the hospital with indications of multiple organ failure. She was heavily sedated, and she would not last long. My cousin Danny picked me up at the airport and drove us straight to the hospital. When we walked into the room I saw that she was lying very still with her mouth partly open. Jack stood up from his chair and told me she had been gone for twenty minutes.

My first thought was that she must have died at almost the exact moment that I had been looking down from the plane onto that spot where she had posed for my father all those years ago. Of course she had been on my mind for the entire journey, ever since I had gotten the call to come earlier that day. But I couldn't help thinking now—as I suppose everyone does in such moments, when we feel a need to pull extraordinary meaning out of ordinary events—that something extra had occurred just then while I sat in the plane, that some powerful calming force had passed through me as I looked down at that turnout in the road below. The airplane had very suddenly stopped shaking—this I remembered quite clearly. No doubt it was because we had just cleared the ridge of the mountains and were simply gliding into the smoother air of the valley. But still.

I went to Helmi's bedside and put my hand on her forehead, which was cold to the touch. Her face appeared smooth and devoid of suffering, and this was a relief. Perhaps her friends had been right. Perhaps she had willed herself to die in order to spare everyone more pain. More likely she had simply died of organ failure, brought on by complications from the massive stroke she had suffered two months before. It didn't matter any more, if it ever had. Her eyes were closed now.

My brother flew in the next morning, and my wife later that day, and we went through the details of dealing with a death in the family. It was quickly decided to hold an informal gathering at the house rather than any sort of formal memorial service. She had long ago made it plain to Jack, and to Terry and me even earlier, that when this day came she wished there to be no service for her. However, we all felt that she wouldn't have minded a gathering of friends and family in her home, with no set agenda.

The task of writing an obituary was given to me. Out of all of us, including Jack, Helmi's husband for thirty-four years, it was decided that I had the clearest sense of her life's trajectory and timeline. I was the one who, years before, had initially coaxed her into sitting still to answer questions and had transcribed her words. Yet once I began, I realized that there were many gaping holes in my understanding. I knew she had been born in Japan and raised in Shanghai, and that she and her mother ended up back in Japan, where after the end of the war she had met the American soldier from Reno who would become Terry's and my father after she came to the United States. I put down these basic facts, and I also made an attempt to describe the qualities of her personality that had enabled her to fully embrace a new life in Reno—her humor; her appreciation of other people; her energy, intelligence, and strength of will. Once the obituary ran in the local newspaper, many people—including some who thought they knew her well—pressed us for more information about her past life. They were learning these details for the first time. Why did Russian Jewish refugees end up living in the Far East? How did they survive the years of war? Why had Helmi been universally perceived as sophisticated and worldly and thoroughly American, if she had actually been a foreign immigrant and victim of poverty and privation?

The non-memorial gathering of friends and family was attended by a great many people. I had conversations with some of Helmi's oldest American friends who in fact had little or no understanding of her past before she came to Reno. One couple, former neighbors who had lived right across the street during the years I was growing up, sat me down and told me that not once, in the forty years that they knew her, did she ever tell them a single thing about her previous life. This was a common theme that day. My mother had been widely admired and greatly loved, but much about her, it turned out, was completely unknown to those who admired and loved her. A common remark around that crowded room was that she should have told her story. She should have written it down. She could have written a book, for heaven's sake.

～

AFTER I UNDERWENT A PERIOD OF GRIEVING—missing her deep voice on the phone, her raucous laughter, her withering gaze of disapproval which usually morphed into a smirk of amusement—at some point, maybe a year or so after her death, it struck me again that, yes, of course, she should have told her story. It would have been vivid, harrowing, probably funny, no doubt better told than the version I have told. But she didn't, because she didn't want to. It also dawned on me that if her story were ever going to be told, it would have to be told by me. Somehow, by default, it fell to me to expend the time and energy necessary to dig through family albums and archives, track down distant relatives, roam the internet for facts and figures, and plow through a shelfload of books to fill in the missing pieces of her tale and get it down as best I could.

I wonder what she would think of my version. I have tried hard to be faithful to what I know to be true, what appears with reasonable evidence to be true, and what ought to be true. No doubt she would find plenty to correct.

All I would say to her is that I'm sorry, but it's too late. Her story doesn't belong to her anymore. It belongs to me now.

Epilogue

November, 1946

T HE SHIP, an American freighter, moved forward slowly through dense fog in the early morning light. Moments ago, the captain had announced that anyone wanting a first view of their destination, the west coast of the United States, should make their way up on deck. There were only a handful of passengers on board. They had been required to pay their fee in cash directly to the captain after embarking from the port of Kobe, Japan.

It had been a journey of twelve days, with consistently rough seas. Most of the passengers spent their time holed up belowdecks, contending with their discomfort, keeping to themselves. Today the only one who climbed out of bed and came upstairs to see the coast of America was twenty-three-year-old Helmi Koskin. She had never felt seasick on the trip, not even once. In fact, while the others had appeared miserable and anxious for the trip to end, she had actually enjoyed the quiet days, the solitude, and the freedom from all responsibility. She even liked the food, which everyone else seemed to think terrible. She was well aware, by how tight her clothes had become, that she had gained several pounds.

She was surprised to be alone. Apparently this was nothing special to the others, civilians who had been in postwar Japan for one reason or another and were merely returning home. But for Helmi, who already knew a great deal about America from books and movies and had long dreamed of coming here, it was different. Somewhere close up ahead, invisible so far, was the city of San Francisco.

She stood on the deck near the bow, gripping the rail with both hands, peering out at the fog. The ship rose and fell on the waves, as it had for all these days, and the engines continued to hum. Occasionally the fog would break for a few seconds, opening narrow paths up ahead that would abruptly end in new walls of cloud. The sun must have risen, but it wasn't breaking through. The water was a uniform color, a darker shade of gray than the fog.

Suddenly a break appeared ahead. A ray of sunlight stabbed the water. A couple of larger breaks opened up, revealing patches of blue sky overhead. Then, nearly straight above, emerged a huge structure—a ladder into the cloud, gleaming orange in the sunlight, partially framed by a still larger patch of blue, hung with thin wires like the strings of a gigantic musical instrument.

"*Bozhomoi!*" Helmi cried out. *My god.* In her amazement, she had reverted to her mother's native Russian. She had seen plenty of pictures in magazines. She knew what it was. The Golden Gate Bridge.

The fog continued breaking up. The bridge—she could see more of it now—was enormous, its span so long that it disappeared completely into the mist on the far side, and the tops of its double towers were lost in the remnants of cloud. The ship passed under the bridge's deck, which was held in the air by thin strands hung from two huge looping cables. The clouds, as if on cue, separated some more, like curtains opening to display a wide expanse of sky.

And then off to the right appeared the city, San Francisco, shining and impossibly white in the morning sunshine. Nothing had prepared her for the alabaster beauty of this place. She laughed out loud. If this were a movie, now would be the time for dramatic music to swell. The heroine, leaning on the ship's rail, would have a close-up, perhaps even shed a tear. But this was not a movie. It was real, and at this moment Helmi was in no mood for tears.

The ship moved forward gently, the rough open sea and the fog now far behind, into the clear light of San Francisco Bay. Helmi stayed, gripping the rail and looking out at the blue bay and the white city and what might be beyond. Somewhere further out there was the rest of America. Somewhere out there was her future.

Helmi and the author, in Reno, 1969.

Acknowledgments

My THANKS to the University of Nevada Press, particularly Clark Whitehorn, Margaret Dalrymple, JoAnne Banducci, and Jinni Fontana. Mr. Whitehorn, the former director, met with me over lunch at Louis' Basque Corner in Reno, listened with interest to my description of the project, and started it down the path toward publication. After his departure from the press, Ms. Dalrymple, Ms. Banducci, and Ms. Fontana took over and shepherded the book to completion. Lynne Ferguson, a wonderful editor, helped to improve the manuscript in a host of ways.

Monique Laxalt has been the book's guardian angel, and I cannot thank her enough. After reading an early draft, she suggested that I offer the manuscript to the University of Nevada Press. The book came to life because of her steadfast friendship and support.

Kirk Johnson skillfully took charge of the widely varying images and photos and made significant improvements, and also designed the custom maps.

A number of people read the manuscript at various stages and helped make it better. Dianne Horgan, who knew Helmi and Rachel across several decades, provided many crucial insights. Richard Opper and Sally Mueller read multiple drafts and offered valuable comments and encouragement. Richard Drake, Patrick Herz, Mark McHenry, Deirdre McNamer, Tia Lombardi, Michael and Gretchen North, Ginnie Lo, Colleen Powell, Rob Sanders, and Diana Simpson all read drafts of the story and provided helpful feedback. Tai Horgan used his sharp eye in the early stages to help prevent the story from slipping off the rails. My beloved cousin and lifelong pal, Dan Horgan, read the manuscript while confined in the hospital in Reno, and over the phone, while still bedridden, he helped clarify some key details. He did not live to see the book in its final form, but his spirit lives on in its pages.

My research led me to discover lost relatives and make new friends. My cousin Maryanne Carthew, who spent her early years in Shanghai, provided me with invaluable photographs and family lore. George Sidline, his wife Simonne, and Simonne's brother Gregory Moiseeff, who knew my mother and grandmother in Kobe during the years of World War II, invited me to visit and provided wonderful stories and photographs. George Sidline's memoir, titled *Somehow We'll Survive*, was an excellent additional source on the living conditions of Japan's wartime foreign refugees. George passed away of COVID-19 in November 2020, and will be greatly missed. Anita Manley, Helmi's first friend in the United States and the matron of honor at her first wedding, also welcomed my brother and me into her home in Los Angeles and offered fascinating memories.

Cliff McCorkle located the scrapbook of Helmi and Jack's return trip to the Far East that had been lost for many years, containing crucial information about locations in both Shanghai and Kobe, which enabled me to tell a much more complete story.

My brother Terry, who grew up beside me and lived through many of the stories on which the book is based, corroborated my memories and provided more of his own. He participated in interviews with Helmi and helped prod her to keep talking. The expeditions he and I made together to Los Angeles and Toronto, hunting for some of Helmi's relatives and friends, were by far the most enjoyable and rewarding aspects of the research process.

Finally, my deepest thanks go to my wife, Beth, whose love and encouragement have carried me through the process of putting this project together. With her artist's eye and musician's ear, she helped make it a much better book.

Bibliography

THE FOLLOWING WORKS were helpful in insuring the accuracy of my information. Any remaining errors are mine alone.

ODESSA

King, Charles. *Odessa: Genius and Death in a City of Dreams.* New York: W. W. Norton & Company, 2011.

Weinberg, Robert. *The Revolution of 1905 in Odessa: Blood on the Steps.* Bloomington: Indiana University Press, 1993.

Weinberg, Robert. "The Pogrom of 1905 in Odessa: A Case Study." In *Pogroms: Anti-Jewish Violence in Modern Russian History*, edited by John D. Klier and Shlomo Lambroza, 248–89. Cambridge: Cambridge University Press, 1992.

HARBIN

Bakich, Olga Mikhailovna. *Valerii Perelshin: Life of A Silkworm.* Toronto: University of Toronto Press, 2015.

Epstein, Israel. *My China Eye: Memoirs of a Jew and a Journalist.* San Francisco: Long River Press, 2005.

Gamsa, Mark. *Harbin: A Cross-Cultural Biography.* Toronto: University of Toronto Press, 2020.

Meyer, Michael. *In Manchuria: A Village Called Wasteland and the Transformation of Rural China.* New York: Bloomsbury Press, 2015.

Stephan, John J. *The Russian Far East: A History.* Stanford: Stanford University Press, 1994.

Wolff, David. *To the Harbin Station: The Liberal Alternative in Russian Manchuria, 1898–1914.* Stanford: Stanford University Press, 1999.

SHANGHAI

Bacon, Ursula. *Shanghai Diary: A Young Girl's Journey from Hitler's Hate to War-Torn China.* Milwaukee: Milestone Books, 2002.

Bergere, Marie-Claire. *Shanghai: China's Gateway to Modernity.* Translated by Janet Lloyd. Stanford: Stanford University Press, 2009.

Dong, Stella. *Shanghai, 1842–1949: The Rise and Fall of a Decadent City.* New York: HarperCollins, 2000.

Eber, Irene. *Wartime Shanghai and the Jewish Refugees rrom Central Europe.* Berlin/Boston: Walter de Gruyter, 2012.

French, Paul. *The Old Shanghai from A to Z*. Hong Kong: Hong Kong University Press, 2010

Hahn, Emily. *China to Me*. Philadelphia: The Blakiston Company, 1944.

Holland, Gail Bernice. *For Sasha with Love: The Anne Bashkiroff Story—An Alzheimer's Crusade*. New York: Dembner Books, 1985.

Jordan, Donald. *China's Trial by Fire: The Shanghai War of 1932*. Ann Arbor: University of Michigan Press, 2001.

Kaufman, Jonathan. *The Last Kings of Shanghai: The Rival Jewish Dynasties That Helped Create Modern China*. New York: Viking Press, 2020.

Krasno, Rena. *Strangers Always: A Jewish Family in Wartime Shanghai*. Berkeley: Pacific View Press, 1992.

Ling, Pan. *In Search of Old Shanghai*. Hong Kong: Joint Publishing Co., 1982.

Mitter, Rana. *Forgotten Ally: China's World War II*. New York: Mariner Books/Houghton Mifflin Harcourt, 2013.

Ristaino, Marcia Reynders. *Port of Last Resort: The Diaspora Communities of Shanghai*. Stanford: Stanford University Press, 2001.

Sergeant, Harriet. *Shanghai: Collision Point of Cultures, 1918–1939*. New York: Crown Publishers, Inc., 1990.

Tuchman, Barbara W. *Stillwell and the American Experience in China, 1911–45*. New York: The Macmillan Company, 1970.

Willens, Liliane. *Stateless in Shanghai*. Hong Kong: China Economic Review Publishing Limited for Earnshaw Books, 2010.

Zia, Helen. *Last Boat Out of Shanghai*. New York: Ballantine Books, 2019.

JAPAN

Bacon, William. *Ed and Ivet: The True Story of a World War II POW Romance*. Bennet and Hastings Publishing, 2010.

Bix, Herbert P. *Hirohito and the Making of Modern Japan*. New York: HarperCollins, 2000.

Cohen, Stan. *Destination Tokyo: A Pictorial History of Doolittle's Historic Raid*. Missoula: Pictorial Histories Publishing Company, 1983.

Craig, William. *The Fall of Japan: A Chronicle of the End of an Empire*. New York: Galahad Books, 1967.

Gordon, Beata Sirota. *The Only Woman in the Room: A Memoir of Japan, Human Rights, and the Arts*. Chicago and London: University of Chicago Press, 1997.

Shapiro, Isaac. *Edokko: Growing Up a Foreigner in Wartime Japan*. Bloomington: iUniverse, Inc., 2009.

Sidline, George. *Somehow, We'll Survive: Life In Japan during World War II through the Eyes of A Young Caucasian Boy*. Vera Vista Publishing, 2007.

Tokayer, Marvin, and Swartz, Mary. *The Fugu Plan: The Untold Story of the Japanese and the Jews during World War II*. Jerusalem: Paddington Press, Ltd., 1979.

Besides the above publications, many websites have been helpful. Here are several that were particularly useful to me:

Virtual Shanghai, virtualshanghai.net. A wonderful online storehouse of images, maps, and documents pertaining to the history of Shanghai, operated by the French Agence Nationale de la Recherche.

U.S. Army Signal Corps archives; https://catalog.archives.gov/id/531473. Somewhat difficult to navigate, but loaded with photos, films, and documents pertaining to historic U.S. military activity.

The United States Holocaust Memorial Museum, https://www.ushmm.org. Vast archive of Jewish history from all over the world.

The Hoover Institution, Stanford University, https://www.hoover.org. Another large archive of material pertaining to U.S. history, politics, conflicts, and diplomacy.

University of Nevada Special Collections, https://library.unr.edu/resources/digital-archive/special-collections. Excellent archive of material on the social and cultural history of Nevada.

ADDITIONAL NOTE

Fictional depictions of places and events can sometimes augment historical accounts in powerful ways. Here are three that I can recommend:

Odessa Stories by Isaac Babel. The Russian writer (1894–1940) wrote a series of ironic tales in the 1920s that vividly portray a completely lost world—the lives of Jews, from gangsters to ordinary citizens, in Odessa, his birthplace.

When We Were Orphans by Kazuo Ishiguro. The supposed glamour and intrigue of colonial-era Shanghai have become well-worn clichés. A rare exception is this wonderful surreal novel, by a Japanese-born author who writes in English, which features a harrowing account of the Shanghai street war during the Japanese invasion of 1937.

Grave of the Fireflies, a 1988 Japanese animated film directed by Isao Takehata, from a short story of the same name by Akiyuki Nosaka. With dreamlike passages and graphic realism, this film is an unstinting depiction of the American bombardment of Kobe in 1945 as experienced by two terrified children.

About the Author

DAVID HORGAN is a writer and professional musician. Born in 1951 and raised in Reno, Nevada, he received a BA in English from Stanford University in 1973 and an MFA in creative writing from the University of Montana in 1987. His stories and essays have appeared in a number of magazines and anthologies. His book of short stories titled *The Golden West Trio Plus One* received the Merriam-Frontier Award from the University of Montana.

Horgan plays several musical instruments in a variety of styles. One of his groups, the Big Sky Mudflaps—a jazz, swing, and rhythm & blues ensemble— has been in continuous operation for forty-five years. He lives in Missoula, Montana, with his wife, artist and musician Beth Lo. They have one son, Tai Horgan, who lives in Portland, Oregon.